JAN 4 '80	DATE DUE		

THE STATES AND THE NATION SERIES, of which this volume is a part, is designed to assist the American people in a serious look at the ideals they have espoused and the experiences they have undergone in the history of the nation. The content of every volume represents the scholarship, experience, and opinions of its author. The costs of writing and editing were met mainly by grants from the National Endowment for the Humanities, a federal agency. The project was administered by the American Association for State and Local History, a nonprofit learned society, working with an Editorial Board of distinguished editors, authors, and historians, whose names are listed below.

Connecticut

A Bicentennial History

David M. Roth

W. W. Norton & Company, Inc.
New York

American Association for State and Local History
Nashville

Author and publisher make grateful acknowledgment to the following for permission
to quote from previously published material.

The Center for Connecticut Studies of Eastern Connecticut State College, for permission to quote from *From Revolution to Constitution: Connecticut from 1763 to 1818,* by
David M. Roth and Freeman Meyer (Chester, Conn.: Pequot Press, 1975). Copyright
1975 by The Center for Connecticut Studies.

Yale University and Yale University Press, for permission to quote from *Connecticut
for the Union: The Role of the State in the Civil War,* by John Niven (New Haven: Yale
University Press, 1965).

W. W. Norton & Company, Inc., for permission to quote from *The New England
States,* by Neal R. Peirce (New York: W. W. Norton & Company, Inc., 1976). Copyright 1976, 1972 by Neal R. Peirce.

Library of Congress Cataloguing-in-Publication Data

Roth, David Morris, 1935–
    Connecticut, a bicentennial history.

    (The States and the Nation series)
    Bibliography: p.
    Includes index.
    1. Connecticut—History. I. Title. II. Series: States and the Nation series.
√ F94.R67   974.6   79–16262
ISBN 0-393-05676-7

Published and distributed by
W. W. Norton & Company, Inc.
500 Fifth Avenue
New York, New York 10036

Printed in the United States of America

1 2 3 4 5 6 7 8 9 0

In Memory of My Mother and My Father

Delia Gannon Roth
(1910–1947)

Irwin E. Roth
(1908–1979)

Contents

Illustrations

Invitation to the Reader

IN 1807, former President John Adams argued that a complete history of the American Revolution could not be written until the history of change in each state was known, because the principles of the Revolution were as various as the states that went through it. Two hundred years after the Declaration of Independence, the American nation has spread over a continent and beyond. The states have grown in number from thirteen to fifty. And democratic principles have been interpreted differently in every one of them.

We therefore invite you to consider that the history of your state may have more to do with the bicentennial review of the American Revolution than does the story of Bunker Hill or Valley Forge. The Revolution has continued as Americans extended liberty and democracy over a vast territory. John Adams was right: the states are part of that story, and the story is incomplete without an account of their diversity.

The Declaration of Independence stressed life, liberty, and the pursuit of happiness; accordingly, it shattered the notion of holding new territories in the subordinate status of colonies. The Northwest Ordinance of 1787 set forth a procedure for new states to enter the Union on an equal footing with the old. The Federal Constitution shortly confirmed this novel means of building a nation out of equal states. The step-by-step process through which territories have achieved self-government and national representation is among the most important of the Founding Fathers' legacies.

The method of state-making reconciled the ancient conflict between liberty and empire, resulting in what Thomas Jefferson called an empire for liberty. The system has worked and remains unaltered, despite enormous changes that have taken

ix

place in the nation. The country's extent and variety now surpass anything the patriots of '76 could likely have imagined. The United States has changed from an agrarian republic into a highly industrial and urban democracy, from a fledgling nation into a major world power. As Oliver Wendell Holmes remarked in 1920, the creators of the nation could not have seen completely how it and its constitution and its states would develop. Any meaningful review in the bicentennial era must consider what the country has become, as well as what it was.

The new nation of equal states took as its motto *E Pluribus Unum*—"out of many, one." But just as many peoples have become Americans without complete loss of ethnic and cultural identities, so have the states retained differences of character. Some have been superficial, expressed in stereotyped images— big, boastful Texas, "sophisticated" New York, "hillbilly" Arkansas. Other differences have been more real, sometimes instructively, sometimes amusingly; democracy has embraced Huey Long's Louisiana, bilingual New Mexico, unicameral Nebraska, and a Texas that once taxed fortunetellers and spawned politicians called "Woodpecker Republicans" and "Skunk Democrats." Some differences have been profound, as when South Carolina secessionists led other states out of the Union in opposition to abolitionists in Massachusetts and Ohio. The result was a bitter Civil War.

The Revolution's first shots may have sounded in Lexington and Concord; but fights over what democracy should mean and who should have independence have erupted from Pennsylvania's Gettysburg to the "Bleeding Kansas" of John Brown, from the Alamo in Texas to the Indian battles at Montana's Little Bighorn. Utah Mormons have known the strain of isolation; Hawaiians at Pearl Harbor, the terror of attack; Georgians during Sherman's march, the sadness of defeat and devastation. Each state's experience differs instructively; each adds understanding to the whole.

The purpose of this series of books is to make that kind of understanding accessible, in a way that will last in value far beyond the bicentennial fireworks. The series offers a volume on every state, plus the District of Columbia—fifty-one, in all.

Each book contains, besides the text, a view of the state through eyes other than the author's—a "photographer's essay," in which a skilled photographer presents his own personal perceptions of the state's contemporary flavor.

We have asked authors not for comprehensive chronicles, nor for research monographs or new data for scholars. Bibliographies and footnotes are minimal. We have asked each author for a summing up—interpretive, sensitive, thoughtful, individual, even personal—of what seems significant about his or her state's history. What distinguishes it? What has mattered about it, to its own people and to the rest of the nation? What has it come to now?

To interpret the states in all their variety, we have sought a variety of backgrounds in authors themselves and have encouraged variety in the approaches they take. They have in common only these things: historical knowledge, writing skill, and strong personal feelings about a particular state. Each has wide latitude for the use of the short space. And if each succeeds, it will be by offering you, in your capacity as a *citizen* of a state *and* of a nation, stimulating insights to test against your own.

James Morton Smith
General Editor

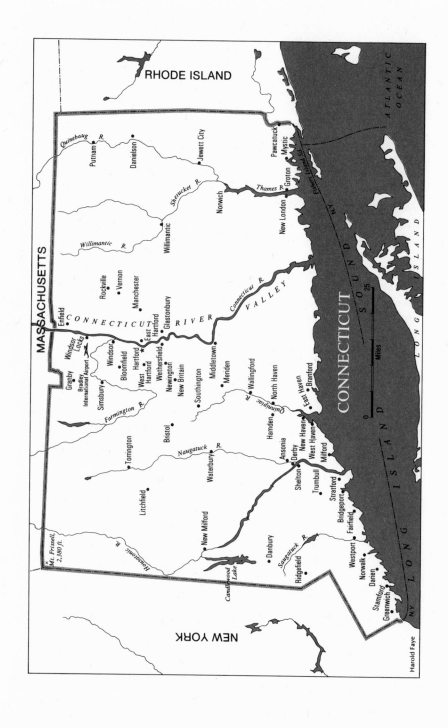

Harold Faye

ACKNOWLEDGMENTS

Because the format of the States and the Nation Series keeps scholarly paraphernalia to a minimum, the footnotes in this essay have generally been used only for direct quotations. They therefore do not reflect the heavy use I have made of a number of previously published studies in the field of Connecticut history. Albert E. Van Dusen, *Connecticut* (New York: Random House, 1961), was indispensable, providing me with a mine of information on a host of topics. Harold J. Bingham, *History of Connecticut* (4 volumes; New York: Lewis Historical Publishing Company, 1962), was also of great help. My chapter on colonial Connecticut was greatly strengthened by material from Albert E. Van Dusen, *Puritans Against the Wilderness: Connecticut History to 1763* (Chester, Conn.: The Pequot Press, 1975), and from Charles McLean Andrews, *Connecticut's Place in Colonial History* (New Haven, Conn.: Yale University Press, 1924). The chapter on Revolutionary Connecticut was taken in good part from the chapters I contributed to David M. Roth and Freeman Meyer, *From Revolution to Constitution: Connecticut 1763 to 1818* (Chester, Conn.: The Pequot Press, 1975). My treatment of Connecticut in the late eighteenth and first half of the nineteenth centuries owes much to Roth and Meyer, *From Revolution to Constitution;* Janice Law Trecker, *Preachers, Rebels, and Traders: Connecticut 1818 to 1865* (Chester, Conn.: The Pequot Press, 1975); and Jarvis Means Morse, *A Neglected Period of Connecticut's History, 1818–1850* (New Haven, Conn.: Yale University Press, 1933). My survey of Connecticut during the era of the Civil War drew heavily from John Niven, *Connecticut for the Union: The Role of the State in the Civil War* (New Haven, Conn.: Yale University Press, 1965). The chapter on Connecticut from 1865 to 1914 reflects a great deal of material in Ruth O. M. Andersen, *From Yankee to American: Connecticut 1865 to 1914* (Chester, Conn.: The Pequot Press, 1975), and Frederick M. Heath, "Politics and Steady Habits: Issues and Elections in Connecticut, 1894–1914" (unpublished Ph.D.

dissertation, Columbia University, 1965). I could not have dealt adequately with Connecticut in the decades since 1914 without Herbert F. Janick, Jr., *A Diverse People: Connecticut 1914 to the Present* (Chester, Conn.: The Pequot Press, 1975), and the essay on Connecticut in Neal R. Peirce, *The New England States: People, Politics and Power in the Six New England States* (New York: W. W. Norton and Company, 1976).

There are a number of people to whom I have the pleasure of tendering thanks. Gerald George and Timothy C. Jacobson of the American Association for State and Local History were uniformly helpful and supportive. Dr. Charles R. Webb, Jr., the president of Eastern Connecticut State College, contributed much to the completion of this essay by his understanding in relieving me of a series of institutional chores. Dr. J. Parker Huber, a colleague at Eastern Connecticut State College, was a steady source of support during the long months of research and writing. Dr. Albert E. Van Dusen, professor of history at the University of Connecticut at Storrs and the Connecticut state historian since 1952, graciously shared with me his masterful grasp of the main currents and forces in Connecticut history, and both he and his wife Wilda offered the warm encouragement of good friends. Lucy Bartlett Crosbie, the publisher of *The* [Willimantic, Connecticut] *Chronicle* and an enthusiastic student of Connecticut history, provided helpful research tips and thoughtful comments on the manuscript. Anne Alling not only typed the manuscript but did so with tireless good cheer—even during those hectic days when the deadline was approaching. I trust it is understood that none of these good people bears any responsibility for deficiencies in my presentation.

And finally, words alone cannot express my appreciation of the loving encouragement I received from my wife Sandra and my daughter Deborah Anne.

D.M.R.

Connecticut

Introduction:

Historic Connecticut

Connecticut's history, measured by that of most states, is a long one. Moreover, the descendants of many of its original Puritan settlers still live here, and in their names—*Hale, Trumbull, Baldwin, Bulkeley*—the figure of Thomas Hooker still seems to cast a shadow. From the beginnings, caution and conservatism have shaped the Connecticut character and have made its nickname, "The Land of Steady Habits," truly descriptive of life here. Yet not everyone in Connecticut shares either that ancestry or that disposition. In the nineteenth and twentieth centuries, people of decidedly different backgrounds and outlooks joined the scions of old Puritans and Yankees to enrich—and to complicate—the state's history. The author, for one, came only recently; and accordingly, his family tree does not have its roots in Connecticut's Puritan past.

My mother (from Louisville, Kentucky) had roots in Ireland's County Galway, and my father (a New Yorker) traced his family's American beginnings to his parents' participation in the Eastern European rush to the United States at the turn of the century. These two treated their son to the sometimes bewildering but always fascinating experience of growing up in cities in Pennsylvania, New York, Maryland, Delaware, Massachusetts, Kentucky, Illinois, Indiana, and Tennessee. As for Connecticut, my wife and daughter and I came only seventeen years ago—when I was a young academic taking but his second full-time teaching job. I came to teach American history at

Eastern Connecticut State College in Willimantic, and we settled in Mansfield.

In the years since, Connecticut—especially rural, northeastern Connecticut—has had its effect on us. We never lock
our car and often not our home. We think a traffic jam is
when three cars are waiting at a stop sign, and we rarely—even
my impatient, teenage Deborah—honk at the car in front of us
no matter how odd the driver's performance. We have come to
know the mountain laurel on Connecticut's hillsides, the blue
and white violets in the lowlands, and meadows sprinkled with
daisies and buttercups in June. Each autumn we are stunned
again by the spectacular display that the state's foliage pro-
vides—the scarlets of the woodlands blending with the yellow
of goldenrod and the flaming red of sumac. From December
through March we wait for those winter nights after a snowfall
when the sounds of man are muffled and the rest of the world
is remote and almost forgotten. But most of all, we have come
to appreciate the unending riches of the state's historical heritage. Whether one settles in the New York City bedroom communities of Fairfield County, in Yale-dominated New Haven,
in the state capital of Hartford with its array of banks and insurance buildings, in one of the serene, colonial-rooted towns
of Litchfield County, or—as we did—in rural, northeastern
Connecticut (which airline pilots report is one of the relatively
few dark spots at night on the East Coast between Boston and
Washington, D.C.), one is constantly struck by ever-present
reminders of Connecticut's long and unique history.

The towns of western Connecticut, the area between the
Connecticut River and the border of New York State, abound
with historic sites. In Guilford on Long Island Sound is the
Henry Whitfield House, begun in 1639 and said to be the oldest stone house in the United States. Built in late medieval English style and furnished as it was in the seventeenth century,
the Whitfield House spurs the visitor to remember that when
Connecticut was first settled by Englishmen in the 1630s the
only other English habitations in the howling North American
wilderness were in Massachusetts, Rhode Island, Virginia, and

Maryland. In Ansonia in the Naugatuck Valley one finds another seventeenth-century home—that of the Reverend Richard Mansfield. The good pastor tended his flock for over seventy years and in the process established a record of service that Connecticut clergymen then and since have regarded with awe and admiration.

Wethersfield—near Hartford—is a community that is distinguished as one of Connecticut's first towns: one which boasts a cluster of colonial homes including the Webb House, a twin-chimney, gambrel-roofed dwelling. In it General George Washington and the Count de Rochambeau met in 1781 to lay plans for the southern campaign that resulted in the surrender of Cornwallis at Yorktown in 1781. The Glebe House in Woodbury in Litchfield County was the site of another historically important meeting—that in 1783 of ten Anglican clergymen who elected Dr. Samuel Seabury of Ledyard the first Episcopal bishop in the United States.

In East Granby, not far from Connecticut's major air terminal, is Old Newgate Prison. In the early 1770s the Connecticut authorities transformed an abandoned copper mine into what must have been one of the most uncomfortable penal institutions in all of American history. Newgate was used during and after the Revolution to house common criminals, and during the Revolutionary War it also held Tories and captured British troops. As one descends the old mine shaft and creeps along the dark tunnels, it seems that one can almost hear the groans and curses of Newgate's inmates—British and American—who suffered chains, rats, darkness, and a damp cold that must have numbed the soul as well as the body.

In Southbury in New Haven County is the Bullet Hill School. Built in 1778, the school is said to be one of the oldest preserved school buildings in the nation. In the Long Island Sound community of Stratford stands Christ Church, on the top of which is a weathercock that was used for target practice by British officers quartered in the town during the French and Indian War; in East Haven one comes upon the Old Stone Church, which has survived since 1774 despite having been ransacked by the British during the Revolutionary War, hit by a tornado, and subjected to various architectural alterations through the years.

Perhaps one's sense of the state's rich past is most jogged in the western Connecticut cities of New Haven and Hartford. The historical and physical heart of New Haven is the Green, on and around which the city's three-hundred-year history has been acted out. Ringing the Green are three churches, each of which is central to the New Haven experience. Trinity Church (Episcopal), designed by Ithiel Town and built in 1815, is one of the oldest Gothic Revival Churches in the United States; Center Church (United Church of Christ) is a Georgian brick-and-wood building—the third that the congregation built on the Green—which, although built in 1812, has a crypt with 139 stones dating back to 1687; and the United Church (United Church of Christ), which was built in 1814 and remains one of the classic examples in the nation of Georgian colonial church architecture. A few blocks from the Green is the Grove Street Cemetery (1797), one of the first American cemeteries to be laid out in family plots and the resting place of such worthies as Noah Webster, Eli Whitney, and Samuel Morse. On New Haven's outskirts in West Rock Park is the "Judges' Cave," the hiding place in the Restoration Period of two judges —Edward Whalley and William Goffe—who were sought dead or alive by Charles II for their role in the arrest and execution of Charles I in the late 1640s.

But the center of historic New Haven is certainly Yale, founded in 1701, established in New Haven between 1717 and 1719, and after Harvard and William and Mary the third institution of higher education founded in the British colonies in North America. Located north and west of the New Haven Green, Yale consists of a combination of Georgian, Gothic, and "modern" buildings ranging from Connecticut Hall, built in 1752 and the residence of such distinguished Yale graduates as Nathan Hale, Eli Whitney, and Noah Webster, to modern buildings including the School of Art and Architecture designed by Paul Rudolph, Morse and Stiles colleges designed by Eero Saarinen, and Gordon Bunshaft's striking Beinecke

Rare Book and Manuscript Library. As one strolls through the campus it is impossible not to be struck by this awe-inspiring institution that has contributed such a wealth of talent and leadership to Connecticut, the American nation, and the world.

Although not possessing such an intellectually and physically inspiring institution as Yale, the state capital of Hartford boasts sites reflective of Connecticut's rich history. The state capitol, designed by Richard M. Upjohn and completed in 1879 at a cost of two and a half million dollars, is made of New England marble and granite and is topped by a twelve-sided dome finished with gold leaf. Throughout the capitol and its grounds are statues of such Connecticut heroes as Nathan Hale; Thomas Knowlton, the gentleman who commanded the Connecticut troops at the Battle of Bunker Hill and who died during the Battle of Harlem Heights in 1776; and Israel Putnam, who at the Battle of Bunker Hill while commanding the New England troops ordered: "Men, you are all marksmen—don't one of you fire until you see the white [*sic*] of their eyes." The capitol overlooks forty-one-acre Bushnell Park, laid out in 1853 by two Hartford gentlemen: Dr. Horace Bushnell, nineteenth-century Protestant leader who did much to liberalize Congregational thought, and Frederick Law Olmsted, designer of New York City's Central Park and the first landscape architect in the United States.

Across the street from the State Capitol is the Connecticut State Library, an Italian Renaissance structure built in 1910. The west wing of the building houses the Connecticut Supreme Court and the east wing—the Library proper—contains a half-million volumes, two million manuscripts, and a million pamphlets, microfilms, maps, pictures, and other memorabilia. The central wing of the building, Memorial Hall, is the state historical museum. Among the treasures of Memorial Hall are portraits of Connecticut's governors, a Gilbert Stuart painting of Washington, the table on which Lincoln signed the Emancipation Proclamation, a collection of Colt firearms, the original Charter of 1662 that Charles II granted to Connecticut, and the Connecticut constitutions of 1818 and 1965.

Another important historic site in Hartford is the Old State

House, a Charles Bulfinch Federal-style building that served as the Connecticut capitol from 1796 to the 1870s when the Connecticut government sat in alternate years in New Haven and Hartford. Sessions of the constitutional conventions of 1818 and 1965 met in the Old State House, as did the Hartford Convention of 1814, a famous assemblage of disgruntled New England Federalists angry at the Madison Administration during the War of 1812. Also in Hartford—or its suburbs—are the homes of three Connecticut natives or residents who played a telling role in American cultural development: Samuel Clemens (Mark Twain), a resident of Hartford from the 1870s to the 1890s; Litchfield's Harriet Beecher Stowe; and West Hartford's Noah Webster.

In eastern Connecticut, the area between the Connecticut River and the Rhode Island border, one also finds historic sites that pull one back into the past. In Marlborough in Hartford County stands an impressive 1740 tavern that had among its guests Presidents James Monroe and Andrew Jackson, and in Stafford in Tolland County are located springs of sulfur and ironwater that attracted John Adams in 1771. In the town of Enfield on the Connecticut–Massachusetts border, theologian Jonathan Edwards in 1741 sparked the religious revival known as The Great Awakening with a sermon entitled "Sinners in the Hands of An Angry God."

The eastern Connecticut community of Lebanon displays the 1735 home of Jonathan Trumbull, Sr., Connecticut's governor during the Revolutionary era. The Trumbull house, a large central-chimney residence, contains a second-floor study with a window placed high on the wall so that the governor, on whose head the British put a price during the Revolutionary War, would not be picked off by a British or Tory sniper. The town of Columbia, not far from Lebanon, was the original site of the educational institution that ultimately evolved into Dartmouth College. In 1755 the Reverend Eleazer Wheelock began Moor's Indian Charity School. When neither Columbia nor Connecticut proved terribly supportive of the school, Wheelock relocated the enterprise in Hanover, New Hampshire, with the aid of the Earl of Dartmouth.

In Lyme in New London County, towering on a hilltop, is a splendid castle built by actor William Gillette during World War I. The forty-two-room structure built of granite, field-stone, and timber was designed to resemble a Rhine Valley castle. Close by in East Haddam is the restored Goodspeed Opera House. Built in the nineteenth century along the Connecticut River in a period when river steamboats were the rage, Goodspeed brings to mind the restrained elegance of a past age.

New London on the Thames River (pronounced in Connecticut Thaymes, not Tems), each June the scene of the Harvard–Yale regatta, boasts the Shaw Mansion, Captain Nathaniel Shaw's home, which served as the state's naval headquarters during the Revolutionary War; the Nathan Hale Schoolhouse in which the young Yale graduate taught from March 1774 to July 1775 before he joined Washington's forces and was subsequently hanged as a spy by the British in New York City; and a house at 325 Pequot Avenue in which Eugene O'Neill lived and wrote his first plays. Across the Thames from New London in Groton stands Fort Griswold, an American strongpoint attacked by the British on September 6, 1781, during a raid led by the turncoat Benedict Arnold—who himself was born but a few miles up the Thames in Norwich.

Nearby in North Stonington rises Lantern Hill, a 580-foot mass of rock on the top of which the locals burned barrels of tar during the War of 1812 to warn the countryside of the approach of British ships on Long Island Sound. In Stonington itself is Mystic Seaport, a forty-acre site devoted to the celebration of Connecticut's past ties to the sea. Coopers and sailmakers practice their crafts in period buildings and vessels such as the *Charles W. Morgan,* one of the last of the great American wooden whalers, remind one of the state's maritime heritage.

But the historic riches of Connecticut are not restricted to sites and landmarks. It sometimes appears that each of the state's 169 towns treasures a legend or a tale—some of which may even be rooted in fact—that reflects Connecticut's apparently inexhaustible historical lore. In Franklin in eastern

Connecticut one hears of the "Bloody Apple Tree." A Yankee peddler was murdered, his pack looted, and his body found under an apple tree on Michah Rood's farm. According to the tale, the dying peddler drew down a curse on his murderer, Michah Rood. Although no evidence was found which might have served as a basis for Rood's prosecution, the curse did its work. Rood's affairs deteriorated, he died a pauper, and the apple tree under which the peddler's body was found bore fruit whose pulp was stained with red spots.

A far less grisly tale is told in Windham in northeastern Connecticut. It seems that during the French and Indian War of 1756 to 1763—when all Americans were jumpy over Indian forays—a Windham farmer decided to drain his pond. By nightfall, the pond's frogs, left high and dry, began a thundering chorus of complaint that the townspeople took for the whoopings of Indians on the warpath. Men grabbed their muskets, hid away their women and children, and set out trembling to face the dreaded aboriginal enemy. Although everything soon quieted down when the Windhamites discovered the source of the noise, Connecticuters[1] ever since have taken great delight in telling of the quaking Windham farmers thrown into a tizzy by a chorus of bullfrogs. Indeed, as late as the nineteenth century one Connecticut author wrote: "Let a son of Windham penetrate to the uttermost part of the earth, he will find that the story of the frogfight preceeded him." [2]

The townspeople of Meriden in New Haven County take rather perverse pleasure in recounting the legend of the "Black Dog." It is said Meriden's "Hanging Hills," formed by two tilted lava flows, are haunted by a black dog. According to the legend one's first glimpse of the creature, who leaves no tracks in either snow or dirt and is possessed of a soundless howl, will always be followed by two more. The first view of the dog

1. While the word "Connecticuters" is not often used by the people of Connecticut to describe themselves, I shall use it in this volume because the use of phrases such as "the people of Connecticut" and "the residents of Connecticut" constitutes a nuisance, especially for the author.

2. Quotation cited in William Bixby, *Connecticut: A New Guide* (New York: Charles Scribner's Sons, 1974), p. 295.

will result in financial gain. However, the legend relates that things deteriorate badly from this point. A second meeting with the dog will bring illness; a third, death. For the sceptics: one hears in Meriden that several people who have seen the black dog have died mysteriously.

A much more pleasant tale revolves around "Bride's Brook" in East Lyme along the Connecticut shore. The story has it that in 1647 one Jonathan Rudd and his fiancée were awaiting the magistrate who was to marry them when a great blizzard struck. Apparently too eager for marriage to have the ceremony postponed, the couple appealed to Governor John Winthrop in nearby New London to come out to East Lyme and perform the ceremony. Although the good governor assented and made the journey to the restless couple, he was unable to cross a swollen brook in his path. As a result, Winthrop stood on one side of the brook and performed the ceremony while Rudd and his lady stood on the other side and said their vows.

Obviously, however, Connecticut is not alone in boasting a multitude of folk tales and an array of such historic places. Other states, especially in New England and elsewhere along the eastern seaboard, enjoy a rich folk tradition and the physical remains of seventeenth- and eighteenth-century life. I mention these manifestations of Connecticut's past for two reasons. First, because Connecticut is a place where a long past has meant much to its people, and where the traditions, habits, and faith that grew in its three centuries of history still matter to the way people live today. And second, because the richness of Connecticut's past has come to mean much to me. As an American colonial historian, I find Connecticut—with its history-laden atmosphere and its manuscript-filled historical depositories, like the Connecticut Historical Society, the Connecticut State Library, and Yale's Sterling and Beinecke Libraries—an invigorating environment in which to practice my craft. And as a man with decidedly itinerant beginnings, I draw more sustenance from Connecticut's roots than I am willing to admit—at least publicly.

1

Economic Eminence

$\mathcal{T}$HE conservative character that so long marked Connecticut history is only one of the twin themes that together truly describe what the state has been and how it became what it is now. "Yankee inventiveness" is one of the great cliches of American history, but unlike some others ("southern laziness" or "frontier violence," for example), it is one that demonstrates how fact occasionally can outdistance fiction. The people of Connecticut from colonial times onward have distinguished themselves as enthusiastic and talented purveyors to the nation of a variety of goods and services, and consequently contemporary Connecticut occupies an impressively high economic standing among the states of the American union.

As of the mid-1970s, Connecticut had the third-highest percapita income in the nation (after Alaska and Illinois); the lowest percentage of poor people; the highest federal income tax payment; the highest percentage of homes with telephones; the second-highest assessed value of property per person; and the third-highest average of life insurance per family. Connecticut's impressive economic standing is all the more remarkable because the state's enviable statistics can hardly be explained on the basis of its physical endowments.

Take, as a prime example, the weather to which the state is subjected. It is true that the state has a good many clear, comfortable days in all of the four seasons. Moreover, Connecticut certainly does not have the number of 90-degree summer days experienced by most of the central and southern states, nor the consistently brutal winters of the central and northern Midwest. What Connecticut does have is a climate of remarkable changeability that includes some of the most taxing weather known to man.

Perhaps the best characterization of the New England weather of which Connecticut is an often reluctant recipient was given by Samuel Clemens on December 22, 1876, when he was the featured speaker at the seventy-first annual dinner of the New England Society. Clemens lived in Hartford from 1874 to 1891 (because his publisher was there) and there wrote *Huckleberry Finn, Tom Sawyer, The Prince and the Pauper,* and *A Connecticut Yankee in King Arthur's Court.* He demonstrated a rapidly learned understanding of his adopted region by speaking on "New England Weather." He soothed his audience by references to New England's "bewitching" autumn foliage and to its unique ice storms, which left trees sparkling "cold and white, like the Shah of Persia's diamond plume." He went to the heart of his subject when discussing the uncertainty of New England's weather, especially in the spring:

There is a sumptuous variety about the New England weather that compels the stranger's admiration—and regret. The weather is always doing something there; always getting up new designs and trying them on the people to see how they will go. But it gets through more business in spring than in any other season. In the spring I have counted one hundred and thirty-six kinds of weather inside of four and twenty hours. . . . You take up the paper and observe how crisply and confidently [the weatherman] checks off what today's weather is going to be on the Pacific, down South, in the Middle States, in the Wisconsin region. See him sail along in the joy and pride of his power till he gets to New England, and then see his tail drop. *He* doesn't know what the weather is going to be in New England. Well, he mulls over it, and by and by he gets out something about like this: Probable northeast to southwest winds, varying to the southward and westward and eastward, and points between, high and low barometer swapping around from place to place; probable areas of rain, snow, hail, and drought, succeeded or preceded by earthquakes, with thunder and lightning.

> . . . Yes, one of the brightest gems in the New England weather
> is the dazzling uncertainty of it. There is only one thing certain
> about it: you are certain there is going to be plenty of it—a perfect
> grand review; but you can never tell which end of the procession
> is going to move first.[1]

Clemens could afford to make light of that notorious New
England climate perhaps because he made his weather observa-
tions from behind the sturdy brick walls of his Farmington Avenue mansion, a wonder of turrets, balconies, verandas, and
embrasures in which even in the dead of winter one could
enjoy a fountain playing amidst calla lilies and flowering vines;
but most residents of Connecticut—before and since Clemens's
time—would hardly affect such humor in the face of the
weather shenanigans to which the state is subjected.

Tropical storms have been but one of the weather features
that have tested Connecticut. Hurricanes, originating as far
north as Cape Hatteras but usually generated in the Caribbean,
have provided remarkable demonstrations of nature's fury. On
August 23, 1683, a hurricane ripped through the colony
"blasting all the trees" and raising the Connecticut River
twenty-six feet above normal. No less potent was the "New
London Hurricane" of August 30, 1713, "a violent storm of
wind and rain . . . which blew down several buildings and
fruit trees such as hath not been known." The weather diary
for October 20, 1770, of the Reverend Ezra Stiles (who would
serve as the president of Yale from 1778 to 1783) recorded:
"A violent hurricane. Wind N or NE. Rain violent—hail—
vane of church steeple blown off." [2] Nineteenth-century Connecticut experienced its share of havoc-bringing hurricanes, but
those of 1856 and 1893 were perhaps the most memorable.
August 21, 1856, brought the "Charter Oak Storm," so
named because Hartford's Charter Oak—in which, legend has
it, the Connecticut Charter of 1662 was hidden in 1687 when
demanded by Sir Edmund Andros representing the Dominion

1. Quoted in David Ludlum, *The Country Journal New England Weather Book* (Boston: Houghton Mifflin Company, 1976), pp. viii–ix.

2. Quotations cited in Ludlum, *New England Weather Book,* p. 121, p. 41, p. 41.

of New England—snapped off six feet from the ground after standing for three hundred years. The storm of August 24, 1893, was an exceptionally potent one, leveling hundreds of elm trees in New Haven and seriously damaging the tobacco crop in the Connecticut Valley.

Connecticut's hurricanes of the twentieth century, however, have made the previous storms seem rather insignificant. Carol in 1954, Diane in 1955, and Donna in 1960 all left their mark on the state, but *the* hurricane in Connecticut history was that of September 21, 1938. The storm, called "the greatest single event in the meteorological history" of New England,[3] ripped into Connecticut about ten miles west of New Haven and followed the Connecticut Valley northward. The death toll in Connecticut was eighty-five, property loss more than $125 million. The region suffered over six hundred deaths and property damage of almost $400 million.

As memorable and often as destructive as Connecticut's tropical storms have been its brutal winters, which have brought bitter cold and awesome snowfalls. The hardest winter of the seventeenth century was said to be that of 1697–1698. Connecticut was hit by snowstorms from November 20 to April 9 and one observer considered it "the terriblest winter for continuance of frost and snow, and extremity of cold, that was ever known." [4]

That the winter of 1697–1698 was no fluke was proven by Connecticut's experience in the eighteenth century. In 1717 Connecticut was hit by what has been called New England's most legendary storm. The "Great Snow" of that year consisted of four storms between February 27 and March 7 that deposited between three and five feet of snow throughout the region. The winter of 1740–1741 was considered by some more severe than that of 1697–1698 and left central Connecticut buried under three feet of snow. Troops in Connecticut during the Revolutionary War were immobilized in the winter of 1780 when the snow in southern Connecticut was measured

3. Ludlum, *New England Weather Book,* p. 42.
4. Quoted in Ludlum, *New England Weather Book,* p. 121.

at forty-two inches on level ground. Perhaps no other winter snow in eighteenth-century Connecticut was so spectacular as that of early December 1786. At Hamden, near New Haven, five inches fell on December 4–5; nine inches on December 7–8; and eight inches with sleet on December 9–10. Following the snow and sleet, the temperature fell to twelve below zero, leaving the state paralyzed under an unyielding covering of snow and ice.

Throughout the nineteenth and twentieth centuries Connecticut has experienced little relief from winter's frozen displays. There was, for example, the "Cold Friday" of January 19, 1810, when the temperature in the early morning hours dropped from a balmy 41 degrees to a deadly −13 degrees. The first week of January 1835 brought bitter cold to New England, and by January 5 thermometers had plunged to 27 below zero in Hartford. But the most stunning winter phenomenon in nineteenth-century Connecticut was the "Blizzard of '88." Unparalleled in the records of modern New England snowstorms, the storm of March 11–14, 1888, brought a monumental snowfall, gale-force winds, and near-zero cold. The snow, accumulating on the ground at the rate of an inch per hour, fell for more than forty-eight hours, leaving New Haven with forty-six inches and Middletown with fifty inches.

Connecticut's twentieth-century winter annals have been marked by bitter cold weather in December–January, 1917–1918; February 1934; and February 1943, when a night of radiational cooling plunged thermometers to nine below zero in New Haven. Connecticut winters have not lost their kick in the contemporary period, as demonstrated by an awesome ice storm in December 1973. Freezing precipitation for over thirty-six hours slicked over roads, tree branches, and power and telephone lines. As utility lines collapsed under the weight of ice up to one half inch thick, hundreds of thousands of homes were left for almost a week without heat, electricity, and telephone service. The Connecticut Light and Power Company reported 145,000 customers without power, and the Hartford Electric Company had 103,000 customers in the same plight. The Southern New England Telephone Company was swamped with calls for service. It was estimated that the damage to trees was greater than that which occurred during the hurricane of 1938.

Nature, as if to compensate Connecticut for its winter discomfort, has also provided the state with stifling summer heat. The Reverend Ezra Stiles had just set up his thermometer in New Haven in June 1778 when the temperature on successive days stood at 94°, 97°, 95°, and 94°.[5] Other enervating stretches of 90°-plus days were recorded in Connecticut in July 1825, July 1911, June 1925, August 1948, and July 1955. The hottest day known in Connecticut's history took place on August 2, 1975. A northwest wind carried across New England a furiously hot air mass that raised temperatures near Hartford to between 105° and 107°.

As Samuel Clemens intimated in his delightful characterization, a chronicle of Connecticut's weather that mentions only slashing hurricanes, numbing winters, and torrid summers would hardly be giving the state its meteorological due. An adequate survey would have to include some truly extraordinary phenomena—such as the oft-recounted "Dark Day" of May 19, 1780. Ezra Stiles recorded:

there fell . . . a singular and very remarkable Darkness, which overspread the Hemisphere for about five hours. In the morning were showers attended by distant Thunder. About Ten o'clock A.M. a Darkness came on, which by Eleven was perceived to be very unusual and extraordinary, and in half an hour was considered as what was never before seen in these Northern Climates in America. The Darkness became and continued so intense from a little before noon to near Two o'clock, as that persons could not read, and it became necessary to light candles. . . . A little after Two P.M. it became somewhat lighter, but the Darkness soon returned. About Three o'clock it began to go off, and at Four P.M. the Heavens resumed their usual Light as in a cloudy day, although the cloudiness continued all the rest of the Afternoon.[6]

5. This was the notorious heat wave during which the Battle of Monmouth was fought on June 28, 1778, in New Jersey.

6. Quoted in Franklin B. Dexter, ed., *The Literary Diary of Ezra Stiles,* 3 volumes (New York: Charles Scribners' Sons, 1901), 2:424–425.

Eighteenth-century Connecticuters, who were terrified by their darkness at noon and quite understandably feared that the end of the world was at hand, did not have the benefit of the analysis of modern meteorologists who have concluded that the legendary "Dark Day" was the result of smoke from western forest fires obscuring the sun's rays.

Although there has perhaps been nothing in Connecticut's meteorological history to rival the mystery of the "Dark Day," there have been other indications of the state's unique weather. Take, for example, the "Wallingford Tornado" of August 1878: a powerful tornado—a rarity in the Northeast—ripped through the north side of Wallingford, near New Haven, destroying a church, killing thirty-four, injuring over one hundred, and causing damage of $200,000. Drought conditions have periodically plagued Connecticut since the colonial period. Particularly severe droughts—causing fires among field crops and woodlands—hit Connecticut in 1749 and 1762, and in the twentieth century the state was hard hit in 1929–1933, the early 1940s, 1948–1950, and 1956–1957. The worst drought in modern Connecticut took place from 1963 to 1966, when the crop yield was seriously hurt, the forest-fire hazard was high, and water for human and industrial use was so scarce that it was rationed.

No catalog of Connecticut's unique weather events would be complete without the flood of 1936. Through the winter of 1935–1936 the state was held fast by a coating of snow and ice. Then, between March 9 and 22, the state experienced rising temperatures and a series of downpours. Melting snow, thawing ice, and rainwater were too much for ice-jammed waterways to take. Dams were smashed, bridges battered and demolished, factories destroyed, and highways and railroads cut by rampaging water. Hartford, on the Connecticut River, had water almost nine feet higher than at any time in the city's three-hundred-year history, and the downtown commercial area was inundated. Damage from the flooding was estimated at over $100 million throughout New England, although loss of life was small because of early warnings.

Such weather as I have described—and in some instances suffered through—has obviously not been a feature of Connecticut life that has contributed to the state's prosperity. Yet it must be pointed out that Connecticut's weather is an important element in the social life of the state's population. In offices, factories, schools—wherever people congregate—a Connecticuter will invariably begin a conversation with: "Well, how do you like this for weather?" But all of this bantering about the weather hides a quiet pride the Connecticuter has in his ability to withstand the worst of weather. "The Yankee's survival in his isolated war against the elements has . . . given him his special tight-lipped and proud aloofness; he feels slightly superior to people who have not been toughened by such a rigorous exposure." [7]

Nor has Connecticut been blessed—by nature or man—with respect to its size. It is a small state. From east to west it extends but ninety-five miles, from north to south about sixty miles. Its area of 5,009 square miles—bounded on the north by Massachusetts, on the east by Rhode Island, on the south by Long Island Sound, and on the west by New York—makes Connecticut the third-smallest state in the Union, just ahead of Rhode Island and Delaware. Indeed, Connecticut could be placed in Texas some fifty-three times. Moreover, all its land borders have been sources of contention with its neighbors.

Connecticut and Massachusetts were at odds over their border for some 185 years. The two colonies attempted unsuccessfully to resolve the issue in 1642, 1649, 1695, 1702, 1713, 1716, and 1724. By the 1740s the principal point of contention was whether the towns of Woodstock, Suffield, Enfield, and Somers were to be under the jurisdiction of Connecticut or Massachusetts. Disliking the higher taxes of Massachusetts, the four towns in 1724 and 1747 petitioned Connecticut for admission. The Connecticut General Assembly appointed a committee of distinguished statesmen to meet with representatives of Massachusetts to resolve the matter. But Massachusetts, probably recognizing that it had nothing to look forward to from talks with Connecticut but the possible loss of

---

7. Joe McCarthy, *New England* (New York: Time Incorporated, 1967), p. 11.

the four towns, refused to negotiate. Finally in 1749 the Assembly voted to accept the four towns and once again gave Massachusetts the opportunity to negotiate. The Bay State continued its objections until 1800, when it ceased to complain of Connecticut's incorporation of the four border communities. Peace officially came to the Connecticut–Massachusetts border in 1827 when the claims of Southwick, Massachusetts, to parts of Granby and Suffield were adjusted and minor changes were made on the boundary to the east.

Colonial Connecticut experienced more serious boundary difficulties with Rhode Island. The root of the problem was the Charter of 1662 granted to Connecticut by Charles II, which provided for an eastern boundary at "the Narragansett River, commonly called Narragansett Bay, where the said river falleth into the sea"—thus ceding to Connecticut nearly all of Rhode Island. John Winthrop, Jr., who had secured the charter, shared with his fellow Connecticuters a hearty dislike for non-Puritan Rhode Island and thus agreed with a Rhode Island representative that the boundary between the two colonies would in fact be at the Pawcatuck River. Various attempts in the 1660s and 1670s to nail down the border came to nothing. The issue flared in the 1680s when Rhode Island arrested Stephen Richardson, a Connecticut constable who was exercising his authority in Westerly. Connecticut in turn seized one Joseph Clarke, a Rhode Islander, in Westerly. Through the next forty years English commissioners, the royal governor of the Dominion of New England, and the Earl of Bellomont of New York all failed to bring the disputants successfully to the conference table. Finally in 1720 the British Board of Trade, disgusted at the Connecticut–Rhode Island contention, recommended that both colonies lose their charters and be annexed to New Hampshire. Such a shocking prospect apparently cooled both parties, and ultimately in 1742 Connecticut and Rhode Island accepted the Pawcatuck as their common border.

Connecticut's most serious boundary dispute involved New York. When the English took New Netherland from the Dutch in the 1660s, Charles II granted the newly acquired colony of New York to his brother James, Duke of York, and included the land from the Connecticut River to Delaware Bay. This arrangement would have left Connecticut only a narrow strip of land east of the Connecticut River. In May 1675 Sir Edmund Andros, the royal governor of New York, demanded Connecticut's concession of the land west of the Connecticut River, and the following July he appeared at Saybrook to reinforce his claim. When Captain Thomas Bull and two companies of the Connecticut Militia contested his claim, the governor withdrew. By 1683, when Thomas Dongan was New York's governor, an agreement was worked out between New York and Connecticut that set the boundary twenty miles east of and parallel to the Hudson River. Controversy continued nonetheless over the exact placement of the boundary, and not until 1881 did New York, Connecticut, and Congress settle on a line between Connecticut and the Empire State.

Although Connecticut settled its boundary disputes with little damage to itself, the state was left with a relatively small amount of land—and, more important, land that has little potential for economic exploitation.

The state's economic success has certainly not been determined by mineral wealth. While Connecticut has had garnet and iron mines in Roxbury; nickel mines in Litchfield; iron mines at Salisbury; copper mines at Granby, Bristol, and Cheshire; brownstone works at Portland; and granite quarries at Roxbury, such enterprises have never played a decisive role in the state's economy. Currently, Connecticut's mineral resources are limited to lime and silica used to make low-grade glass.

Nor has Connecticut been blessed with a substantial amount of fertile farmland. It is ironic that the first English settlers in Connecticut in the 1630s were lured by the rich bottomland of the Connecticut River Valley, for land so fertile is not common in the state. Adjacent to Connecticut's central lowland, of which the Connecticut and Housatonic river valleys are a part, are the western and eastern highlands. These ranges of north–south hills—rising 1,300 feet in northeastern Connecticut and 2,380 feet on Mount Frissel in Salisbury in northwestern Connecticut—provide lovely scenery; but the rugged, heavily forested land with thin soils, strewn with stones and boulders, has never proven very useful for tillage.

Connecticut's paucity of fertile farmland presented no great problems in the seventeenth and first half of the eighteenth centuries. Connecticut's small population managed very well with the land available. Farmers grew corn, rye, oats, barley, and the vegetables that constituted an important part of the colonial diet: beans, peas, squash, turnips, and pumpkins. Wethersfield specialized in onions, and settlers in the Connecticut River Valley were well on their way to becoming noted cultivators of tobacco. About 1750 a good many Connecticuters shifted from tillage to the raising of livestock in order to satisfy expanding markets in the West Indies and mainland colonies.

In the last half of the eighteenth century, however, Connecticut began to experience problems because of its scanty agricultural resources. The population rose from 130,000 in 1756 to over 250,000 in 1800. Large families constituted the principal factor in the state's population growth. "Travelers passing houses frequently noticed ten or twelve little heads peeping out of doors and windows. According to some writers, eight to twenty children to a family were not uncommon." [8] The resultant division of the state's better farmland among numerous heirs brought a falling standard of living, for it is a basic economic maxim that: "As more labor is applied to the same area of land, the soil cultivated tends to yield less." [9] In addition, more and more people were forced onto the rugged and hilly land of northwestern and northeastern Connecticut, and the cultivation of this marginal or submarginal land added little to the state's agricultural viability.

As late-eighteenth-century Connecticut was confronted with inadequate fertile land for an expanding population, it also became evident that despite the efforts of agricultural reformers such as Killingworth's Jared Eliot (1685–1763), Connecticut's colonial agricultural practices had left a good portion of the state's soil exhausted and of little use. As Timothy Dwight described the situation:

8. Albert Laverne Olson, *Agricultural Economy and the Population in Eighteenth-Century Connecticut*. Tercentenary Commission of the State of Connecticut, Pamphlet Number 40 (New Haven: Yale University Press, 1935), p. 18.

9. Quoted in Olson, *Agricultural Economy*, p. 26.

The husbandry of New-England is far inferior to that of Great
Britain. . . . The principal defects in our husbandry . . . are a
deficiency in the quantity of labor, necessary to prepare the ground
for seed; insufficient manuring; the want of a good rotation of crops;
and slovenliness in cleaning the ground. The soil is not sufficiently
pulverized; nor sufficiently manured. We are generally ignorant of
what crops will best succeed each other; and our fields are covered
with a rank growth of weeds.[10]

Repercussions from Connecticut's dismal agricultural situation at the beginning of the nineteenth century were many.
Thousands of Connecticuters, unable to afford good farmland
and incapable of supporting their families on the hilly terrain of
the western, northern, and eastern portions of the state, quit the
game altogether and participated in a mass migration from Connecticut. Those who stayed on the land in Connecticut fought
the soil for a living but were hard pressed to compete with the
products of western virgin lands, particularly during the era of
rapid expansion of canals, railroads, and highways throughout
the nineteenth and twentieth centuries. Statistics for the period
since World War II reveal the relative insignificance of agriculture in the state's contemporary economic framework. Connecticut farms decreased from 22,241 in 1945 to some 4,490 in
1969; and although Connecticut's gross state product in the
early 1970s was over $20 billion, farm sales were only $200
million—based generally on poultry and dairy products and the
tobacco production of the Connecticut River Valley, which accounts currently for wrappers for about ninety percent of the
eight billion cigars smoked each year in the United States.

The most significant repercussion of Connecticut's paucity of
fertile farmland in the late eighteenth and early nineteenth centuries was a recognition that Connecticuters would have to effect economic diversification if the state were not to become a
wasteland. Of course the thrust toward diversification did not
begin all at once at the turn of the nineteenth century. From the
beginning of the colony Connecticuters turned to a variety of
pursuits with great flair and success.

10. Quotation cited in Albert Van Dusen, *Connecticut* (New York: Random House,
1961), p. 112.

Trade began when farmers with a surplus exchanged their stock or grain with shopkeepers and sea captains for a variety of goods: lace, salt and pepper, sugar, paper, pots and pans, needles, knives, thimbles, buckles, tea, buttons, spectacles, combs, and cord. By the eighteenth century, when farmers were regularly producing a surplus, the colony had spawned a host of merchants who traded Connecticut beef, pork, hay, oats, bread, hoops, and staves in Boston, Providence, Newport, New York, Halifax, Salem, Nantucket, Philadelphia, Annapolis, and the Carolinas. A particularly lucrative commerce was trade with the West Indies. Up until 1800, when Connecticut's West Indian trade began a slip from which it never recovered, its citizens traded their agricultural surpluses and wood products for molasses, sugar, salt, and tropical fruits.

Other Connecticuters either gave up agriculture entirely or supplemented their agricultural incomes by turning to shipbuilding. Utilizing Connecticut's stands of oak, pine, and spruce, shipbuilders emerged in the seventeenth century and flourished in the eighteenth century in towns such as Branford, Guilford, Glastonbury, Hartford, Middletown, New Haven, Rocky Hill, and Stratford. In the nineteenth century the village of Mystic developed as the center of the state's shipbuilding industry. Shipbuilders like Charles Mallory and George Greenman produced ships for the sealing and whaling fleets and constructed famous packets and clipper ships. During the Civil War Mystic builders launched more than 30,000 tons of shipping for the Union Navy, including over fifty steamers.

The most hardy of nonagricultural occupations adopted by early Connecticuters was whaling. From the early eighteenth century until after the Civil War, when American whaling declined, whalers cleared from Connecticut ports such as Bridgeport, East Haddam, Mystic, New Haven, and Stonington. In the 1840s and 1850s, the heyday of American whaling, New London ranked behind only New Bedford and Nantucket among American whaling ports. Between 1784 and 1876 over 800 whalers cleared from New London. Whaling voyages were financed by sharp businessmen who saw profits to be acquired from whale oil, spermaceti candles, and whalebone. The

whalers were manned up until the 1820s by adventure-hungry
New England Yankees and later—as the demand for whalemen
increased—by Indians, blacks, Portuguese, and Pacific is-
landers. Undaunted by low pay, miserable food, and iron-tough
captains and mates, Connecticut whalemen faced disaster from
killer whales, rough seas, and ice floes—and in the process
wrote a unique chapter in American maritime history. Although
the last Connecticut whaling voyage was in 1909, Connecticuters still drawn to the state's whaling past visit Mystic Seaport
to study its artifacts.

Connecticut's most successful attempt at economic diversification—the one most clearly related to the state's agricultural
problems in the late eighteenth and early nineteenth centuries,
as well as the foundation of Connecticut's contemporary economic eminence—was manufacturing. An idea of what Connecticut achieved in the field of manufacturing in the nineteenth
century was provided by William A. Countryman, a former editor of the Hartford *Post,* who was a statistician in the Census
Bureau in Washington in 1902 when he wrote:

I have been much pleased as a native and citizen of Connecticut,
now residing in Washington, D.C., to observe the evidence on
every hand of the importance of our state as a manufacturing center.
At my boarding-house I find the plated ware to be of Connecticut
manufacture. The clock that tells me the time from the mantelpiece;
the watch my friend carries; the hat he wears; his pocket knife, are
all from Connecticut. At the office I write with a Connecticut pen
and when I need an official envelope I find that the original package
from which I take it bears a Connecticut mark. If I make an error
and wish to erase it, I do so with a steel eraser made in Connecticut,
and my letter finished I deposit in a corner letter box, stamped
"New Britain, Conn." This letter I am sure, when it reaches its
destination, is delivered from a post-office box locked with a Yale
key. My desk has a Connecticut lock and key although perhaps
made in Michigan. In looking about the city I am attracted to a
shopwindow glittering with swords, and read on an ugly looking
machette this inscription: "Hartford, Conn., U.S.A." A Winchester
or a Marlin rifle, or a Colt's revolver, all made in Connecticut, I
find in another window, and in still another a supply of fixed
ammunition from New Haven and Bridgeport. Axes, hammers,

augurs, all kinds of builders' hardware, and in a shop close by—all made in Connecticut. Foulards, cottons, woolens, worsteds, rubber goods of all kinds, are near by—they are standard makes from Connecticut. The gas and electric fixtures that show them off are of our manufacture, I doubt not. Do I want a button? Made in Connecticut. "Hand me a pin." The box tells me it is from "Waterbury, Conn., U.S.A." That automobile rushing by came from Connecticut. That bicycle, those tires, these novel call and door bells—all from Connecticut. Typewriters on every side from our little state. And if I lounge through residential streets summer evenings, I hear from many open doors and windows the sound of music. This may not be from a Connecticut piano, although in most cases the ivory keys would be found to have been made in our state, but in many instances emanates from a Connecticut-made gramaphone or phonograph. And what of the sewing machine? Everybody knows that the earliest ones were made in Connecticut, and the latest improved are made there now in great numbers. And last let me say that where my trousers are put away at night they go into a hanger of the best kind—made in Connecticut. This is really a brief catalogue of the glories of Connecticut seen in its manufactures.[11]

The key to Connecticut's emergence in the nineteenth century as a manufacturing giant was a remarkable inventiveness on the part of its Yankee sons. That inventiveness, like many things in Connecticut, is easier to describe than to explain. Perhaps, as Samuel Goodrich asserted in his *Memoirs* in 1856, the explanation can be traced to the Connecticuter's fondness for whittling:

For my own part, I can testify that during my youthful days, I found the penknife a source of great amusement and even of instruction. Many a long winter evening, many a dull, drizzly day . . . have I spent in great ecstasy, making candle-rods, or some other simple article of household goods, for my mother, or in perfecting toys for myself and my young friends, or perhaps in attempts at more ambitious achievements. . . . My mind was stimulated to inquire into the mechanical powers, and my hand was educated to mechanical dexterity.[12]

11. Quoted in Ruth O. M. Andersen, *From Yankee to American: Connecticut 1865 to 1914* (Chester: The Pequot Press, 1975), pp. 43–44.
12. Quoted in David M. Roth and Freeman Meyer, *From Revolution to Constitution: Connecticut 1763 to 1818* (Chester: The Pequot Press, 1975), pp. 71–72.

Or perhaps the explanation for the inventiveness of the Connect-icuter was simply that the Yankee hated the drudgery that made up so much of his life. In an attempt to escape it he tinkered endlessly and came up with "some clever contrivance that would do a distasteful chore quicker and better than the old method—shaping a lighter cradle for mowing wheat, making a gadget for paring apples, cracking nuts, or shelling corn, build-ing a hand-cranked blower for winnowing grain, putting together a tougher horse harness, devising a pump to make water-drawing easier." [13] Whatever the explanation, Connecti-cuters early manifested an inventiveness that would figure sub-stantially in the state's nineteenth-century transformation from a sleepy, agrarian society into a bustling, manufacturing giant.

David Bushnell, of Westbrook, as a student at Yale had con-tended with his professors that it was possible to destroy ships by exploding gunpowder under water. Undaunted by ridicule during the Revolution, he built a strange product that resembled two turtle shells placed together. The "vessel," capable of as-cending and descending by the use of a foot-operated valve to admit and eject water, was armed with a torpedo that could be screwed into the hull of a ship. Although Bushnell's "Turtle" failed in attempts to destroy British ships in Boston Harbor, New York Harbor, and the Delaware River, he had taken the first steps toward the development of the submarine. Two later Connecticuters, John P. Holland and Simon Lake, contributed to the design of submarines that were adopted by the United States Navy in 1900 and 1912. Also in 1912, the New London Ship and Engine Company of Groton made the first use of the Diesel engine for submarines.

Connecticut became the original home of the American rub-ber industry as a result of the successful vulcanizing process worked out by Charles Goodyear. As he grew up watching his New Haven father tinker with and improve upon various farm tools, Goodyear became obsessed with finding a substance that would keep rubber from melting in summer and freezing in win-ter. Plagued by family debts, Goodyear was in and out of

13. W. Storrs Lee, *The Yankees of Connecticut* (New York: Henry Holt and Com-pany, 1957), p. 110.

debtor's prison most of his life but nevertheless managed to continue to experiment. In 1843 he hit upon the vulcanizing process that was the basis for the evolution of the Goodyear Tire and Rubber Company.

The American brass industry had its roots along the Mad River in Waterbury in the Naugatuck Valley. Between 1806 and 1809 Abel Porter and Company made the first successful castings of brass bars. The firm, bought out in 1811 by Frederick Leavenworth, James Scovill, and James Mitchell Lamson Scovill, evolved by 1850 into the Scovill Manufacturing Company, whose brass sheet output in 1860 was 663,000 pounds. The giant International Silver Company of Meriden, which was formed in 1898, developed from the efforts of Connecticut silvermakers such as Asa, Simeon, and William Rogers, who in 1847 devised a method of silver plating.

The roll of Connecticut's premier inventors and manufacturers goes on and on. John Fitch of South Windsor in 1787 built the first steamboat to make a successful trip. Dr. John I. Howe ended the shaping of pins by hand with a pinmaking machine in 1832. Glastonbury's J. B. Williams in 1840 sold the first American soap made exclusively for shaving. In 1858 Eli Whitney Blake developed a stone-crusher that has been used in road building ever since. Alonzo House of Bridgeport produced a steam-propelled horseless carriage in 1866. Linus Yale, Sr., and Linus Yale, Jr., led in the development of flat-keyed, dial, and combination locks that served as the basis for the Yale and Towne Manufacturing Company, formed in 1869. In the 1880s Frank J. Sprague of Milford was responsible for a series of inventions that led to the building of the first American street railway in Richmond, Virginia. William Gray in 1889 patented the first coin-operated telephone.

No discussion of Connecticut's inventive genius would be complete without reference to the towering figure of Eli Whitney, often called "the father of American technology." Born in Westboro, Massachusetts, in 1765, Whitney as a young man was an undistinguished scholar whose only enthusiasm was working in his father's shop with tools and a turning lathe. During the Revolutionary War at the age of fifteen he manufactured nails and, when after the war the demand for nails fell off, he monopolized the production of hatpins in central Massachusetts. After teaching school to obtain funds for college, he entered Yale at age twenty-three in 1789. Graduating in 1792, he went south to work as a tutor and to read law. While visiting with the widow and family of General Nathanael Greene of Revolutionary War fame, Whitney learned that southern agricultural development could be facilitated by a machine that would clean short-staple upland cotton. Within ten days Whitney designed the cotton gin to do the job and thus changed the course of both southern and American history. Whitney's cotton gin resulted in a tremendous leap in cotton production and a predictable expansion of the South's utilization of slave labor. As for Whitney, he reaped perhaps a total of $90,000 from his invention and spent years immersed in patent infringement suits. Regarding one of the trials in which he was involved, Whitney wrote: "I had great difficulty in proving that the machine had ever been used in Georgia, although at the same moment, there were three separate sets of this machinery in motion within fifty yards of the building in which the court sat, and all so near that the rattling of the wheels was distinctly heard on the steps of the courthouse." [14] Whitney did not waste his life immersed in lawsuits over his claim to the invention of the cotton gin. From the late 1790s until his death in 1825 he operated a firearms factory near New Haven, where he devised the system of interchangeable parts. Whitney's concept, the basis for modern American mass production, was later used in the production of Isaac Singer's sewing machine and Cyrus McCormick's reaper and was the crucial element in the evolution of Connecticut's firearms industry.

The list of Connecticut's firearms manufacturers reads like a *Who's Who* of the industry. While Whitney began to produce muskets for the federal government at his factory near New Haven, at Middletown in 1799 Simeon North began to fill government requests for arms. By 1853 North had supplied Washington with 50,000 pistols and 33,000 rifles. Horace Smith and

14. Quoted in Lee, *The Yankees of Connecticut*, p. 112.

Daniel Wesson of Norwich, skilled in the production of repeating firearms, played a role in the evolution of the Winchester Company of New Haven, whose "Winchester" became famous around the globe. Samuel Sharps invented a breech-loading rifle and subsequently opened a factory in Hartford in 1851. But the premier firearms manufacturer of nineteenth-century Connecticut was Samuel Colt, whose "Peacemaker" had such an impact on the winning of the West in the decades after the Civil War.

Colt, born in Hartford in 1814, weathered early years wracked by his father's business failure, his mother's death from consumption, and his own checkered attempts to emerge as a leading entrepreneur. Finally, utilizing Whitney's system of interchangeable parts and a program of aggressive promotion in the United States and abroad, he was able to build a great armory in Hartford in 1855. A 250-horsepower steam engine drove some 400 machines that allowed him to turn out 250 guns a day by 1857. Although Colt drove himself to a premature death in 1862, during the Civil War his armory turned out almost 400,000 revolvers, 6,500 rifles, and 114,000 muskets.

Another Connecticut industry that owed much to the system of interchangeable parts was clockmaking. Eli Terry, who did for clockmaking what Whitney did for the arms industry, was born in East Windsor. In 1793 he opened a shop in Plymouth where he made brass and wooden clocks that he sold door to door. By 1808 Terry had developed machines run by water power to do much labor formerly done by hand, and in 1816 he obtained a patent for a thirty-hour wood-movement shelf clock that could be sold far more cheaply than hand-produced, taller models. Further strides in the production of inexpensive clocks were made between 1818 and 1832 by Joseph Ives of Bristol, who was noted for the development of an eight-day rolled-brass movement. By the mid-nineteenth century Connecticut clockmaking firms such as Seth Thomas of Plymouth, William L. Gilbert of Winsted, E. N. Welch of Bristol, and the New Haven Clock Company dominated the American clockmaking industry with an annual production of 400,000 clocks.

While such manufacturing eminence was in great measure the result of the inventiveness of Connecticut's sons, the state's emergence as a manufacturing giant was based on other factors as well. From the early nineteenth century to World War I Connecticut was able to develop adequate transportation facilities to distribute its products and to transport coal when water power was no longer sufficient to drive its machines. In the first half of the nineteenth century Connecticut's transportation needs were served by plank toll roads; the Farmington Canal, which between 1835 and 1847 connected New Haven to Northampton, Massachusetts; and steamboats that operated on the Connecticut River and on Long Island Sound. Although the steamboats were to continue to operate until the 1930s, the last half of the nineteenth century saw Connecticut transportation dominated by railroads. Hartford and New Haven were connected in 1839; the New Haven line was completed to Northampton, Massachusetts, in 1856; the Housatonic Railroad linked Bridgeport to the Massachusetts Western Railroad in 1842; the New Haven and Hartford line was extended to Springfield, Massachusetts, in 1844; and in the 1840s and 1850s a network of lines connected Hartford with such eastern Connecticut communities as Manchester, Willimantic, Plainfield, Putnam, Norwich, and New London. The giant in Connecticut railroading was the New York, New Haven, and Hartford Railroad, which between the 1880s and World War I expanded to include competing railroad lines as well as coastal freight and passenger boat lines.

Another factor in the expansion of Connecticut manufacturing was the growth of capital in the state, as reflected in the emergence of banks and insurance companies. Banks were begun in Hartford and New London in 1792, in New Haven and Middletown in 1795, and in Norwich and Bridgeport between 1795 and 1805. By 1850 the state had forty-three commercial banks and fifteen savings banks; by 1974 the state's 169 towns had more than 175 banks. Connecticut's eminence in the insurance industry and Hartford's title of the "insurance capital" of the nation can be traced to the 1790s, when Hartford businessmen agreed to bear a portion of a shipowner's financial risks in return for a share of the profits. The first insurance company as such was formed in Norwich in 1795 and provided protection for losses from fire. Soon afterward, marine insurance companies were established in New Haven (1797); in Hartford, Middletown, and Norwich (1803); and in New London (1805). The state's oldest active fire-insurance company is the Hartford Fire Insurance Company, formed in 1810. The firm, as well as Hartford's reputation, was strengthened by the company's response to the New York fire of December 1835, which destroyed hundreds of buildings:

> When the news reached Hartford, Eliphalet Terry, president of Hartford Fire Insurance Company, rushed to the Hartford Bank, obtained a blanket promise to honor all drafts which he might make on his company, and in turn pledged his personal fortune as security. Going to New York on a sleigh in below-zero temperatures, he found that most insurance companies had collapsed and the populace was demoralized. Terry immediately announced that his company would pay every just claim in full. He also opened his books for new business. In response, he was deluged with applications. The Hartford Company was well on the road to booming prosperity. In the process, it had greatly boosted Hartford's reputation as the best place to obtain insurance.[15]

Since the mid-nineteenth century scores of fire, life, and multiple-line insurance companies have located in Hartford, including Aetna and the Travelers. As of 1974 there were forty-six national insurance companies centered in Connecticut with assets of some $40,000,000,000.

Thus, utilizing the inventive genius of its sons, varied transportation developments and the capital of its banks and insurance companies, and eventually with massive numbers of immigrants to supply needed labor, Connecticut emerged in the nineteenth century as a bustling manufacturing center. Its manufacturing eminence has continued into the twentieth century. In the 1970s Connecticut was first in the nation in the number of people employed in the manufacture of aircraft engines and parts, submarines, bearings, and helicopters. Connecticut was second in workers involved in the production of typewriters, office machines, and electrical equipment; third in the manufacture of hardware, guns and ammunition, optical instruments, and watches and clocks.

15. Van Dusen, *Connecticut*, p. 331.

Yet, a curious feature of Connecticut is that the inventiveness that the state has demonstrated in the factory and the laboratory has not generally been visible in its political history. While Connecticut has certainly had its share of social and political mavericks, a goodly number of political upheavals, and a truly unique record of integrating ethnics into the political structure, the state's history, as we shall see in the remaining chapters of this volume, is essentially a tale revolving around the retention of a conservative political atmosphere. Puritanism and the Congregational Church; mass population emigrations—especially in the late eighteenth and early nineteenth centuries; rural domination of the General Assembly; and the assumption of conservative political patterns by ethnics integrated into the body politic have all contributed to the establishment and maintenance of a political order characterized principally by a respect for order and stability and a marked fiscal cautiousness.

2

Colonial Connecticut

$\mathcal{T}$HE chronicles of the American colonial era—the period between the founding of Jamestown in 1607 and the Treaty of Paris of 1763, which ended the French and Indian War—abound with spectacular occurrences in almost every American colony. One thinks, for example, of John Smith's heroics and Bacon's Rebellion in Virginia; of the rise of John Coode's Protestant Association in Maryland; of the "Regulators" in North Carolina; of Leisler's Revolt in New York; and of the controversies surrounding Roger Williams, Anne Hutchinson, and suspected witches in Massachusetts Bay. Yet, as one examines the annals of "His Majesty's Colony of Connecticut," one finds little that could be termed "spectacular" or even dramatic. Except for a hair-raising—in literal terms—confrontation with the Pequot Indians in the 1630s, Connecticut's colonial history rather reveals a remarkable placidity. Throughout its colonial career Connecticut was a small, conservative, agricultural society essentially isolated from the main currents and forces of the Anglo-American world. Connecticut was indeed—as so many of its historians have pointed out—a "Land of Steady Habits." That such was the case was largely due to the colony's commitment to Puritanism. For Connecticut, it must always be remembered, was an English colony whose settlement and development were rooted in that stern Puritan faith introduced and sustained by its founders and subsequent leaders.

Puritanism was a response to the limited nature of England's Reformation in the sixteenth century. The Anglican Church, which was created in 1534 when Henry VIII broke from Rome over the issue of his marriage to Catherine of Aragon, differed little in structure or dogma from the Roman Catholic Church. Henry replaced the Pope as the head of the ecclesiastical system and introduced an English version of the Bible; but he did not move toward called-for Protestant reforms like altering the sacramental system and rejecting medieval Catholic innovations such as the invocation of saints, a complicated liturgy, and the veneration of relics. During the reign of Edward VI (1547–1553), however, a more distinct move toward Protestantism was effected—priests were permitted to marry; images were abolished; the sacraments were repudiated except for Baptism and the Lord's Supper; and the Anglican Church replaced the Catholic conception of salvation through works with the Lutheran doctrine of salvation by faith. These Protestant reforms were obliterated when Queen Mary (1553–1558) returned England to Catholicism and the Roman fold; and even when England was guided back to Protestantism under Elizabeth (1558–1603), the Anglican Church that was revived was not sufficiently "cleansed" of Catholic remnants to satisfy England's most ardent Protestants—the Puritans.

The Puritans sought to complete the Reformation by demonstrating that salvation could be achieved only by returning to the simplicity of the early Christian Church and the truth of God as revealed in the Bible. A break from the Roman Catholic Church, the Puritans believed, had been imperative. Catholicism had burdened Christianity over the centuries with a complicated liturgy, incense, vestments, stained-glass windows, adoration of saints, veneration of relics, and a hierarchy of bishops at the head of which was the Pope. But the Anglican Church constructed by Elizabeth was viewed by the Puritans as little better.

Elizabeth had made the Church Protestant, but the "Elizabethan Compromise" effected by 1570 had resulted in an Anglican Church that retained the episcopal form of organization and much of Catholic ritual. The Puritans sought to rid the Anglican Church of episcopal government and to develop worship composed of plain services, with substantial study of the Bible and tough-minded sermons on moral duty. The prospects for Puritan reform of the Anglican Church, however, were not bright. Elizabeth, fearing that her cherished kingdom would be wracked by sectarian strife, refused to satisfy determined Puritans or uncompromising Catholics. Her reign brought repression of Puritans as well as the hounding of Jesuits into "priest-holes" on the estates of Catholic county squires.

The situation of the Puritans hardly improved under the Stuarts—James I (1603–1625) and Charles I (1625–1649). At the Hampton Court Conference in 1604, James I, enraged at a Puritan request for a reform of the episcopal form of church organization, shouted "No Bishop, No King" and threatened to harry out of the land all those who did not conform to the Anglican Church. Puritan ministers were instructed to accept the ceremonies and trappings of the Established Church or give up their positions. Charles I was equally committed to the unreformed Anglican Church and punished those Puritans who spoke in protest. Puritan ministers were deprived of their pulpits, and Puritan writings were banned. At the same time, Charles's taxation policies fell heavily upon the Puritan middle class, strongest in the eastern and southern counties of England. As a result, English Puritans by the late 1620s and early 1630s were convinced that England and its Established Church were not capable of redemption. Facing an unreformed church and an arbitrary government, the Puritans looked abroad to the New World as a site on which to complete the work of the Lord.

After selecting New England for their colonizing activity, the Puritans formed the Massachusetts Bay Company and by a shrewd maneuver secured from Charles I a charter to the land between the Merrimac and Charles rivers. Between 1630 and the outbreak of the Puritan Revolution in England in 1642, over twenty thousand Puritans in some two hundred ships made the treacherous Atlantic crossing to New England. Although the major thrust of the Puritan migration was along the shores of Massachusetts Bay and nearly thirty miles into the interior, the concern here will be with those hardy Puritans who left the relative security of Massachusetts Bay to settle in the area the Indians called Quinnehtukqut—''Beside the Long Tidal River.''

While Rhode Island was settled by Massachusetts Bay Puritans—such as Roger Williams and Anne Hutchinson—who did not find the theocratic atmosphere of the Bay Colony congenial, Connecticut's early communities were planted by orthodox Puritans who were very much in accord in matters of faith with their former neighbors in Massachusetts. It appears that the first Connecticuters were displeased only by the limited economic opportunities in and around Boston. The first Puritan thrust from Massachusetts Bay into Connecticut was undertaken by Bay residents of Watertown, Dorchester, and Cambridge who found the quantity and lushness of the land in the Connecticut River Valley far superior to that in their former communities. By the mid-1630s settlements had been established in Windsor, Wethersfield, and Hartford, and the Reverend Thomas Hooker—the guiding force behind the settlement at Hartford—gradually emerged as the spiritual leader of the River Towns.

Another major Puritan thrust into Connecticut centered on the settlement of New Haven in 1638. Inspired by the Reverend John Davenport, former vicar of St. Stephen's in London, and Theophilus Eaton, a successful Puritan merchant who had served as commercial agent of Charles I at Copenhagen, two boatloads of English Puritans arrived in Boston in 1637. Although originally intending to reside permanently in the Massachusetts Bay Colony, the Davenport–Eaton group was disturbed by the Anne Hutchinson controversy that was shaking the Bay Colony and unimpressed with the sites near Boston that might serve as trading ports. When word came to Boston of the splendid harbor at Quinnipiac, the party resolved to relocate. Landing in April 1638 on the shores of what would be christened New Haven Bay, these sturdy Puritans planted the nucleus of the New Haven Colony, which by 1643 would also include the towns of Milford, Guilford, Branford, Stamford, and Southold (the last on Long Island). Although New Haven sought desperately to maintain itself as an autonomous colony, economic difficulties and a fear of incorporation into Anglican New York drove the community in 1665 to become a part of the Colony of Connecticut.

Such were the beginnings of the Connecticut colony, which by the eve of the Revolution would consist of seventy towns and a population of nearly two hundred thousand. As Puritanism was the key to the settlement of the colony, so it continued to be the force that largely determined the society's values and characteristics.

Central to Puritan theology, and a principle that contributed significantly to the evolution of Connecticut society, was the Puritan concept of "the Elect." The Puritan believed that few residents of this earth would ever achieve a state of grace. He held, following the theology of John Calvin of Geneva, that God had promised Adam and his posterity life and salvation in return for obedience to His laws. With Adam's fall in Eden, God's pledge had been withdrawn and mankind doomed to physical suffering, spiritual corruption, and death. Yet Calvinist theology qualified this depressing view of mankind's condition by holding that God in His infinite mercy promised salvation to a select group of men and women. These few, referred to by Calvinists as "the Elect," would undergo a spiritual rebirth. Although the Puritans knew—Calvin so stated—that the number of Elect would be small, they were nevertheless sure that they would be counted among that holy group. The Puritans came to this rather immodest conclusion by discerning that God had singled them out for His special attention in much the same way He had chosen the Israelites in the time of Abraham.

The Puritan thus lived his life constantly searching for evidence that he had undergone the spiritual awakening that would signify his election. As a result the Puritan image is of a person turned inward, ever taking his spiritual temperature to discern the condition of his soul. Meditating, praying, castigating himself when he believed that his thoughts or actions were such as to indicate that he had not yet been included among the Elect, the Puritan conceived of this life as a time of trial during which he must maintain the purity of thought and deed that was a manifestation of his reception of God's saving grace.

Unlike most, however, the Puritan did not relegate his theological condition to a corner of his life while he focused on earthly concerns; rather, the Puritan ordered his society on the basis of his concept of the Elect. If it were true that this life was but a preparation for the next and that God sought on this earth a society that approached His own purity, it followed that any sane man would recognize that human society had to be organized around the leadership of the Elect. Thus when the Puritan had the opportunity to order society according to his inclinations, as he had in Connecticut, he created a theocracy—a social organization led by God's chosen, the Elect.

Strangely enough, rule by a religious elite had not been the intention of Connecticut's founding father, the Reverend Thomas Hooker. Born in Leicestershire, England, in 1586, Hooker was educated at Queen's and Emmanuel Colleges, Cambridge University, receiving his A.B. in 1608 and his A.M. in 1611. He was converted to Puritanism while he was a fellow at Emmanuel from 1611 to 1618, and his subsequent ecclesiastical career in England was conducted under the disapproving glare of James I and the Anglican clergy. Persecuted by William Laud, the Bishop of London, and his agents, Hooker fled to Holland, where he preached in Amsterdam, Delft, and Rotterdam. But he saw only limited opportunities for himself in Holland and none in Stuart England, so Hooker decided for America, arriving in Boston in September 1633. Although chosen as a pastor at Newtown and selected by the Bay leaders to answer Roger Williams in debate, Hooker was apparently restless in Massachusetts Bay. When members of his Newtown congregation looked beyond the Boston area for better land, Hooker supported the decision to transfer his flock to the Connecticut Valley.

Once he was in Connecticut, Hooker made clear that he had in fact nourished opposition to the principles of the Massachusetts Bay leadership, for Hooker's preaching in Hartford indicated that he thought the people should play a greater role in their government than they had enjoyed in the Bay Colony.

In a sermon preached on May 31, 1638, Hooker laid down the principle on which the colony's framework of government—The Fundamental Orders of 1639—would be based. Hooker maintained that the foundation of authority rested in the consent of the people expressed through the electoral process. Yet despite Hooker's call for popular participation in government and the fact that the Fundamental Orders clearly called for separation in Connecticut of civil privilege from church membership, there was erected in the colony a system of government based on membership in and leadership by the Puritan Congregational Church.

Connecticut's founding fathers erected their system of government on the proposition that the mass of mankind, the non-Elect, was evil, corrupt, and hardly fit for political participation. Connecticut's leaders held that "the making of rulers of the lower sort of people will issue in contempt, let their opinion be what it will." [1] One sermon held that government by common men "directly tends at once to destroy both the Rectitude and Success of Government . . . and to enervate the Force of all their Administrations." If the common sort should gain political control, government would "sinke into the mire of popular confusion." [2] Functioning on the basis of such assumptions, Connecticut's leaders erected barriers to mass participation in the government. To participate in town affairs, one had to be an "admitted inhabitant": an adult male, possessing a freehold estate rated at fifty shillings a year or forty pounds in the common list, of "Honest Conservation," and regarded as acceptable by a majority of the town's voters. To be a freeman and serve in and vote for colony-wide offices, one had to meet property qualifications of a freehold estate of forty shillings or forty pounds personal, be of "Quiet and Peaceable Behaviour and Civil Conservation," and be approved by the town's freemen and selectmen. In the early years of the colony an individual's chances of becoming either

1. Quoted in Richard L. Bushman, *From Puritan to Yankee: Character and the Social Order in Connecticut, 1690–1765* (Cambridge, Massachusetts: Harvard University Press, 1967), p. 12.

2. Quoted in Bushman, *From Puritan to Yankee*, p. 13.

an admitted inhabitant or a freeman were nonexistent if he was not a member of the Congregational Church. Thus Connecticut's Puritan fathers not only excluded from political participation all women, children, apprentices, indentured servants, slaves, blacks, and Indians but a good portion also of the white, adult male population. The number of admitted inhabitants in the towns was small—as late as the 1760s only twenty-five percent of the adult males in New Haven took part in town meetings. The evidence indicates that the number of freemen was small as well. In 1669 there were but 1,789 freemen out of an adult male population of 3,000, and in 1740 only 4,000 when the male population was 15,000.

The principal result of these political arrangements—as indeed was intended—was government by the colony's elite. At both the town and colony levels, Connecticut's leaders were devoted Congregationalists, often Yale graduates, tended to come from the families with the largest landholdings, and frequently were active in law and business. A study of the towns of Hartford, Norwich, and Fairfield during the period 1700 to 1784 indicates that each community was in effect presided over by its leading families—in Hartford the Pitkins; in Norwich the Huntingtons and the Traceys; and in Fairfield the Burrs.[3] The same families that provided leadership for the towns dominated the colony-wide offices—governor, deputy governor, and members of the General Assembly. Moreover, the men who filled the colony's highest offices could generally count on almost lifetime tenure. Of the 111 men who served as governors, deputy governors, and members of the Council (the upper house of the Assembly) between the early 1660s and 1776, the average individual was elected and reelected fourteen times. Members of the Pitkin family served for ninety-eight years, the Allyn family for seventy-seven, the Wolcott family for sixty-nine, and the Stanley family for sixty-six. Jonathan Trumbull, Sr., Connecticut's governor during the Revolution, entered the General Assembly in the 1730s and proceeded to

3. Bruce C. Daniels, "Large Town Power Structures in Eighteenth-Century Connecticut: An Analysis of Political Leadership in Hartford, Norwich, and Fairfield" (Dissertation, University of Connecticut, 1970), *passim*.

occupy colony-wide office until his retirement in 1784 at seventy-four. It is clear that an individual of religious and economic substance could, upon entering public life in colonial Connecticut, expect to be reelected for as long as he wished to bear the burdens of office.

But what of the voters within this system, those whose principal responsibility apparently was "to vote and to vote, as a rule, to continue in office those who were already there." [4] Was there not a sense of resentment on the part of substantial farmers and traders as they saw their more prosperous neighbors monopolizing society's positions of honor? It would appear not.

Connecticut's Puritans were presented as weekly fare with sermons which made clear that leaders held their charge to rule directly from God. On the first page of every law book in the colony was printed the scriptural declaration: "There is no Power but of God, the Powers that be are ordained of God." Magistrates were told that they were God's "Viceroyes," given authority by His will to keep order among fallen man. Moreover, the congregations were warned that disobedience constituted "resistance of the Ordinances of God." [5] Such sermons admonished all to respect the civil leadership of those persons whom God had placed at the top of the social scale.

Connecticut's Puritans did just that. They were not only certain that the colony's Elect should rule; they were just as certain of the principal responsibilities which that leadership should bear. Foremost among those responsibilities was accomplishment of the Puritan mission in the New World. The Puritans, unlike their fellow Englishmen who came to America for gold or fish or land or trade, embarked on their American venture in order to complete the Reformation. Anguishing over the unwillingness of the Stuarts and their clergy to reform the impurities in Anglicanism, the Puritans were struck by the notion that God was calling them to establish a truly Christian Church and society that would serve as a model for the rest of

4. Charles McLean Andrews, *Connecticut's Place in Colonial History* (New Haven: Yale University Press, 1924), p. 32.

5. Quotations cited in Bushman, *From Puritan to Yankee*, p. 10.

Christendom. Since it was obviously impossible to succeed in such an undertaking in Stuart England, the Puritans removed to a new land where their experiment might succeed without Stuart obstacles. Hence the Puritan concept of mission. The Puritans were to journey to the wilderness to do the Lord's work; and, they were convinced, God would sanctify and promote the venture by providing His protection. The Puritans' concept of their mission was nowhere more clearly stated than by John Winthrop aboard the *Arbella* in 1630, as one of the first Puritan contingents sailed toward New England:

> The Lord will be our God and delight to dwell among us, as his own people and will command a blessing upon us in all our ways, so that we shall see more of his wisdom, power, goodness, and truth than formerly we have been acquainted with, we shall find that the God of Israel is among us, when ten of us shall be able to resist a thousand of our enemies, when he shall make us a praise and glory, that men shall say of succeeding plantations: the Lord make it like that of New England: for we must Consider that we shall be as a City upon a Hill, the eyes of all people are upon us; so that if we shall deal falsely with our God in this work we have undertaken and so cause him to withdraw his present help from us . . . we shall shame the faces of many of God's worthy servants, and cause their prayers to be turned into Curses upon us till we be consumed out of the good land whither we are going. . . .[6]

One result of this Puritan sense of mission was the manner in which Connecticut's seventeenth-century Puritan dealt with the Pequot menace. When Thomas Hooker and his small band reached Hartford in 1636, there were sixteen Indian tribes in Connecticut, all members of the Algonkin Confederation. Because of their fear of the Mohawks to the west, Connecticut's Indians, who numbered between six and seven thousand, sought the friendship of the newcomers. The Indians sold land to the English and provided instruction in New World agricultural, hunting, and fishing techniques.

The generally harmonious Puritan–Indian relationship in the

6. John Winthrop, "A Modell of Christian Charity," in Gerald N. Grob and Robert N. Beck, eds., *American Ideas: Source Readings in the Intellectual History of the United States,* 2 volumes (New York: The Free Press, 1963), 1:37–38.

colony was disturbed by the Pequots, a tribe that had migrated from the Hudson River Valley to the southeast corner of Connecticut in the region of the Mystic River. From the outset of white intrusion in Connecticut, the Pequots, whose name according to Roger Williams meant "destroyers of men," clearly indicated that they were spoiling for a fight. In 1633 the Pequots wiped out a small group of English traders near the mouth of the Connecticut River, and in 1636 they gave refuge to a band of Block Island Indians who had killed an English trader on Long Island Sound. When such provocations were followed by a Pequot attack on the English fort at Saybrook, and by evidence to indicate that the Pequots were seeking an alliance with the Narragansets to drive the whites from Connecticut, the Puritans mounted an offensive.

In 1637 Connecticut's River Towns assembled a force of ninety men under the command of Captain John Mason to deal with the Pequot menace. After some deft maneuvers during which Mason apparently convinced the Pequots that he was reluctant to join in battle, the Connecticut force managed to surprise the Indians with a night attack on the Pequot fort at Mystic. There then took place as horrible a slaughter as one is likely to find in all of American history. The English set fire to the fort, and those Pequots who were not burned to death were shot down by the Puritans who surrounded the burning enclosure. Mason calculated that six to seven hundred Pequots—including women and children—were slain.

The Puritans were not yet through with the Pequots. The remaining members of the tribe were tracked to a swamp in Fairfield, where once again they were surrounded. After scores of Pequots were killed trying to break through the Puritan lines, a pitiful remnant of the tribe surrendered, to be ultimately given as slaves to tribes friendly to the English. In his account of the confrontation with the Pequots, Mason concluded: "Thus the LORD was pleased to smite our Enemies . . . and to give us their Land for an Inheritance." [7] But while the initial Puritan at-

7. Quoted in Albert Van Dusen, *Connecticut* (New York: Random House, 1961), p. 40.

tack on the tribe may have been justified by Pequot provocations and intentions, the subsequent tracking down and decimation of the Pequots was a dramatic indication of the cultural and racial blindness not only of the seventeenth-century Englishman, but of the Connecticut Puritan so struck with his uniqueness as one of God's "Chosen."

One can see a similar cultural and racial blindness in the attitude of the Connecticut Puritan to the black. Africans were first introduced into Connecticut as slaves early in the colonial period. Prominent early settlers such as Edward Hopkins of Hartford and John Davenport and Theophilus Eaton of New Haven owned slaves. Subsequently Connecticut's coastal ports and inland river communities received loads of slaves, and major town merchants sent surplus slaves to the southern colonies. The Connecticut Puritan was clearly not squeamish about the practice of slavery.

There were no great numbers of black slaves in colonial Connecticut. Because extensive agriculture was limited in Connecticut, the colony did not require the gangs of black field hands that were used on the rice and tobacco plantations of the southern colonies. The average slaveholder in Connecticut had one to three slaves and often worked with the slave both in agriculture and in pursuits like fishing, lumbering, and shipbuilding. The oft-quoted journal of Mrs. Sarah Kemble Knight of Boston gives insight to the white–slave relationship in Connecticut in an entry for 1704–1705:

> And they Generally lived very well and comfortably in their famelies. But too Indulgent (especially the farmers) to their slaves: sufering too great familiarity from them, permitting them to sit at Table and eat with them, (as they say to save time,) and into the dish goes the black hoof as freely as the white hand. They told me that there was a farmer . . . who had some difference with his slave, concerning something the master had promised him and did not punctualy perform; w[hi]ch caused some hard words between them; But at length they put the matter to Arbitration and Bound themselves to stand to the award as such as they named—w[hi]ch done, the Arbitrators Having heard the Allegations of both parties, Order the master to pay 40s to black face, and acknowledge his

fault. And so the matter ended: the poor master very honestly standing to the award.[8]

On the other hand, there was no doubt that the black slave in colonial Connecticut led a life bounded by definite restrictions. In 1660 slaves were exempted from military duty; by 1690 "black codes" existed that required blacks to have passes when they travelled from their homes and prohibited their being sold intoxicating beverages without their owner's permission; in 1708 blacks were denied the privilege of selling goods to whites, were prohibited from striking or arguing with a white, and were prohibited from being out at night after 9:00 P.M.; and in 1730 black slaves were enjoined against speaking harshly to any white. At the same time, free blacks in colonial Connecticut did not have the status of white freemen and were often included in the slave codes. Free blacks had to carry passes when travelling outside their town's limits; could not meet socially with slaves; could not serve on juries; and, although they were taxed the same as whites, could not vote or hold office. The black man in colonial Connecticut—whether free or slave—was hardly judged or treated as an equal with whites. Indeed, blacks were often placed in the same category as animals. The Reverend Daniel Wadsworth's inventory for his 1746 will included "one Black cow, one Red cow, one Brindle Whiteface, 21 sheep, [and] one old Negro woman named Rose. . . ."[9]

Perhaps the most significant result of the Puritan sense of mission was the energy that each Puritan colony in America expended in order to maintain its theological and ecclesiastical purity. It clearly made no sense to journey to the wilderness to escape the corruptions of Christianity in England, only to permit such corruptions to be transplanted to the Wilderness Zion. It is ironic to note how frequently nineteenth-century New England historians celebrated their colonial ancestors for establishing religious liberty in America. The Puritans did no such thing. While they were ardent advocates of religious liberty for them-

8. Quoted in Albert Van Dusen, *Puritans Against the Wilderness: Connecticut History to 1763* (Chester: The Pequot Press, 1975), p. 99.

9. Quoted in David O. White, *Connecticut's Black Soldiers: 1775–1783* (Chester: The Pequot Press, 1973), p. 11.

selves, they were certainly not proponents of such liberty for those not within the Puritan fold. Perhaps the most memorable statement of the Puritans' approach to the subject of religious liberty was presented in 1647 by Nathaniel Ward, a Puritan pastor who migrated to New England in 1634 and became minister of the Congregational church in Ipswich, Massachusetts. Ward, in *The Simple Cobler of Aggawam in America,* laid down the Puritan position regarding toleration for non-Puritans: "Polypiety is the greatest impiety in the World. . . . He that is willing to tolerate any Religion, or discrepant way of Religion, besides his own, unless it be in matters merely indifferent, either doubts of his own, or is not sincere in it." [10] Regarding such convictions as fundamental to the success of their mission, New England's Puritans consistently sought to close off their holy commonwealths from intrusions by non-Puritans.

The first step taken to insure the purity of New England's Wilderness Zion was to put the Puritan Congregational churches on a firm legal footing. The Fundamental Orders of 1639 had charged the colony's magistrates with "preserving the disciplyne of the Churches, which according to the truth of the said gospel is now practiced amongst us," and the Code of 1650, the first codification of Connecticut's laws, directed the "Civil Authority to see the peace, ordinances, and rules of Christ be observed in every Church." Attendance at one's local Congregational church on Sundays and days of fasting and thanksgiving was required on penalty of a five-shilling fine. Heavy penalties awaited the individual who interrupted or challenged the minister. A first offense brought censure, while a second transgression called for a five-pound fine. If the fine were not paid, the offender might be put on display on lecture day "with a paper fixed on his breast written with Capital Letters, AN OPEN AND OBSTINATE CONTEMNER OF GODS HOLY ORDINANCES." [11] Finally, the Code of 1650 restated a law of 1644 that made the financial maintenance of the ministers of the

10. Nathaniel Ward, *The Simple Cobler of Aggawam in America* in Grob and Beck, eds., *American Ideas,* 1:47, 49.

11. Quotation cited in Albert E. Van Dusen, *Connecticut* (New York: Random House, 1961), p. 67.

Puritan Congregational Church an obligation upon everyone, Congregationalist or not. This provision was strengthened many times in Puritan Connecticut, notably in 1691, 1697, 1699, and 1717.

Having erected the Congregational Church as the "established church" in the colony, Connecticut's Puritans had to contend with various challenges to their ecclesiastical control by increasing numbers of non-Puritan newcomers. The most spirited of such challenges in the seventeenth century came from the Quakers and the Rogerenes.

The Society of Friends, better known as Quakers because they "quaked [or trembled] at the word of the Lord," was a sect born in England in the first half of the seventeenth century. Rejecting rites, ceremonies, and a formal priesthood as unnecessary for the understanding of God's will, the Quakers concluded that religion was an individual, inward matter that came from a perception of one's "inner light." In the belief that such "inner light" was a sure reflection of God's presence, the Quakers rejected all forms of earthly control— secular or ecclesiastical. Quakers damned existing churches and did their best to disrupt services by cantankerous methods such as references to the clergy as "Priests of Baal" and bearing "conclusive evidence of the fall of man [by running] up the broad aisle of the meeting house in a costume which that event put forever out of fashion." [12] Toward the authority of the civil magistrates the Quakers manifested comparable disrespect, refusing to pay tithes, bear arms, or take oaths. Driven out of England in the 1650s and 1660s because of what was regarded as their obnoxious troublemaking, the Quakers came to America, where they were generally subjected to fines, whippings, and banishment. In Massachusetts Bay, four zealous Friends were hanged on Boston Common when they persisted in returning after banishment.

The Puritan fathers of Connecticut, dedicated to the purity of their Wilderness Zion, were predictably determined that

12. Quotations cited in Oscar Barck, Jr., and Hugh Lefler, *Colonial America* (New York: The Macmillan Company, 1968), p. 182.

Quakers would gain no foothold in the colony. New Haven's Puritans maintained:

> If after they have suffered the law . . . and shall presume to come into this jurisdiction again, every such male Quaker shall for that second offence be branded on the hand with the letter H [for Heretic], be committed to prison and kept to work till he can be sent away at his own charge, and every Quaker woman that hath suffered the law here and shall presume to come into this jurisdiction again, shall be severely whipt . . . and for every Quaker, he or she, that shall a fourth time again offend, they shall have their tongues bored through with a hot iron.[13]

The New Haveners, distinguished as the most fanatical Puritans in New England, were as good as their word. One Humphrey Norton, who returned to New Haven after banishment to follow his Quaker leanings, paid the price. He was "whipped severely, burnt in the hand with the letter 'H,' and banished. . . ."[14] Three of Norton's cohorts who spoke out against his treatment were apprehended by the New Haven authorities and forcibly removed to Rhode Island.

While less brutal than the New Haveners, Hartford's Puritans were no less determined that the Quakers not spread their pernicious doctrines. The River Towns decreed that punishment be left to "the discretion of the magistrates . . . where any [Quaker] shall be found fomenting their wicked tenets . . . to punish the said heretics by fine or banishment or corporal punishment as they judge meet."[15] Quakers in Hartford in the 1650s and 1660s were hustled out of town and east into Rhode Island as quickly as could be managed, and in 1676 one William Edmundson was dragged out of a Congregational meeting in Hartford with an arm hurt "so that it bled."[16] As a result of such

13. *New Haven Colonial Records, 1653–1665*, p. 239, quoted in Thomas Jefferson Wertenbaker, *The Puritan Oligarchy* (New York: Grosset and Dunlap, 1947), pp. 213–214.

14. M. Louise Greene, *The Development of Religious Liberty in Connecticut* (Freeport, New York: Books for Libraries Press, 1970), p. 165.

15. *Colonial Records of Connecticut, 1636–1665*, pp. 303, 324, quoted in Wertenbaker, *The Puritan Oligarchy*, p. 214.

16. Quoted in Greene, *The Development of Religious Liberty in Connecticut*, p. 167.

forcefulness by Connecticut's authorities, the Quakers obtained no foothold in the colony until the Revolutionary era.

Connecticut had a much harder time with the Rogerenes. Organized by John and James Rogers, Jr., of New London in the 1670s, the Rogerenes were Seventh Day Baptists who repudiated Sunday worship and infant baptism. Ignoring whippings, fines, imprisonments, and various other harassments, the Rogerenes manifested their disdain for the Puritan establishment by immersing new converts in public, travelling on the Sabbath, and working on Sunday to show their contempt for the laws of the Puritan community.[17] Such challenges to the Puritan order by the Rogerenes continued for decades, leading in the 1720s to a series of measures by the Congregational establishment to frustrate zealous demonstrations by the radical sect. Legislation in 1721 required persons accused of non-attendance at Congregational worship to provide proof that they had attended some church and provided punishment of a fine or a public whipping for persons guilty of "prophanation of the Lord's Day" or "any disturbance" of public worship. An act in 1723 "for preventing disorders in the worship of God" punished persons for conducting unauthorized religious meetings and administering the sacraments by a fine or a whipping.[18] Although not intimidated by such measures, the Rogerenes, too fanatical to obtain a large following, eventually died out in the Revolutionary period.

Dissent from the Puritan Congregational order, however, did not die out. In the eighteenth century Connecticut's Puritans had to contend with Baptists and Anglicans who proved to be more substantial opponents of the Congregationalists than were the Quakers and Rogerenes.

Baptists began to hold meetings in Groton in 1705 under the leadership of Valentine Wightman, who formerly had preached at the Baptist church in North Kingston, Rhode Island. Al-

17. By the time of his death in 1721, John Rogers spent a total of fifteen years in jail for his opposition to the Puritan order. See William G. McLoughlin, *New England Dissent, 1630–1833: The Baptists and the Separation of Church and State*, 2 volumes (Cambridge, Massachusetts: Harvard University Press, 1971), 1:252.

18. Quotations cited in McLoughlin, *New England Dissent*, 1:252.

though harassed by the Connecticut authorities, the Baptists, less flamboyant than the Quakers or the Rogerenes, managed to hold on and even expand the number of their congregations. In 1726 Stephen Gorton became pastor of a Baptist flock in New London, and soon afterward Baptist groups appeared in Wallingford, Farmington, Lyme, and Saybrook. Such Baptist expansion was not carried forward without the bitter scorn of the representatives of the established religious order. John Bulkley, a champion of Congregationalism, said of the Baptists:

> [They were obsessed with the desire] to bring an Odium on the Ministry in the Land, and hurt their Reputation and Interest with the People. . . . If they can but gain [the people] to their *Senseless Opinions,* furnish them with some Objections against the Established Religion of the Country, render them prompt and ready at Invective and Railery against Ministers, and prevail on them to forsake our Assemblies, neglect Family Prayer, Prophane the Sabbath etc., Tis enough, and there they leave them, they are now good Christians.[19]

The Baptists, no mean hands at invective, charged that the Puritan ministers were "hirelings, they teach for Hire and Divine for Money . . . Yea and what is worse, they are Greedy Dogs and Ravenous Wolves that devour their Flocks: Therefore come not nigh them." [20]

If Puritan Congregationalists were disturbed by the existence of determined Baptists in their midst, they were absolutely incensed by the eighteenth-century growth of Anglicanism in the colony. Anglican missionaries representing the Society for the Propagation of the Gospel in Foreign Parts spearheaded the penetration of Puritan Connecticut. The Reverend George Muirson, a Society missionary at Rye, preached at Stratford in 1707 and succeeded in converting one John Reed, a Congregational minister. Subsequent conversions followed, including in the 1720s that of the Reverend Samuel Johnson of West Haven. By the 1730s there were Anglican congregations in Stratford, Fairfield, New London, Newtown, and Redding. More than a score

19. Quoted in Bushman, *From Puritan to Yankee,* p. 169.
20. Quoted in Bushman, *From Puritan to Yankee,* p. 169.

of Anglican parishes were formed in the 1740s and 1750s when divisions among the Congregationalists caused by the Great Awakening caused many to seek the security of the Anglican Church. The Anglicans' success was, of course, a bitter pill for the Puritans to swallow. Although London watched benevolently over the status of Anglicans in the colony, it appears that the Puritan Congregationalists nevertheless harassed adherents to the English church in various ways, in particular demanding that Anglicans pay taxes for the support of the Congregational Church while denying the use of such churches for Anglican services. George Muirson wrote to the Society's headquarters in London:

> And though every Churchman in that Colony pays his rate for the building and repairing their [Congregationalist] meeting-houses, yet they are so maliciously set against us, that they deny us the use of them, though on week days. They tell our people that they will not suffer the house of God to be defiled with idolatrous worship and superstitious ceremonies. They are so bold that they spare not openly to speak reproachfully, and with great contempt, of our Church. They say the sign of the cross is the mark of the beast and the sign of the devil, and that those who receive it are given to the devil. And when our people complain to their magistrates of the persons who thus speak, they will not so much as sign a warrant to apprehend them, nor reprove them for their offense.[21]

Not content with such harassment, the Puritans punished those Anglicans who refused to pay taxes toward the support of Congregationalism with imprisonment. The Reverend William Gibbs, an Anglican missionary in Simsbury, reported in 1749: "The [Congregationalists] do oblige them [Anglicans] to pay to the dissenting [Congregationalist] minister, and which they have refused, and for their refusal were, four of them, committed to Hartford gaol, and in a place where they keep malefactors." [22]

21. Quotation cited in Origen Storrs Seymour, *The Beginnings of the Episcopal Church in Connecticut.* Connecticut Tercentenary Commission Publications, Number 30 (New Haven, Connecticut: Yale University Press, 1934), p. 3.

22. Quoted in Seymour, *Beginnings of the Episcopal Church . . . ,* p. 11. Such action was apparently in contradiction to the exemption from Congregational taxes that was granted by the Connecticut General Assembly to Anglicans, Quakers, and Baptists in the late 1720s. See McLoughlin, *New England Dissent,* 1:263–270.

In addition to securing the establishment of the Puritan Congregational Church and attempting to keep the colony free of dissenting sects, Connecticut's Puritan fathers, on behalf of their sense of mission, labored to keep their Wilderness Zion free from sin. Remembering that God's blessing would be maintained only if the colony heeded the Lord's admonitions, the Puritans sought to legislate sin out of existence, and thus prevent any manifestations of God's wrath. Hence came the Blue Laws.

While contemporary America would find disagreeable any diminution of individual liberty comparable to what was found in Puritan statutes, the laws themselves, as well as their application, were far less onerous than might be imagined. A great deal of the misunderstanding regarding the Blue Laws proceeds from an eighteenth-century history of Connecticut written by Samuel Peters, an Anglican priest in Hebron who was run out of the colony during the Revolutionary era because of his unrestrained Toryism. Peters described his unplanned departure from Connecticut in a letter to a friend:

> For my telling the Church people [Anglicans] not to take up arms,
> . . . the Sons of Liberty have destroyed my windows, rent my
> clothes, even my gown, crying down with the Church, the rages of
> Popery, etc.; their rebellion is obvious—treason is common—and
> robbery is their daily diversion: the Lord deliver us from anarchy.[23]

Peters had his revenge for such discomfort. When safely established in London during the Revolution, he wrote a furiously distorted history of Puritan Connecticut, drawing a slanderous account of life under the dreadful Blue Laws. According to Peters the people of Connecticut were daily subjected to banishment, confiscation, fines, whippings, losses of ears, burning of tongues, and death for the most trivial departures from the Puritan system. The historian Benjamin Trumbull, who knew Peters, dismissed the Hebron minister's "history" with the assertion: "Of all men with whom I have ever been acquainted, he is the least to be depended upon as to any matter of fact." [24] But in England, where Connecticut's stern Puritans did not have a

23. Quoted in Lee, *The Yankees of Connecticut*, p. 27.
24. Quoted in Lee, *The Yankees of Connecticut*, p. 28.

good press to begin with, Peters's account of the Blue Laws seemed plausible, and the belief grew that Connecticut's founders and leaders had established a system which bristled with severity and brutality.

In truth, the legal code of England during the American colonial era was far more harsh than that which existed in Puritan Connecticut. Between 1603 and 1819 the number of offenses in England that brought the death penalty rose from 31 to 223. Englishmen could be executed for larceny above twelve pence, for killing a deer in the King's preserve, or for the theft of a horse. Hartford during the colonial period never had more than twelve capital crimes. Yet, even given the excesses of Peters's history and the fact that the English system was hardly a model of humanitarianism, it is nevertheless true that Connecticut's Puritan fathers did undertake a concerted attempt to control human behavior with a harshness that contemporary Americans find repugnant. New Haven's lawgivers led the way with a legal system based on the word of God. Almost every statute was backed up with Biblical reference, and the New Haven code was introduced by the assertion: "The Laws for holiness, and Righteousness, are already made and given us in the scriptures, which in matters moral or of moral equity, may not be altered by human power. . . ." [25] Sanctity of the Sabbath was emphasized:

> Whosoever shal profane the Lords day, or any part of it, either by sinful servile work, or by unlawful sport, recreation, or otherwise, whether wilfully, or in careless neglect, shal be duly punished by fine, imprisonment, or corporally according to the nature, and measure of the sinn, and offence. But if the court upon examination, by clear, and satisfying evidence find that the sin was proudly, presumptuously, with a high hand committed against the known command and authority of the blessed God, therein despising and reproaching the Lord, such a person, shal be put to death. . . .[26]

25. Quoted in Lee, *The Yankees of Connecticut*, p. 24.
26. Quoted in Lee, *The Yankees of Connecticut*, pp. 24–25.

Capital punishment was also established for adultery, sodomy, lesbianism, harlotry, rape, incest, bestiality, and withdrawal as a form of birth control.

Swearing was another practice frowned upon by the Puritan authorities. A ten-shilling fine was drawn for the first offense, and one of twenty shillings for the second. If the offender could not pay the fine, he was placed in the stocks for one to two hours for the first offense and for three to four hours for the second. "But if the same person, notwithstanding such former proceedings, shal offend the third time, by such swearing, or cursing, he shal be whipped, for his incorrigible profaneness." Long after the Puritan vigor in Connecticut had declined, such Blue Laws were still operative. P. T. Barnum, of later circus fame, told of a confrontation in the 1820s between one Crofut of New York—"a man of property, and equally noted for his self-will and his really terrible profanity" [27]—and a magistrate in the community of Bethel near New Haven:

> One day he [Crofut] was . . . engaged in conversation when Nathan Seelye, Esq., one of our village justices of the peace, and a man of strict religious principles, came in, and hearing Crofut's profane language, he told him he considered it his duty to fine him one dollar for swearing. Crofut responded immediately with an oath that he did not care a damn for the Connecticut blue-laws. "That will make two dollars," said Mr. Seelye. This brought forth another oath. "Three dollars," said the sturdy justice. Nothing but oaths were given in reply, until Esquire Seelye declared the damage to Connecticut laws to amount to fifteen dollars. Crofut took out a twenty dollar bill, and handed it to the justice of the peace, with an oath. "Sixteen dollars," said Mr. Seelye, counting out four dollars to hand to Mr. Crofut as his change. "Oh, keep it, keep it," said Crofut, "I don't want any change, I'll damn soon swear out the balance." He did so, after which he was more circumspect with his conversation, remarking that twenty dollars a day for swearing was about as much as he could stand. [28]

Although Connecticut's Puritan fathers were probably as unsuccessful in eliminating immorality as they were in cleansing the

27. Quotations cited in Lee, *The Yankees of Connecticut*, p. 25.
28. Quoted in Lee, *The Yankees of Connecticut*, p. 25.

vocabulary of people like Crofut, their efforts at combating sinfulness nevertheless continued. The Puritan Elect labored under the charge by Hooker that the "true convert" seeks to destroy all sin: "What ever sins come within his reach, he labors the removal of them, out of the familyes where he dwells, out of the plantations where he lives, out of the companies and occasions, with whom he hath occasion to meet and meddle at any time." [29]

Another responsibility of the Puritan Elect in the cause of their mission was to establish an adequate program of education for the colony's children. Believing that the only true source of God's will was the Bible, the Puritan colonies in America made a concerted effort to foster literacy. Just six years after the founding of Massachusetts Bay, the Bay Puritans in 1636 established Harvard College "to advance Learning and perpetuate it to Posterity; dreading to leave an illiterate Ministry to the Churches, when our present Ministers shall lie in the dust." [30] In 1647 the Massachusetts General Court enacted legislation which in its justification and outline served as a model for other Puritan colonies:

It being one chief project of that old deluder, Satan, to keep men from the knowledge of the Scriptures, as in former times by keeping them in an unknown tongue, so in these latter times by persuading them from the use of tongues, that so at least the true sense and meaning of the original might be clouded by false glosses of saint-seeming deceivers [it is ordered] that every township of this jurisdiction, after the Lord hath increased them to the number of fifty householders, shall then forthwith appoint one within their town to teach all children as shall resort to him to read and write [and requires also] that where any town shall increase to the number of one hundred families or householders, they shall set up a grammar school, the master thereof being able to instruct youth as far as they may be fitted for the university. [31]

29. Quoted in Edmund S. Morgan, *The Puritan Family* (New York: Harper and Row, 1966), p. 6.

30. Quoted in Grob and Beck, eds., *American Ideas*, I, 79.

31. Quoted in Francis J. Bremer, *The Puritan Experiment: New England Society from Bradford to Edwards* (New York: St. Martin's Press, 1976), p. 181.

Such pioneering educational efforts while communities were but tiny islands in a howling wilderness leads one to appreciate the assertion of Moses Coit Tyler in *A History of American Literature* regarding the Puritan communities in seventeenth-century New England: "Probably no other community of pioneers ever so honored study, so reverenced the symbols and instruments of learning. Theirs was a social structure with its corner-stone resting on a book." [32]

The Connecticut colony made comparable efforts to foil "that old deluder" and make certain that its population could understand the Bible. The Code of 1650 required a town of fifty families to employ a teacher to instruct in reading and writing and a town of one hundred families to operate a grammar school to prepare students for college. Subsequent legislation suggests that the towns were not taking their educational tasks with sufficient seriousness. The preamble to a 1690 law asserted that there were "many persons unable to read the English tongue." [33] The law went on to establish free schools in Hartford and New Haven to teach reading, writing, arithmetic, Latin, and Greek and ordered the towns to operate an elementary reading and writing school for six months a year. In 1700 the General Assembly established grammar schools in four county seats (Hartford, New London, Fairfield, and New Haven); required towns of seventy families to operate an elementary school the full year and smaller towns to operate such schools for six months yearly; and provided support of 40 shillings per £1,000 of the polls and estates. The towns could secure supplementary funds via gifts or taxation or by charging tuition. By 1717, when the society or parish rather than the town was the unit for schools, the General Assembly provided for an eleven-month school year for the larger parishes and a six-month school plan for the smaller ones. Finally in 1733 the Assembly, in an attempt to supplement school funds, added monies from the sale of western Connecticut lands to existing school revenues.

32. Quoted in McCarthy, *New England,* p. 140.

33. Quoted in Albert E. Van Dusen, *Puritans Against the Wilderness: Connecticut History to 1763,* p. 103.

The mode of instruction in Puritan Connecticut was based on the assumption that the child, like all mankind since the fall in Eden, was born of God's wrath and hence was "a poor, wicked, miserable, hateful creature." [34] Because the natural impulses of the child were thought to be sinful, the pre-eminent function of education was restraint—there was "no question of developing the child's personality, or drawing out or nourishing any desirable inherent qualities which he might possess, for no child could by nature possess any desirable qualities." [35] Instruction was aimed at the inculcation of obedience "in point of good manners, and dutiful behavior towards all." Academic subjects were taught through rote memorization, and all education was based on limiting self-expression and promoting uniformity.

Central to the education system in the colony was the catechism—a summary of orthodox Puritan beliefs set in the form of questions and answers. The catechism, like rules for reading and writing, presented no opportunities for intellectual creativity. Drilled on "right" answers that were forever fixed, the child was schooled in the Puritan intellectual rigidity that was perhaps the natural corollary of the Puritan sense of uniqueness. Such a child grew to adulthood believing that God's writ was clear and bold and offered no conceivable justification for tampering. The Puritan child became a person who not only saw just the black and the white; he was intellectually incapable of recognizing that a gray might exist.

A comparable Puritan tone was characteristic of the education offered at the colony's college—Yale—founded in 1701 and finally settled in New Haven in 1717-1719. Supported by the General Assembly and by contributions from the affluent such as Elihu Yale (who had made a fortune in the employ of the East India Company and especially as governor of Madras), Yale demanded that "every student shall consider the main end of his study to wit to know God in Jesus Christ and answerably

34. Quoted in Michael Zuckerman, "Socialization in Colonial New England" in Michael B. Katz, ed., *Education in American History: Readings on the Social Issues* (New York: Praeger Publishers, 1973), p. 29.

35. Edmund Morgan, quoted in Katz, ed., *Education in American History,* p. 29.

to lead a Godly sober life.'' Although the Yale student body was instructed in Latin, Greek, Hebrew, logic, metaphysics, mathematics, and physics, a student's life was ringed with prayer and meditation. In addition to ''secret prayer wherein every one is bound to ask wisdom for himself,'' a student was required to be present ''morning and evening at publick prayer in the Hall.'' [36] An even more strenuous regimen of prayers and services was required on the Sabbath, for which students prepared on both Friday and Saturday:

> All students after they have done resciting rhetorick on fridays recite Wolebius theology and on saturday morning they shall Rescite Ames theologie thesis in his Medulla, and on saturday evening the Assemblies shorter Chatechism in lattin and on Sabbath Day attend the explication of Ames's Cases of Conscience.[37]

On the Sabbath itself there were morning prayers at the college; two services at the meetinghouse on the New Haven Green; and then evening prayers back at the College.

The impact of such religiously oriented education was substantial in Connecticut because of the numbers of Yale men in positions of power in the colony. By the time of the Revolution there were almost one thousand Yale graduates in the colonies, two-thirds of whom not only resided in Connecticut but occupied key positions in the colony's power structure.

> In 1775, of the twelve members serving in the House of Assistants (upper house of Connecticut's legislature), eight were Yale graduates. The Colony Secretary was a Yale graduate, as were all of the judges of the county court. The General Assembly abounded with Yale graduates. On the local level, many served in such influential positions as moderator of the town meeting, town clerk or justice of the peace. Nearly one-half of the field officers of the Connecticut militia in 1775 were Yale graduates, as was the majority of the powerful Council of Safety.[38]

36. Quotations cited in Brooks Mather Kelley, *Yale: A History* (New Haven: Yale University Press, 1974), p. 42.

37. Quotation cited in Kelley, *Yale,* p. 42.

38. Louis Leonard Tucker, *Connecticut's Seminary of Sedition: Yale College* (Chester: The Pequot Press, 1974), p. 15.

But the true significance of Yale lay beyond its production of public officials; it molded the men who in fact ruled colonial Connecticut, the Congregational clergy. Contemporary Americans who relegate the clergy to performances on the Sabbath and on special occasions must labor to appreciate the immense power of the Puritan clergy in early Connecticut. Trained at Yale or occasionally at Harvard, these men were hard thinkers, good orators, skilled at exercising carefully the power they wielded, and most probably the best that Puritan society created. The Reverend Lyman Beecher has left us a picture of these clergymen and their power on Election Day:

> All the clergy used to go, walk in the procession, smoke pipes, and drink. And, fact is, when they got together, they would talk over who should be governor, and who lieutenant governor, and who in the Upper House, and their counsels would prevail. . . . The ministers had always managed things themselves, for in those days the ministers were all politicians, they had always been used to it from the beginning.[39]

The minister, however, was more to the town and the colony than simply a political manipulator who called the shots on Election Day. That he could in fact exercise such power was a reflection of his overall immersion in and significance to the society:

> At every occasion he was expected to be on hand ready with a prayer and a few profound remarks, whether it was the town meeting at the church or a dinner party at the deacon's. There was the routine of pastoral calls, funerals, and patriotic rallies. Before high schools came into existence, his mornings and evenings were taken up with tutoring boys for entrance to Yale, supplementing the learning that went beyond the scope of the schoolmaster. All travelers of distinction called at his door expecting an invitation for dinner or for the night. His bookshelves became a lending library until he organized one in the village. . . . The local pastor had knowledge of every phase of life. . . . It was from that orientation that his power grew. He was a man of vitality, stamina, and consequence.[40]

39. Quoted in Lee, *The Yankees of Connecticut*, pp. 22–23.
40. Lee, *The Yankees of Connecticut*, pp. 42–43.

Although he was indeed the central figure around which the affairs of the community revolved, the pastor assumed his most significant role on the Sabbath. During his Sunday sermon, the pastor was the community's newspaper columnist, TV star, and keeper of morals. While his sermon contained "erudite treatises on the wisdom of Isaiah, the acts of Jeroboam, and the teachings of Hosea," [41] there were also references to and judgments on local and colonial political doings, commentaries on economic news and prospects, and not altogether guarded references as to which members of the congregation were straining the Lord's patience by carousing, paying excessive attention to the upstairs maid, or "sharping" their neighbors in business transactions. But the main thrust of his sermon was always the statement and restatement of the Puritan concept of mission. For one hundred fifty years the Puritan Congregational clergy in Connecticut asserted that never in Puritan society was the inclination of the individual to take precedence over the aspirations of the community. Society, it was maintained, was not an aggregation of individuals but an organism in which all parts were subordinate to the whole. The individual had as his primary responsibility contributing to the success of the community's mission. He was to live within the confines of God's word, do that labor to which he was "called" by God, educate his children in the ways of the Lord, and, most important, adhere to the teachings and admonitions of his spiritual leaders. Told constantly that the erection and maintenance of "the City upon a Hill" was his basic obligation, the Puritan accepted his roles as defined by his ever present and seemingly all-knowing pastors.

The Congregational clergy's ability to maintain its influence in colonial Connecticut was a reflection of the fact that Connecticut, more than any place on earth during the American colonial period, approached the spirit and structure of the Wilderness Zion. While the original Puritan zeal in old England had long since become the victim of latitudinarianism encouraged by a theologically lukewarm Anglicanism, and the strident Calvinism of Massachusetts had deteriorated to a detectable secularism,

41. Lee, *The Yankees of Connecticut*, p. 40.

Connecticut held scrupulously to the doctrines of Hooker's generation.

Connecticut's retention of an essentially undiluted Puritanism well into the eighteenth century emanated from the political and economic isolation of the colony. The charter granted by Charles II in 1662 had established Connecticut as a corporation with authority entrusted to an elected governor and the freemen. On the basis of the Stuart grant, Connecticut continued to chart its own political course as it had done since the settlement of the colony in the 1630s. While the British government periodically attempted to tighten its control, its efforts were usually isolated and unsustained. Except for Connecticut's brief inclusion in the Dominion of New England under Sir Edmund Andros from 1686 to 1689, the colony was a principal American beneficiary of the uncoordinated approach to colonial management that characterized London's policy between the reign of James II (1685–1689) and the accession of George III in 1760. Thus the Connecticut Puritan leadership functioned as a law unto itself and was able to maintain the structure of the Wilderness Zion without significant disturbance from Britain.

The colony's economic as well as political condition contributed to its dominant Puritanism during the greater part of the colonial period. The outstanding characteristic of the colony was its inability to conduct comprehensive direct trade with the mother country. Lacking an exportable product such as Massachusetts cod, Carolina rice, or Virginia tobacco with which to trade directly with England, and unable to import significant quantities of manufactured goods because of its limited market, Connecticut drifted through the colonial period relying generally on Boston and New York City for the marketing of its agricultural products and its purchases of foreign goods. While a number of Connecticut merchants such as Nathaniel Shaw of New London and Jonathan Trumbull of Lebanon were able to conduct sizable mercantile operations with Great Britain, Connecticut as a whole never managed to become a member of the imperial trading community. The colony thus did not effect those social and intellectual ties with the mother country that would have been the natural concomitants of extensive trading within the structure of the British empire—and undoubtedly would have threatened the viability of Connecticut's Puritan system and atmosphere.

Therefore, while a member of an empire that stretched the globe and included some thirty colonies in America from Nova Scotia to Barbados, Connecticut functioned throughout the colonial period much like an independent republic.[42] Made up of isolated rural communities in which the local clergy and magistrates ruled according to Puritan principles, Connecticut was "cut off from very much contact with the outside world, knew little of [its] neighbors, less of other colonies, and almost nothing of what was going on in England or the Continent."[43] It was the only colony that generally did not follow English practices in its legislative proceedings nor allow a considerable amount of English common and statute law into its legal code. Its participation in four intercolonial wars with France between 1689 and 1763 was willing enough, but its leaders on four separate occasions resisted the orders of English commanders who sought troop integration and centralization of command.

Such were the values and institutions that characterized Puritan Connecticut during the colonial period. This environment, permeated by Puritan values, principles, and institutions, produced people who believed without question in the omnipresence of God in the disposal of man's fate. Life for the Connecticut Puritan was no succession of chance occurrences: it was the unfolding of God's will. Through personal gain, through personal failure, through family joys, through crushing family tragedies, and through the trials and tribulations of life in a primitive environment, the Connecticut Puritan's most distinctive characteristic was an unbreakable will, a rock-like ability to take what life gave without once doubting that all—pain and pleasure alike—was God's will.

Such people were tough-minded. They purged from their religious worship all that was soft and comfortable. As Harriet Beecher Stowe, a daughter of Litchfield, put it:

42. The following discussion of the characteristics of colonial Connecticut and its people owes much to Andrews, *Connecticut's Place, passim.*

43. Andrews, *Connecticut's Place,* p. 18.

They shut out from their religious worship every poetic drapery, every physical accessory that they feared would interfere with the abstract contemplation of hard, naked truth, and set themselves grimly and determinately to study the severest problems of the unknowable and the insoluble. . . . They never expected to find the truth agreeable. . . . Their investigations were made with the courage of the man who hopes little, but determines to know the worst of his affairs. They wanted no smoke of incense to blind them, and no soft opiates of pictures and music to lull them; for what they were after was *truth,* and not happiness, and they valued duty far higher than enjoyment.[44]

Essentially isolated from the rest of the Anglo-American world and living in a harsh, demanding environment, the Connecticut Puritan learned that there was no such thing as success achieved without effort. Land clearing, fence building, road construction, and constant care of fields and stock constituted the core of existence in an essentially agrarian society. The Connecticuter learned to dedicate himself to the task before him with a uniquely New England appetite for sustained labor. Whether he occupied a pulpit, anguished over the rocky New England soil, or bore the burdens of the mercantile maelstrom, the Connecticuter gave almost sacramental attention to his labors, knowing that the survival of his family and the salvation of his eternal soul were at stake.

The Puritan system in colonial Connecticut also produced a man who was accustomed to going his own way politically. His autonomy was challenged only occasionally, and then usually weakly, by the mother country. The Connecticut Puritan in his town meeting and General Assembly bore the responsibility of lawmaking, taxation, land distribution; in short, the entire range of duties necessary for the management of his society. Such responsibility naturally bred a spirit of self-reliance, an absolute detestation of "meddling" by outside forces or persons.

While this instinct for self-government would become a crucial force in the evolution of both Connecticut and the emerging American nation, it would also trigger a number of negative

44. Quoted in McCarthy, *New England,* p. 32.

repercussions. For example, the autonomy of the towns and the colony gave rise to men of strong minds and contentious dispositions who were not much given to cooperative efforts. An atmosphere of censoriousness resulted in very little getting done. Men of strong opinions and angular personalities were rarely able to agree among themselves about anything, and the business of making roads and clearing rivers in colonial Connecticut went on very slowly. But it is crucial to understand that the Connecticut Puritan was not at his core a person who really cared much about "progress." The Connecticut Puritan's fundamental attitude toward "progress" was perhaps best described by Charles McLean Andrews, a distinguished colonial historian who taught at Yale from 1910 to 1931:

> [The Puritans] did not believe in change, much less progress, for men's material betterment was to them a matter of little consequence as compared with his spiritual welfare. They were troubled about their souls not their bodies . . . and preparation for the next world, not improvement in this one, was the lesson . . . impressed upon every individual. Earthly existence was a time of probation . . . and to pay attention to ameliorating the material conditions under which man lived and worked was to imperil the happiness that only the kingdom of Heaven could bestow. Comfort and enjoyment were but vanities and their pursuit was unbecoming in the sight of God.[45]

Puritanism had indeed left its mark on colonial Connecticut, producing tough-minded men and women who had an unparalleled appetite for sustained labor, were strongly self-reliant, were prone to rigidity in the assertion of their principles, and who were fundamentally suspicious of that which implied change or innovation. Such people, obviously conservative to the core, were predictably not very receptive to the winds of change that blew toward the American colonies from Great Britain in the early 1760s.

45. Andrews, *Connecticut's Place*, pp. 33–34.

3

Revolutionary Connecticut

ONE of the most striking features of the Revolutionary era is the pettiness and factionalism that detracted from American unity. In the period between the Stamp Act of 1765 and the Declaration of Independence in 1776 Americans ranted and raved at one another with almost as much fury as they vented toward the mother country. Americans assumed positions vis à vis England, abandoned them, and then accused other Americans of deserting the common cause. The situation changed little after the Declaration of Independence: many Americans reacted to demands of their state governments and of Congress much as they had reacted to those of King and Parliament before independence. Citizens suspected state governments; the state governments were fearful of congressional power; and Congress appeared terrified of the possibility of an emerging military aristocracy.

Worse still, many Americans appeared to regard the war as a tremendous opportunity for personal gain and recognition. Merchants had a field day capitalizing on the needs of the Continental and militia troops for meat, flour, grain, horses, and weapons. Shrewd traders cornered the market on urgently required materiel and then charged excessive prices. The records of the American Army reek with petty quarrels over rank, seniority, and promotions. High-ranking officers raged, pouted, schemed, and frequently resigned over minor slights.

The situation in Congress was no better. Its membership included embezzlers, profiteers, and speculators using secret information.

Given the existence of this apathy, greed, and vanity among Americans of the Revolutionary era, how did the American cause ever succeed? The British helped considerably, never recognizing that their task was nothing less than the conquest of a continent. By 1781, after six years of warfare, the British had only 34,000 men in America. Although such a force was sufficient to occupy a portion of the former colonies, it was less than capable of achieving victory. Moreover, the principal British commanders never fully used the military resources that they did possess. Pressing the Americans, assuming that a good blow would end it all, they kept waiting for the collapse that never came. Washington time and time again took the punches—Long Island, Brandywine, and Germantown—covered up, and retreated to fight again.

British blunders alone did not decide the war. The aid of France was crucial. The French, delighted at the prospect of an independent America and thus a weakened British empire, poured aid into the rebelling colonies from the outset of hostilities. In the first two and a half years of the war, and especially after the Alliance of 1778, French aid mounted until by the end of the fighting Louis XVI had donated eight million dollars and more than 9,000 troops to the American cause.

And yet, while British weakness and mistakes and French aid were crucial elements in the achievement of American independence by the Treaty of Paris of 1783, the new nation's birth was ultimately brought about by its own men and women. Enough Americans sacrificed their time, their property, and not infrequently their lives so that succeeding generations could inherit the birthright of independence and liberty proclaimed by the Declaration of Independence. While all geographical areas gave to the Patriot cause these dedicated Americans who did not falter in the "times that tried men's souls," no state had a record of service more distinguished than that of Connecticut.

In the 1760s Great Britain attempted to ease its imperial burdens in North America by passing a series of revenue-raising measures, including the Sugar Act of 1764, the Stamp Act of 1765, and the Townshend Duties of 1767. British officials undoubtedly assumed that the Americans, while perhaps not overjoyed with the legislation, would as loyal subjects of the mother country bend to Britain's judgment. If by chance American colonists protested excessively against the measures, the mother country, fresh from its recent victory over France and Spain and at the peak of its military might, could easily restrain any unseemly colonial conduct.

It was, of course, soon evident that the British had been tragically mistaken in assuming that the colonies would quietly accept the new legislation. Americans, growing strong economically and enjoying a population of a million and a half, were unwilling to see any of their traditions of self-government fade in the face of the newly assertive mother country. A storm of protest, mostly verbal but often physical, burst from the American side of the Atlantic, and powerful Britain found herself embroiled in a losing struggle to retain her hold on the aroused colonies.

Connecticut, rooted in Puritan hostility to Anglican England and conditioned by self-government and economic independence, was hardly inclined in the early 1760s to accept the new British legislation. Factors were at work at the end of the French and Indian War which would make it even more certain that Connecticut's response to the more energetic British colonial policy would be explosive. The colony had made a major contribution to the British victory in that war. Connecticut, seeking to protect its own security in the face of the threat posed by the French and their Indian allies, had spent almost £260,000 in the war effort and had sent five thousand men into battle. Indeed, one in five of Connecticut's males between the ages of sixteen and forty-five had seen service in the war years, a most impressive contribution—especially as the essentially agricultural colony needed as many men as possible to work the land.

Despite its praiseworthy military effort, however, Connecticut found itself in dire economic straits by 1764. While the colony had done well economically during the war by selling its agricultural products to supply Connecticut militiamen and British troops, the end of hostilities had cut off this source of profit. Connecticut plunged into a severe depression. Farmers who no longer had a market for their products could not pay outstanding debts to merchants, who in turn were unable to meet their own obligations to importers of manufactured goods in New York, Boston, and Providence. Both farmers and merchants felt the pinch, and many farms and businesses were on the brink of bankruptcy. The colony could not have been expected to react positively to the news of the Sugar Act of 1764, which would make Connecticut trade with the West Indian sugar islands less profitable.

News of the legislation immediately brought sentiment to a boil. Merchants moaning that Connecticut trade was "embarrassed and Clogged" and farmers who were in debt for "all their Stock and half their Land" complained that the Sugar Act would cut off the last major source of trade left open to the colony. The *Hartford Courant* stated: "Our trade to the French and Spanish islands is stopped. . . . Husbandry is discouraged for there is no vent for that purpose. Merchants and farmers are breaking; and all things going into confusion." [1]

Mounting cries of distress brought prompt official protest of the Sugar Act by the colony. Governor Thomas Fitch, a Yale graduate from Norwalk who had become governor in 1754 after a distinguished legal career, sent to London a closely reasoned paper that noted the colony's economic distress and cited the Sugar Act as unjust. Fitch was concerned that the act, by forcing Connecticut merchants to trade with the British sugar islands, would abruptly cut off trade with the French sugar islands, a major source of specie. Fitch asked the British government if it were fair to satisfy the demands of the British West Indian planters for greater profit at the expense of the economic health of the northern mainland colonies such as Connecticut.

Britain, seemingly concerned only with its imperial and fi-

1. Quoted in Zeichner, *Connecticut's Years of Controversy*, pp. 46–47.

nancial interests, not only did not reconsider the Sugar Act but prepared to establish another revenue-raising operation with the Stamp Act of 1765. That act required that items such as licenses, newspapers, and legal documents carry stamps available only from the British government.

In a very short time, the Connecticut protest over the Stamp Act made the previous outcry seem insignificant. From throughout the colony protests poured into the General Assembly. A committee of the Assembly was set up to cooperate with Governor Fitch in the preparation of the colony's objections to the legislation. The committee's report, promptly approved by the General Assembly, set forth a position that was widely held throughout the American colonies in protests against the Stamp Act. First, the report noted that the proposed tax conflicted with the Englishman's traditional right to be taxed only with his consent. Since residents of Connecticut were not represented in Parliament, the British legislature could not enact taxation measures. Second, the report asserted that by the Charter of 1662 Connecticut's General Assembly was to be responsible for all necessary legislative enactments. Again, Parliament in Connecticut's eyes could not legally enact a measure such as the Stamp Act. Unfortunately for the future of Anglo-American relations, Britain, apparently growing weary of America's legal rhetoric, disregarded colonial protests and enacted the legislation in March 1765 with the provision that the tax go into effect the following November.

As swift packets from Britain and speedy riders from Boston and New York brought word to Connecticut in the spring of 1765 that the Stamp Act was to become law, the colony entered into a period of violent political disagreement. The stormy atmosphere was not caused simply by Connecticut's residents venting their wrath at the mother country and its latest measure; Connecticut's sons and daughters were ranting not at the mother country but at each other. News of the Stamp Act produced bitter debate over how the colony should respond to the new legislation. Opinion in the towns west of the Connecticut River was generally that Connecticut would have to resign itself to the Stamp Act. East of the river, however, the population was seething with outrage.

Governor Fitch's view was typical of that in western Connecticut. While Fitch had taken the position that it was proper for Connecticut to communicate its objections to the stamp legislation while the measure was being considered in London, he held that protest must cease once ''the Parliament in their Superior Wisdom Shall Judge it Expedient and accordingly do pass an Act.'' [2] A similar stand, again typical of western Connecticut's leaders, was taken by Jared Ingersoll of New Haven. Ingersoll, an attorney who had been in London when the stamp bill was proposed and who had been charged to speak against it by Connecticut's General Assembly, finally concluded that the legislation would have to be accepted. In fact, reasoning that there would be less difficulty over the measure if Americans enforced it, Ingersoll had agreed before leaving London to serve as a stamp distributor for Connecticut.

While Fitch, Ingersoll, and other residents of western Connecticut were taking this reasoned, moderate stand on the Stamp Act, the towns of eastern Connecticut were exploding. The particular object of the area's wrath was Ingersoll. When the New Haven attorney returned from London to Connecticut in August 1765, the New London-published *Connecticut Gazette* commented on his decision to become a stampmaster:

> Have three hundred Pounds a Year, or even a more trifling
> Consideration been found sifficient [*sic*] to debauch from their
> Interest those who have been entrusted with the most important
> concerns by the Colonies? . . . No, you'll say, I don't delight in
> the Ruin of my Country, but since 'tis decreed she must fall, who
> can blame for taking part in the Plunder? Tenderly said! Why did
> you not rather say—if my father must die, who can accuse me as
> defective in filial duty, in becoming his Executioner, that so much
> of the Estate, at least goes to the Hangman, may be retained in the
> Family? [3]

The newspaper assault on Ingersoll seemed to encourage expression of even more violent sentiment throughout eastern Connecticut. The not-so-gentle citizens of New London, Norwich, Lebanon, and Windham led the way. A fiery demon-

2. Quoted in Zeichner, *Connecticut's Years of Controversy*, p. 50.
3. *Connecticut Gazette*, August 9, 1765.

stration took place in New London on August 22, 1765. Dr. Benjamin Church, active in Boston protests with James Otis and Sam Adams, sparked the crowd in a speech that condemned Ingersoll as an enemy to American liberty and advised that a delegation should interview the New Haven attorney to convince him of his error in accepting the stampmaster's post. The type of "interview" that Church had in mind was indicated after the oration when an effigy of Ingersoll was hanged from a tree while dancing children shouted: "There hangs a traitor; there's an enemy to his country." [4] Not to be outdone, crowds in Norwich and Windham enjoyed lusty protest meetings during which effigies of Ingersoll were objects of the people's wrath. Lebanon, however, was the eastern Connecticut community warmest in its denunciation of the Connecticut stampmaster. Ingersoll's effigy was tried and convicted by a jury, dragged through the streets while people lashed it with whips, and finally burned before a cheering throng.

That eastern and western Connecticut reacted so differently to the Stamp Act was in part a reflection of each section's historic relationship with the mother country. Western Connecticut had tended in the first half of the eighteenth century to lose the traditional Connecticut suspicion of England. The area had come to conduct substantial business enterprise with the royal colony of New York, and the Anglican Church had experienced rather surprising growth in western Connecticut as a result of heated controversies growing out of the Great Awakening. Thus when the imperial issue was drawn in the 1760s western Connecticut, although certainly not pleased by the taxes called for, was unwilling to repudiate London's leadership.

Eastern Connecticut experienced no such inhibition. Rural, economically underdeveloped, having little contact with London, the area reflected the Puritan Congregational Church's traditional hostility toward mother England. When Britain sought to tax America by the Sugar and Stamp acts, eastern Connecticut viewed the measures as fatal to American liberty. Western Connecticut's passivity in the face of the British legislation drove the already outraged easterners into frenzied protest.

4. Quoted in Zeichner, *Connecticut's Years of Controversy*, p. 51.

Full understanding of the wrath that eastern Connecticut directed toward Ingersoll and Fitch in the summer of 1765 requires recognition that the easterners were reacting to more than a difference of opinion with the westerners on the imperial issue. The fury of eastern Connecticut was a reflection of the area's frustration at having its interests and plans torpedoed by western Connecticut for more than three decades.

One of the issues that had divided eastern and western Connecticut was paper money. As the seacoast towns of eastern Connecticut grew in the eighteenth century, merchants in the area found their operations impeded by a shortage of money. The problem was particularly acute for eastern Connecticut merchants who had long conducted their overseas trade through importing merchants in Boston, Newport, and New York and who were seeking to establish direct contacts with English traders to eliminate the costs of the middleman. Prospects of direct trade with England were dim as long as eastern Connecticut did not have sufficient funds to pay off outstanding debts to Massachusetts, Rhode Island, and New York importers. The region's response to the situation was the formation in 1729 of the "New London Society for Trade and Commerce," which petitioned the General Assembly for the opportunity to issue bills of currency based on mortgages deposited with the company. If this operation were successful, eastern Connecticut would have an expanded supply of currency with which it could pay off past debts and purchase goods directly from Britain.

Western Connecticut, more populous than the towns east of the Connecticut River and thus more powerful in the colony's General Assembly, was successful in the 1730s in destroying the New London Society. Western representatives in the Assembly spoke out against the Society on the ground that the issuance of paper currency would be contrary to Britain's wish to keep paper money, so often insufficiently secured by hard money in the colonial period, out of circulation. More to the point was western Connecticut's unwillingness to stand by while merchants from eastern Connecticut grew strong enough to become substantial competitors. Eastern Connecticut consequently bore great and long-lasting resentment toward western representatives in the General Assembly.

Another element that disturbed relations between eastern and western Connecticut in the decades preceding the Revolution was the religious strife that grew out of the Great Awakening. That religious revival, which rolled through Connecticut in the 1730s and 1740s, brought serious division in the Puritan Congregational Church. The revivalists, called New Lights, attacked the cold formality of traditional Congregational preaching and introduced a personal spontaneity to eighteenth-century Connecticut Puritanism. The anti-revivalists, called Old Lights, were appalled by the "schreechings, faintings, visions, and convulsions" that characterized New Light worship; in 1743 they were strongly enough represented in the General Assembly to pass a measure that banned revivalist preachers from taking the pulpit in a congregation unless so permitted by the local minister. The ban on itinerant preaching only succeeded in enraging the New Lights, who then conducted a bitter pamphlet war on the Old Lights.

The New Lights were centered in the towns east of the Connecticut River, particularly in Windham and Lebanon, while the Old Lights were a majority in western Connecticut. Eastern Connecticut, as a rural and economically underdeveloped area, was fertile ground for the unrestrained emotionalism of the revivalists. Western Connecticut, populated by the more wealthy and aristocratic elements in the colony and influenced in a conservative religious direction by Anglican missionaries, regarded the emotional excesses of the Great Awakening as "disgusting Distortions of True Religious worship." Thus, as New Lights and Old Lights thundered at one another through the 1740s and 1750s, Connecticut's east–west conflict became more bitter.

A third issue that deepened the colony's sectional division was the territorial ambition of the Susquehannah Company. A principal result of Connecticut's population growth in the first half of the eighteenth century, as well as of wasteful agricultural methods, was a shortage of fertile land. In the period between 1730 and 1750 over 300,000 acres of land were gobbled up in Connecticut, and land companies were formed to obtain territory beyond the colony's borders. One of the most significant was the Susquehannah Company, which was formed in Windham in July 1753. Established by some of eastern Connecticut's most distinguished—and land-hungry—citizens, the company wished to use the sea-to-sea clause in the Connecticut charter of 1662 to claim land in Pennsylvania along the Susquehannah River.

The Penn family, alarmed by the prospect of the loss of a portion of the colony which it had held as a proprietary grant from Charles II since 1681, protested both to the Connecticut General Assembly and to London. Opposition to the Susquehannah Company also quickly formed within Connecticut. Leading citizens of western Connecticut, undoubtedly fearful that the success of the proposed settlement in Pennsylvania would result in lower prices for land in their area, lashed out at the founders of the Susquehannah Company. Asserting that the eastern Connecticut land company would succeed only in angering the Penns until the wrath of the mother country would fall upon Connecticut, the anti-Susquehannah faction opposed any step that would link the colony with the plan of the company. Although the Susquehannah project had little chance of receiving royal approval because of the opposition of the Penns, the company's supporters in eastern Connecticut and opponents in western Connecticut racked each other with bitter speeches and pamphlets.

Thus when the eastern Connecticut towns of Windham, Norwich, Lebanon, and New London lashed out at Jared Ingersoll in August 1765, the easterners were doing more than venting their displeasure at western Connecticut's "soft" position on the Stamp Act. Eastern Connecticut was expressing its accumulated frustration at having its plans for paper money, religious revivalism, and territorial expansion deflated by westerners such as Ingersoll. The easterners had tasted the ashes of defeat once too often; now they were determined to have their way regarding the Stamp Act and in the process to effect a political revolution in the colony.

A group of eastern Connecticut's most distinguished leaders came together in that summer of 1765 to organize themselves for the battle. Eliphalet Dyer of Windham, a lawyer and founder of the Susquehannah Company, and Jonathan Trumbull of

Lebanon, a leading merchant and official in the General Assembly since the early 1730s, joined with three militia officers who had seen service in the French and Indian War—Major John Durkee of Norwich, Captain Hugh Ledlie of Windham, and Colonel Israel Putnam of Pomfret. From their meeting came the Sons of Liberty. The organization was to seek two ends: to convince Connecticut's freemen that their liberties could only be secure if the colony's Tory western Connecticut leaders were repudiated and to organize the colony to elect "patriotic" leaders, who, by no accident whatsoever, were to be drawn from eastern Connecticut. The plan was carefully drawn, rapidly executed, and successful beyond the expectations of even the easterners themselves.

Having set their plan in motion by organizing the demonstrations against Jared Ingersoll, the Sons of Liberty moved ahead in September 1765 to eliminate the New Haven attorney as a respected political figure and to intimidate other moderates. As Ingersoll was on his way to a meeting of the General Assembly in Hartford called to discuss Connecticut representation at the Stamp Act Congress in New York, some five hundred Sons, all armed with clubs and staves and some dressed in militia uniforms, intercepted the stamp distributor in Wethersfield. The assembled throng demanded that Ingersoll then and there resign his post. When Ingersoll, a man of no little courage, angrily protested that it was not fair for easterners to dictate policy for the colony, the throng's leaders threateningly responded: "Here is a great many people waiting and you must resign." Faced with the likelihood of considerably more than conversation in the offing, Ingersoll read a letter of resignation the Sons of Liberty had prepared and then obliged the crowd by offering three cheers for "liberty and property." [5] Ingersoll's humiliation was completed when he was escorted into Hartford and forced by the crowd to repeat his performance within hearing distance of the assembled legislature. The Assembly, with the disheveled Ingersoll before it, satisfied the easterners by appointing delegates to the Stamp Act Congress.

5. *Connecticut Gazette*, September 27, 1765; *Connecticut Courant*, September 23, 1765.

Fitch was next on the easterners' list. While the governor had spoken out against the passage of the Stamp Act, he had also made it clear that he would fulfill his constitutional responsibility by taking the oath to uphold the Stamp Act that was required of all American governors. On October 31, 1765, when Fitch assembled the Council to administer the oath to him, the members from eastern Connecticut led by Dyer and Trumbull withdrew from the chamber in indignation, leaving Fitch the company of four westerners. Fitch then took the oath and by doing so sealed his political fate.

In the months that led up to the colony's next election in the spring of 1766, the Sons of Liberty conducted an untiring and vicious campaign to defeat Fitch and the four councilors from western Connecticut. The easterners expanded their organization throughout eastern Connecticut's towns and even penetrated the area west of the river. Exploiting the hard times that all Connecticut had been facing since the end of the French and Indian War, the Sons of Liberty asserted over and over that if Connecticut were to support leaders such as Fitch, the colony would not only lose its liberties but suffer economic devastation. Too, the Sons introduced into partyless Connecticut a ticket of their own, supporting William Pitkin of Hartford, a leading merchant and friend to "liberty," for governor and Jonathan Trumbull for deputy governor. Even though fierce American opposition moved the British to withdraw the Stamp Act of 1766, the easterners kept up their campaigning, always declaring that Connecticut would have to possess leadership willing to oppose any future British tyranny. The campaign paid off handsomely. Sweeping the eastern towns and picking up some support in western Connecticut, the Pitkin–Trumbull slate carried the day. Eastern Connecticut had pulled off a political upset.

The victory of the easterners in the election of 1766 was by far the most important single event in Connecticut history during the Revolutionary era. The election brought eastern Connecticut control of both the Council, the upper house of the Assembly, and the governorship; and that control was maintained throughout the entire Revolutionary Period. William Pitkin served as governor from 1766 until his death in 1769, and Jonathan Trumbull replaced him from 1769 until 1784. The significance of eastern Connecticut's rise to political power was that it made certain that the colony would follow an unyielding Patriot line as the Anglo-American controversy deepened in the late 1760s and early 1770s. In essence, Connecticut made its choice between resistance and obedience to Britain in 1766; all that followed was but a result of that decision.

For example, when Parliament in 1767 enacted the Townshend Duties providing for British taxation on colonial imports, Connecticut's leadership in conjunction with the Sons of Liberty wasted no time in mounting protests. Governor Pitkin declared to Britain that while Connecticut had no desire to free itself from its relationship with the mother country, the colony had to protest the new duties as unconstitutional in light of Connecticut's charter-given privilege of being responsible for its own taxation. While Pitkin was satisfied with protests, the Sons of Liberty were not. They organized meetings in New London, Norwich, and Windham to draw up plans for the nonimportation and nonconsumption of British goods. By 1769 Connecticut's merchants were generally "educated" to respect the necessity of doing without the mother country's merchandise. Nonimportation and nonconsumption were also employed in other colonies, with the result that by 1770 the British had repealed all of the 1767 duties with the exception of that on tea.

The significance of eastern Connecticut's control of the colony's government can best be seen during the critical months between the Boston Tea Party in December 1773 and the outbreak of fighting at Lexington and Concord in April 1775. In the course of the period when the Anglo-American controversy exploded into warfare, the easterners led Connecticut unswervingly along the road to revolution.

The final stage in the imperial crisis began with Parliament's enactment of the Tea Act of 1773. Hoping to bail out the near-bankrupt British East India Company, Britain provided the company with a monopoly of the American tea trade. The colonists once again rose in protest at another indication of British insensitivity to American interests. The Sons of Liberty in the various colonies organized a boycott of tea, thus beginning the American reliance on coffee as the national drink. Ships carrying tea were prevented from landing their cargo in American ports, and finally, on the night of December 16, 1773, John Hancock and Sam Adams organized the Boston radicals to dump East India Company tea in Boston Harbor.

When the Americans had mounted similar protests against the Stamp Act and the Townshend Duties, Parliament had retreated from a confrontation with the colonists by repealing the legislation. As George III frequently discarded prime ministers, the British government had been unable to establish a consistent colonial policy. By 1773, however, George III had firmly established Lord North as prime minister, and, with members of Parliament outraged by such a clear challenge to British authority as the Tea Party, Britain was ready to exert itself. The Coercive Acts of 1774 closed the port of Boston until the dumped tea was paid for, reorganized the government of Massachusetts so that the royal governor exercised virtual control, and ordered that Americans in violation of British trade regulations be tried in Halifax, Nova Scotia, where they would not have the advantage of sympathetic American juries. Britain had drawn the line. Now the Americans would have to decide whether they would support their brethren in Massachusetts and by so doing further intensify controversy with King and Parliament.

With Governor Trumbull and the easterners in command, there really was no question about the course Connecticut would follow. Urged on by radical pamphlets and fiery meetings of the Sons of Liberty, the colony moved briskly to support the Patriot position. In May 1774 the General Assembly passed resolutions repudiating the Coercive Acts and promising aid for Boston. The same month the Assembly accepted an invitation from the Virginia legislature to establish a Committee of Correspondence to facilitate communication among Patriots throughout the colonies. Connecticut's committee soon afterward appointed Roger Sherman, Eliphalet Dyer, and Silas Deane to represent the colony at the First Continental Congress in Philadelphia in September. By October the Assembly, preparing for the worst, ordered intensive training of militia and asked towns to double their supply of powder, ball, and flints. Early in 1775 Connecticut's towns ratified the action of the First Continental Congress that called for the support of Massachusetts and for immediate non-importation of British goods and nonexportation of American products to Britain and her possessions.

While Governor Trumbull and the General Assembly, reflecting the Patriot position of eastern Connecticut, were moving to support Massachusetts and resist the Coercive Acts, Connecticuters acted energetically to silence any Tory opposition. Those residents or visitors in Connecticut who were inclined to condemn the Patriot-Radicals for their "wild and licentious" activities felt the full brunt of popular and official denunciation.

Francis Green, a Bostonian who had pledged his loyalty to the mother country, made the almost fatal error of visiting radical Windham in July 1774. Local Patriots hauled a cannon to the door of the inn where Green was staying, suggesting that unless the visitor moved on, both he and the inn would be immediately restructured. A comparable experience was that of the Reverend Samuel Peters, an Anglican clergyman in Hebron who had antagonized the eastern-Connecticut radicals by his spirited attacks on the Sons of Liberty. In September 1774 a mob of three hundred led by the Sons forced Peters out on the Hebron Green, where he was made to retract his views.

Through all of this mob activity the hapless victims found that appeals to Governor Trumbull for "law and order" did little good. Trumbull, believing that "a man's right to protection by the state was qualified by his political opinions," [6] did not lift a finger to protect the assaulted Tories. When both Green and Peters wrote to him for protection, Trumbull replied that it was beyond his power to restrain people from doing what they considered to be their duty.

When, in January and February 1775, moderates in Fairfield and Litchfield counties joined together to assert their allegiance to the Crown, they too found Trumbull less than appreciative of their views. The governor went before the March 1775 session of the General Assembly to malign such Tories as "depraved,

6. Clifford J. Shipton, "Jonathan Trumbull," *Sibley's Harvard Graduates: Biographical Sketches of Those Who Attended Harvard College* (Boston: Massachusetts Historical Society, 1951), 7:280.

malignant, avaricious, and haughty'' and called for ''Manly action against those who by force and violence seek your ruin and
destruction.'' [7] The radical-dominated Assembly heeded Trumbull's call and passed legislation providing for the investigation
of Toryism in western Connecticut. The westerners, thrown out
of political power by the election of 1766, now found themselves forced into silence or hounded into New York by the
easterners in political control of Connecticut.

Any possible remaining question of Connecticut's course in
the imperial controversy evaporated the next month when word
came of the clash at Lexington and Concord. As the ''Lexington
Alarm'' spread throughout the colony, Connecticut moved un-
hesitatingly in support of the sturdy farmers who had tasted
British steel. Some 3,600 men, Sons of Liberty and militiamen,
drew their weapons and marched to join the Patriot force collecting at Cambridge. The patriotic—and immediate—response
of Connecticut to the ''Lexington Alarm'' was to be characteristic of Connecticut's support of the American cause throughout
the Revolutionary War.

Connecticut's contributions to the American victory were
made possible by a number of factors. First, Connecticut, unlike
such states as Pennsylvania, the Carolinas, and Georgia, did not
experience a Patriot–Tory conflict of any significance during the
Revolutionary War. Connecticut's internal conflict in the Revolutionary era had taken place during the crisis over the Stamp
Act in 1765–1766. With the eastern radicals' victory in the election of 1766, those who placed obedience to the mother country
before the defense of American rights had little influence. Such
persons, especially during the critical days of 1774–1775, were
subjected to brutal assaults by the Sons of Liberty if they drank
tea, failed to participate in days of patriotic fasting or thanksgiving, or actually spoke out against the American cause. Connecticut's Revolutionary generation was clearly not concerned with
minority rights.

Once the war began, unofficial mob violence was replaced by
state action. The General Assembly in 1775 and 1776 enacted

7. The Jonathan Trumbull Papers, 20/1:101a–101c, Connecticut State Library.

legislation providing for loss of property, imprisonment, or death for those who aided, joined, or sympathized with the British. Connecticut's Tories, many of whom were Anglican and almost all of whom were located in western towns such as Norwalk, Stamford, Fairfield, Ridgefield, Newtown, Danbury, Greenwich, Stratford, Redding, and New Haven, came to number some six percent of the adult male population (2,000 to 2,500 out of a total of 38,000 males). The state's Patriots were eager to search out traitors in their midst; Tories were quickly identified, disarmed, subjected to loss of property, and in some cases imprisoned. This process of neutralizing the Connecticut Tories was so swift and so complete that Loyalists had no opportunity to combat the tide and energy of the Patriot majority. Rather, the hapless Tory minority was forced into a grudging acceptance of the Patriot position or, if that could not be swallowed, into fleeing the state. It has been estimated that more than 1,000 Connecticut Tories did leave for the safety of the British forces in New York. Some wound up joining such British regiments as General Montfort Browne's Prince of Wales' American Volunteers, the Queen's Rangers, and Colonel Edmund Fanning's King's American Regiment. While these regiments were to play a role in British raids on Connecticut, such activity probably gave insufficient satisfaction to men who had lost their homes and their homeland—many of these Tories eventually left the United States and settled in England, New Brunswick, and Nova Scotia.

In a sense the ease with which Connecticut's Tories were neutralized worked to their long-range advantage. Since there was no protracted Patriot–Tory conflict and since the Tories could not have served as a threat to the Patriot majority, by 1777 Governor Trumbull and the General Assembly adopted a softer position toward them. The General Assembly offered pardons to Tories who wished to return to Connecticut, and Trumbull provided compassionate treatment to many. Nine Tories held in Lebanon and Coventry were released upon giving bonds and assurances for their good behavior, and large numbers held in Stamford and Norwalk likewise were given freedom. A young Anglican divinity student successfully petitioned Trumbull for permission to journey to London to take holy orders, and a Connecticut Tory physician was given permission to move his family and possessions to the British lines in New York.

Another factor that enabled Connecticut to make a major contribution to American success during the Revolutionary War was the high degree of political stability that it enjoyed during the war years. As an essentially autonomous corporate colony in 1775, Connecticut did not have to go through a difficult period of political reorganization as did most of the emerging American states. In fact, the only action independence demanded from the General Assembly was a resolution of October 1776 that declared:

> The form of civil government in this State shall continue to be as established by Charter received from Charles the second, King of England, so far as an adherence to the same will be consistent with an absolute independence of this State on the Crown of Great Britain; and that all officers, civil and military, heretofore appointed by this State continue in the execution of their several offices, and the laws of this State shall continue in force untill otherwise ordered.[8]

Thus, Connecticut simply dropped all references to Great Britain and continued the representative government that had served its interests throughout the colonial period. Indeed, Connecticut not only did not reorganize her government during the Revolutionary era, but stuck to her traditional governmental framework until the adoption of a new state constitution in 1818.

Connecticut's political leadership and principles as well as its governmental framework remained stable during the Revolutionary War. The easterners who had come to political power as a result of the Stamp Act crisis had by the time of the war become Connecticut's new "Standing Order" of political respectability and power. Throughout the war years Jonathan Trumbull served as governor, Matthew Griswold as deputy governor, John Lawrence as treasurer, George Wyllys as secretary, and William Williams as speaker of the House of Represen-

---

8. Charles J. Hoadly and Leonard Woods Labaree, compilers, *The Public Records of the State of Connecticut, 1776–1784,* 5 volumes (Hartford: 1884–1943), 1:3.

tatives. These easterners stuck to those conservative, Puritan-rooted political principles that had been so evident in colonial Connecticut. While the easterners were "radicals" insofar as they took a hard line with respect to the government of George III, they were far from advocating political innovations that might have threatened the dominance of Connecticut's conservative Congregational order. Hence, while other states had their war effort seriously weakened by political reorganization or by controversies stemming from political innovations, Connecticut, enjoying a smooth transition from a colony to a state and maintaining its conservative orientation, could devote itself without serious distractions to aiding Washington's forces.

Finally, Connecticut's support of the Patriot cause during the Revolutionary War was greatly facilitated by its fortune in escaping British occupation. If Connecticut had experienced the prolonged presence of enemy troops, as did New York and Pennsylvania, clearly Connecticut would have been less able to contribute to Washington's victory.

As it was, Connecticut suffered damage from four British attacks during the Revolutionary War. In April 1777 Major General William Tryon, the royal governor of New York, led some 2,000 troops in an assault on Danbury to destroy supplies stored for the Continental Army. Tryon's forces easily pushed aside a militia unit of less than 200 men and set about burning and ravaging. Although Tryon's men were diverted by supplies of rum and bothered by a militia counterattack led by David Wooster and Benedict Arnold, they still were able before withdrawing to destroy 1,700 bushels of corn and 1,600 tents—provisions and materiel badly needed by the American forces.

The next British assault on the state came in February 1779 when Tryon led an attack on the saltworks at Greenwich. Even though Connecticut militiamen under the command of Israel Putnam drove off the attackers, Greenwich suffered damage later estimated at £6,000.

An even more destructive raid was that of July 1779 when the British commanded by General George Garth and Tryon struck at New Haven, Fairfield, and Norwalk. The enemy contingent of 3,000 swept through New Haven burning, looting, and destroying property valued at £14,000. In Fairfield the British put the torch to the town, burning over 200 buildings. The assault concluded at Norwalk, where the destruction included 2 churches, 40 shops, 130 homes, flour mills, saltworks, almost 100 barns, and 5 ships.

While the first three British attacks brought considerable destruction of property and provisions in Connecticut, they generally did not involve much loss of life. This was not true, however, of the last British assault on Connecticut during the Revolutionary War. With close to 2,000 men under his command, Connecticut-born Benedict Arnold raided New London and Groton in September 1781. Whether because of the British hatred of New London as a nest for privateers, the bitterness of Arnold toward his renounced homeland, or the circumstances of the battle, the episode was one of the bloodiest of the war.

The New London–Groton area was guarded by two forts— Trumbull on the New London side of the Thames River and Griswold on the Groton side. Arnold himself led the attack on Fort Trumbull, which, with its small detachment of men, fell quickly. Griswold, however, proved to be a much more formidable objective. There, some 150 Americans under Colonel William Ledyard held off a British attack force of over 800. Using cannon fire and the fort's stone walls to their advantage, the American defenders inflicted heavy casualties before Griswold was finally carried by a slashing British bayonet charge. Then, as Ledyard surrendered his sword, he was run through by one of the enemy officers. This began an orgy of bloodletting during which the British soldiers, apparently inflamed by the losses they had suffered, massacred over eighty of the surrendering Americans, including those who were wounded.

While Benedict Arnold had played no role in the butchery at Griswold, he was responsible for the catastrophe that was taking place at the same time on the opposite shore. As they set ablaze ships and warehouses, Arnold's forces began fires that ravaged the town. By the time the blaze was brought under control, New London had lost sixty homes, thirty stores and warehouses, eighteen shops, twenty barns, and a dozen public buildings.

The massacre of the surrendering troops at Fort Griswold and the burning of New London were bitter enough events in themselves, but the episode was particularly maddening to Connecticut citizens because of the involvement of the despised Benedict Arnold. Public indignation in Connecticut had not yet subsided at the news that Arnold had turned traitor by attempting to turn over the American fort at West Point to the British. Now Connecticuters were even more inflamed as Arnold completed his descent into dishonor by leading the vicious assault on New London. It is little wonder, therefore, that few in Connecticut—then or even now—have been able to view Benedict Arnold with objectivity.

Given the facts of his life, Arnold's treason can perhaps be understood, if not condoned. Born in Norwich in 1741, Arnold spent a boyhood troubled by a bankrupt and drunken father and a mother who sent the boy to be raised by cousins. These circumstances apparently made Arnold a bitter man—one who attempted to gain success as an adult as compensation for the emotional deprivations of his youth. Throughout his life he was willing to sacrifice all to satisfy his ambition. As one of his critics said early in the Revolutionary War: "Money is this man's god, and to get enough of it he would sacrifice his country." [9]

As a young man, Arnold operated an apothecary's shop in New Haven and was involved in trading ventures with Canada, the West Indies, and Central America. His commercial interests led him to resent the British legislation of the 1760s, and he therefore became a member of radical political circles. Just before the outbreak of the Revolutionary War, Arnold was made a captain of a militia company organized in New Haven as the "Governor's Second Company of Guards."

At the start of the war, Arnold—short, dark, and powerfully built—assumed his military duties with energy and fearlessness matched by few American commanders. In May 1775 he shared

9. John Brown, of Pittsfield, Massachusetts—a patriot leader and Revolutionary War officer who clashed with Arnold at Ticonderoga and at Quebec. Quoted in Willard M. Wallace, "Benedict Arnold: Traitorous Patriot," in George A. Billias, ed., *George Washington's Generals* (New York: William Morrow and Company, 1964), p. 179.

command with Ethan Allen of a Connecticut–Massachusetts–Vermont force that captured Fort Ticonderoga, a crucial outpost on the Lake Champlain route to Canada. Shortly afterward, as a colonel in the Continental Army, Arnold played a leading role in an American offensive action against Canada. Although Arnold's thrust at Quebec did not succeed, he won the praise of Washington by leading a heroic march through the Maine woods during which he kept his troops moving although they were reduced at one point to eating meals of boiled moccasins and a gruel of shaving soap. By 1777, now a brigadier general, Arnold was visiting his family at New Haven when Tryon made his attack on Danbury. Upon hearing of the British thrust, Arnold helped mobilize the militia to complicate Tryon's withdrawal. Although he had two horses shot from under him, Arnold gave no quarter—a performance that shortly afterward led Congress to promote him to major general. By the fall of 1777 Arnold was at Saratoga as General John Burgoyne led his troops toward Albany. Despite the fact that he had been deprived of his command by Gates for insubordination, Arnold entered the battle at a crucial point and succeeded in leading the American troops through Burgoyne's entrenchments.

In spite of his battlefield glories, his promotions, and an appointment as commandant of the city of Philadelphia, by the late 1770s Arnold was a badly frustrated man. His military career had been damaged by quarrels with fellow officers and by charges that he had used his Philadelphia command to aid him in various personal financial schemes. Moreover, a series of war wounds had left him a cripple with one leg shorter than the other—a condition which the always vain Arnold found unbearable. Finally, finding himself unable to satisfy the social aspirations of his second wife—the beautiful, restless Peggy Shippen of Philadelphia—Arnold proved vulnerable to the blandishments of the British. His unsatisfied ambition led him to exchange loyalty to his nation for a payoff of £6,000 and a commission as brigadier general in the British Provincial Army, an arrangement that won for him the curses of every Connecticut Patriot. Even though Connecticut was inflamed by the Benedict

Arnold-led attack on New London and Groton, this raid did no more than the previous ones to seriously weaken the state's ability to contribute to Washington's victory.

Connecticut's war effort was guided by Governor Jonathan Trumbull of Lebanon. Born in 1710 to one of Lebanon's leading merchants, Trumbull was prepared for the Congregational ministry by study with a local clergyman and by attending Harvard College. After his graduation from Harvard, however, Trumbull joined his brother and his father in the family mercantile business, and when his brother was lost at sea in the early 1730s during a trading voyage to Barbados, Jonathan Trumbull took on ever increasing business responsibilities.

Trumbull's turning from the pulpit to the marketplace apparently caused him little regret. He assumed mercantile and later political responsibilities with extraordinary energy and dedication, and in the decades leading up to the Revolution Jonathan Trumbull emerged as one of Connecticut's most prominent citizens. He greatly expanded the family business to include commercial operations in Nova Scotia, Britain, and the West Indies. He won as his bride Faith Robinson of Duxbury, Massachusetts, a beauty whose family was descended from no less than Priscilla and John Alden.[10] Their home became the center of Lebanon's social life, and Trumbull involved himself in the founding of the Philogrammatican Society of Lebanon, one of the earliest American non-academic libraries.

Trumbull's record of achievement in Connecticut public life in the decades before the Revolutionary era was unequaled. He served in one of the two houses of the General Assembly in al-

---

10. The couple had six children, three of whom played important roles in eighteenth-century America. Joseph (1737–1778) served as the Commissary-General of the Continental Army from 1775 to 1777. Jonathan, Jr. (1740–1809), during the Revolutionary War was Pay Master of the Northern Department (1775–1778), Comptroller of the Treasury (1778–1779), and secretary to General Washington (1781–1783) and afterwards was a United States congressman (1789–1794), senator (1794–1797), and the governor of Connecticut (1797–1809. John Trumbull (1756–1843) saw service in the Revolutionary War at Dorchester Heights (1776), at Crown Point and Ticonderoga (1777), in Pennsylvania (1778), and in Rhode Island (1777 and 1778). Subsequently his celebrated paintings based on Revolutionary War scenes came to constitute a landmark in the evolution of American painting.

most every year from the mid-1730s to the mid-1760s; represented Connecticut in intercolonial conferences during King
George's War (1744–1748) and the French and Indian War
(1765–1763); served as a justice in the colony's county, probate, and superior courts; and was appointed a colonel in the
Twelfth Connecticut Regiment. A leading force in eastern Connecticut's surge to political power in the 1760s, Trumbull became deputy governor in 1766 and governor in 1769.

As Connecticut's governor in the Revolutionary era, Trumbull, obviously influenced by his theological background,
viewed the Anglo-American conflict in strikingly religious
terms. America was, to his mind, the most potent instrument of
the divine will in achieving Christianization of the world.
America was to be a just and humane society that by its existence would demonstrate to mankind that salvation could be
gained if only the will of God were followed. Americans since
the generation of Winthrop and Hooker had succeeded in meeting their obligations to the divine will. They had evolved with
God's blessing a fruitful society in which attention to labor and
His word had brought a free and satisfying life. Yet at the
moment when America, this "City upon a Hill," was reaching
maturity, the Lord's enemies had struck. The hosts of Satan, in
the form of British statesmen, had attempted to corrupt and
debase this pristine society; by so doing they were testing the
will and determination of God's chosen to adhere to their mission. If Americans allowed British tyranny and corruption to
emerge triumphant, God's will would once again have been spat
upon by the forces of evil, who would delight in glorying in the
vice and squalor that they regarded as the proper characteristics
of man's existence.

Functioning on the basis of such a Puritan-oriented political
outlook, throughout the war era Trumbull associated the cause
of American nationhood with that of the realization of God's
plan for the salvation of mankind. In June 1776 Trumbull interpreted the struggle to the freemen of Connecticut thus:

> The Race of Mankind was made in a State of Innocence and
> Freedom, subjected only to the laws of God. . . . But through

Pride and Ambition, the Kings and Princes of the World, appointed by the People the Guardians of their Lives and Liberties . . . degenerated into Tyrants. . . . An unnatural King has risen up—violated his sacred obligations, and by the Advice of evil Counsellors, attempted to wrest from us, their Children, the sacred Rights we justly claim, and which have been ratified and established by solemn compact with, and ratified by, his Predecessors.[11]

In calling out the Connecticut militia for service in New York some two months later, his proclamation had the ring of Old Testament verses:

Be roused therefore and alarmed to stand forth on our just and glorious cause. Join yourselves to . . . the companies of militia now ordered to New York. . . . Stand forth for our defence. Play the man for God, and for the cities of our God. May the Hosts, the God of the armies of Israel, be your Captain, your Leader, your Conductor and Saviour. . . .[12]

For Trumbull there could be no compromise with the forces of evil. The British came to represent unadulterated darkness and corruption. Describing their conduct before the evacuation of Boston, he said: "Burning and destroying our towns, robbing our property, trampling on . . . places dedicated to divine worship and service, and cruel treatment of the persons so unhappy as to fall into their hands, are injuries of the first magnitude. Every subtle art, as well as arms, are used against us." [13]

If Trumbull was convinced that the enemy represented evil, he was just as certain that the ultimate design of God was the victory of American arms. Writing to the Connecticut delegates in Congress in July 1775 he advised them "to have your eyes upon the supreme director of Events for protection and Defence. He is good, He is a stronghold in the day of Trouble, He goes with them that put their trust in Him." [14] After Washington's

11. Quoted in Shipton, "Jonathan Trumbull," pp. 285–286.

12. Quoted in I. W. Stuart, *Life of Jonathan Trumbull, Senior, Governor of Connecticut* (Boston: Crocker and Brewster, 1859), pp. 268–269.

13. Quoted in Stuart, *Life of Jonathan Trumbull*, p. 261.

14. Jonathan Trumbull to Roger Sherman, Eliphalet Dyer, and Silas Deane, November 7, 1775, Box 3, Jonathan Trumbull, Sr., Papers, The Connecticut Historical Society.

defeat in the Battle of Long Island in August 1776 when gloom and hopelessness characterized the American cause, Trumbull never doubted that the Lord would rescue America. In a proclamation issued in September 1776 he encouraged his fellow citizens "to supplicate for his Mercy, for Wisdom and Direction . . . so the free and independent States may be radicated, confirmed, established, built up, and caused to flourish, and to become a Praise in the whole earth." [15]

Although he was sixty-five years old in 1775, Trumbull emerged as the heart and soul of the Connecticut war effort. The aged governor turned his former store in Lebanon into the War Office, where he met between 1775 and 1783 with his Council of Safety—a committee of the General Assembly to deal with war matters. Day after day, through news of military defeat, financial chaos, and political confusion at Philadelphia, he sat at his battered desk in the War Office and turned out the directives, and occasionally pleas, that kept the Connecticut war effort functioning until ultimate victory was achieved. He came to be something of a comic figure to the sophisticated French who passed through Lebanon during the War. Remarks were made about the short, unimposing governor whose conversation was saturated with biblical exhortations. But the smiles never lingered very long, for this Old Testament patriarch never appeared anachronistic when the time came for performance. His quotas were very nearly always filled on time. He was the man to whom Washington turned when the shaky Continental Army was on the point of dissolution. In time, as the French came to appreciate the man's total commitment to victory, it was said that "when Louis XV asked Vergennes at Constantinople to send the Sultan's head, Vergennes replied that it would be a very delicate and difficult matter but would nevertheless send the head; Trumbull would not have even discussed the difficulty involved; he would have just sent the head." [16]

Trumbull's contributions to the American cause are perhaps

15. Quoted in Stuart, *Life of Jonathan Trumbull,* p. 273.

16. Quoted in Forrest Morgan, "Jonathan Trumbull—The Evolution of an Administrator," *Americana* 7 (March 1912):247–248.

even more impressive in light of the succession of personal tragedies that he experienced during the war years. His first—and most tragic—loss was that of his first-born daughter, Faith. Born in 1743, she had been educated at a private school in Lebanon and then had been sent to Boston to complete her studies. Faith added to the family's social position by becoming the bride of Jedediah Huntington of Norwich, one of eastern Connecticut's most eligible bachelors. The social and political prominence of the Huntington family was based upon the accomplishments of Jedediah's father, Jabez. The elder Huntington was a Yale graduate (1741) who made a fortune in the West India trade and went on to become a major political figure in Connecticut. Jedediah graduated second in his Harvard class of 1763. He then assisted his father in the family business until he devoted more and more of his time to political questions, becoming one of the most staunch eastern Connecticut Whigs by the late 1760s and early 1770s. Jedediah Huntington developed into a first-class officer during the Revolutionary War and put together an impressive record of service. Faith Trumbull Huntington, however, was not to live to share the honors accorded her husband.

The Trumbull family correspondence indicates that Faith was ill in 1775. Governor Trumbull wrote to his son Joseph, the Commissary-General of the American Army, in October 1775 to request that Huntington, a colonel of the 20th Regiment of Connecticut Militia, be relieved for a few days of his duties with Washington's army outside Boston so that he could visit Faith. It appears that Huntington did make it home to see her, but she died on November 24, 1775. The circumstances of Faith's illness and death are difficult to understand precisely; the only information available is the following excerpt from the autobiography of John Trumbull:

> About noon of that day [June 17, 1775, the day of the Battle of Bunker Hill] I had a momentary interview with my favorite sister, the wife of Colonel Huntington. . . . The novelty of military scenes excited great curiosity throughout the country, and my sister was one of a party of young friends who were attracted to visit the

Army before Boston. She was a woman of deep and affectionate sensibility, and the moment of her visit was most infortunate. She found herself surrounded, not by ''the pomp and circumstances of glorious war,'' but in the midst of all its horrible realities. She saw too clearly the life of danger and hardship upon which her husband . . . had entered, and it overcame her strong, but too sensitive mind. She became deranged, and died the following November. . . .[17]

One of Jonathan Trumbull's biographers, the great-great grandson of the governor, states that Faith took her own life, but the assertion is not supported by any documentation.[18] Faith must have been a person susceptible to emotional distress who suffered a severe psychological trauma while viewing the carnage of battle. The experience may well have so disturbed her that she suffered a state of depression which culminated in her suicide.

As tragic as was the death of Faith, no matter what the exact circumstances, it was only the first of the family's afflictions during the war years. Before Jonathan Trumbull could have adjusted to the loss of Faith, he was faced with the illness and death of his son Joseph. The eldest Trumbull son, a merchant, had enjoyed substantial public recognition in the 1760s and 1770s. He had served in the Connecticut General Assembly (1767–1773), had been a member of the colony's Committee of Correspondence (1773), and was chosen to represent Connecticut as an alternate delegate at the First Continental Congress (1774). On the basis of his mercantile experience and his public record, he was appointed by the Assembly in April 1775 to serve as the Commissary-General of the Connecticut troops assembled near Boston. He was so successful in this capacity that with Washington's urging the Continental Congress appointed him Commissary-General of the American Army on July 19, 1775. Although Joseph Trumbull's efforts as Commissary-

---

17. Theodore Sizer, ed., *The Autobiography of Colonel John Trumbull: Patriot-Artist, 1756–1843* (New Haven: Yale University Press, 1953), p. 21.

18. Jonathan Trumbull, *Jonathan Trumbull: Governor of Connecticut, 1769–1784* (Boston: Little Brown and Company, 1919), pp. 175–176.

General were recognized,[19] the task was fraught with endless difficulties. Transportation was laborious and uncertain; purchasing was impeded by a constant shortage of funds, state embargoes, and wildly fluctuating currency values; and agents of the Continental Commissariat often found themselves in competition for provisions with state agents. In addition to constant complications occasioned by these difficulties, Joseph Trumbull experienced a particularly bitter clash with General Philip Schuyler in 1776 over the prerogative of the Commissary-General in supplying the Northern Army.

While Trumbull's position in the controversy was ultimately supported by both Washington and Congress, he decided to resign his position in the spring of 1777 when Congress put into effect a scheme for the reorganization of the Commissariat that Joseph thought unworkable. Congress had decided to reorganize the commissary department by creating two commissaries-general, one of purchases and the other of issues. Trumbull thought this foolish but was especially angered by the additional provision that deputy commissaries were to be appointed by and made responsible to Congress. He wrote to General Washington: "In my humble opinion the head of every department ought to have the control of it. . . ." In explaining his resignation to Washington, he concluded by saying: "It never shall be said that I was the first American pensioner. I am willing to do and to suffer for my country and its cause, but I cannot sacrifice my honor and principles." [20]

Joseph Trumbull's resignation as Commissary-General did not signify any unwillingness to continue to shoulder public responsibilities, for in November 1777 he accepted an appointment to the Board of War. But his tenure as Commissary-General had so shattered his health that when he was stricken with a cold in the winter of 1777–1778, he underwent a physical decline from which he was not to recover. By February 1778 he

19. Washington was especially enthusiastic regarding the performance of Joseph Trumbull. See John C. Fitzpatrick, ed., *The Writings of George Washington*, 39 volumes (Washington, D.C.: Government Printing Office, 1933–1944), 5:192.

20. Joseph Trumbull to George Washington, July 19, 1777, The Governor Joseph Trumbull Collection, 5:493, Connecticut State Library.

had experienced paralysis of his left side and was suffering from jaundice. Although he appeared to be recovering during the summer from his afflictions, Joseph Trumbull had a relapse and died on July 23, 1778.

A final personal loss that Jonathan Trumbull had to bear during the war was the death of his wife. By the late 1770s, in her sixties, Faith Robinson Trumbull began to suffer from a dropsical affliction that finally took her life on May 29, 1780. She had been not only an affectionate wife and mother, but a woman who had understood and bound herself to the nation's cause for which her husband and sons were laboring. During the Revolutionary War she was a tireless worker on behalf of Connecticut troops and their families. She supported charities, instituted clothing drives, and encouraged soldiers' wives to bear the burdens of loneliness and economic deprivation. It was said that during one of the clothing drives, she inspired others by contributing to the cause "a magnificent scarlet cloak" that had been given to her by Count Rochambeau. The death of Faith Robinson Trumbull deprived Trumbull of a loving and philosophically compatible mate.

Despite these tragedies, Trumbull was throughout the war years a strong, competent statesman who successfully bore the burdens of wartime administration, and who in the process came to be viewed by his contemporaries as one of the most potent instruments in the achievement of American independence.

Trumbull and Connecticut were especially important during the war in supplying Washington's troops. The Connecticut, Housatonic, and Thames river valleys produced large crops of corn, rye, wheat, oats, barley, flax, vegetables, and fruit, and the hillsides of the northeast and northwest sections of the state were excellent grazing lands for cattle, horses, mules, and sheep. Connecticut put together a superior commissary staff under the leadership of such men as Joseph Trumbull, Elijah Hubbard, and Jeremiah Wadsworth. Overcoming poor roads, exposure, uncertain pay, and bitter conflicts with Continental agents, the agents and teamsters of Connecticut's Commissariat proved equal to almost every demand.

At the beginning of the war the Connecticut General Assembly adopted a ration schedule for state troops that was later to serve as a model for the Continental Commissariat. Each soldier was to be provided daily with three quarters of a pound of pork or one pound of beef, one pound of bread or flour, and three pints of beer. In addition, each man was to be supplied with "one jill of rum per day" along with milk, molasses, soap, candles, vinegar, coffee, chocolate, sugar, tobacco, onions, and other vegetables. Each week's ration also included a half-pint of rice or a pint of corn meal, six ounces of butter, and three pints of peas or beans. Connecticut had apparently learned well that an army does indeed travel on its stomach.

The Connecticut system of supply was also exceptionally efficient in providing clothing for state troops in the militia and the Continental regiments. The excellence of the state's efforts was demonstrated throughout the war, but it was especially apparent during Washington's terrible winter at Valley Forge in 1777–1778. More than two thirds of Washington's troops were practically barefoot, and thousands went without blankets in the dead of winter. In March 1778 Washington wrote Governor Trumbull: "Among the troops unfit for duty and returned for want of clothing, none of your State are included. The care of the legislature in providing clothing . . . for their men is highly laudable, and reflects the greatest honor upon their patriotism and humanity." [21]

The recognition that Connecticut received during the Revolutionary War as the "provisions state" was really not accorded on the basis of the state's everyday supplying of troops. Rather, Connecticut was recognized for its distinguished logistical effort in coming to the rescue of the American forces on two critical occasions. While many factors contributed to the American troops at Yorktown in October 1781 being in a position to sing "The World Turned Upside Down" while the troops of Cornwallis stacked their arms, not the least was the service that Connecticut provided to the American cause at crucial stages in the war.

21. George Washington to Jonathan Trumbull, March 3, 1778, Trumbull Papers, *Massachusetts Historical Society Collections*, Fifth Series, 10 (1888):111–113.

The winter of 1777–1778 has been called the Gethsemane of the American Army. Although the American victory at the Battle of Saratoga had had a favorable impact upon the court of Louis XVI, the American Congress sat for months without hearing from its commissioners in Paris whether France had agreed to become an ally of the United States. The so-called "Conway Cabal" was flourishing as members of Congress were disgruntled with Washington's showing at Brandywine and Germantown and Howe's subsequent occupation of Philadelphia. Finally, the American Army was in the process of disintegrating. After starting the campaign of 1777 with almost 10,000 troops, Washington wound up wintering at Valley Forge with a bleeding army of 3,000. The American Commissariat had broken down; Washington received supplies of food and clothing only irregularly, and because Valley Forge was located in a region that the previous campaign had cleansed of cattle and grain, Washington's troops endured an unprecedented trial by cold and hunger.

Housed in crude huts that were wracked by snow, wind, and rain, the troops huddled together around smoky fires. Few of the men had anything resembling adequate clothing. Lafayette described their plight: "The unfortunate soldiers were in want of everything; they had neither coats, hats, shirts nor shoes; their feet and legs froze until they became black and it was often necessary to amputate them." Hunger added to the torture of the troops. On December 20, 1777, it was reported that the men had been without bread for three days. Through January and early February Washington tried to keep his army fed by sending out foraging parties and writing desperate appeals to Congress. The Virginian apparently had little luck, for in February 1778 he wrote: "For some days past there has been little less than a famine in the camp. A part of the army has been a week without any kind of flesh and the rest three or four days." [22]

Under these conditions of exposure and hunger it is not surprising that disease swept through the American ranks. Typhus

22. Quoted in Christopher Ward, *The War of the Revolution*, 2 volumes (New York: The Macmillan Company, 1952), II, 545, 549.

was the principal scourge. With few physicians, less medicine, and no food to strengthen the stricken men, the troops were decimated by disease. Ill men were placed on dirty straw mats in huts and tents while the few helpless physicians watched them die. Of some 1,500 men hit by typhus, 550 died. A physician reported that he had "known four to five patients die on the same straw before it was changed." [23]

With his men hungry, cold, and overcome with typhus and the American Army literally dissolving before his eyes, in early February 1778 Washington sent urgent appeals for food to state governors such as Clinton of New York, Livingston of New Jersey, Read of Delaware, Johnson of Maryland, Henry of Virginia, and Trumbull of Connecticut. While each of these governors made a contribution to the maintenance of Washington's army during its time of crisis, no man labored more diligently than did Trumbull.

After meeting with his advisors in Lebanon, Trumbull delegated to one of the Connecticut commissaries, Colonel Henry Champion of Colchester, the task of collecting cattle to be driven to Valley Forge. Champion set out from Lebanon to round up as many head as possible throughout eastern Connecticut. Aided by endless dispatches from Trumbull to farmers, Champion was able to collect a large herd at Hartford. Then Champion and his son Epaphroditus began the long trek to Valley Forge. Moving into New York, crossing the Hudson at King's Ferry, passing through upper Jersey and over the Delaware, the herd finally reached the famished troops west of the Schuylkill. That Washington's troops were in dire straits at the time is clear: the entire herd was devoured within five days of its arrival. Epaphroditus Champion was said to have remarked that the beef had been eaten so thoroughly that "you might have made a knife out of every bone." [24]

Through the winter and spring of 1778 herd after herd of Connecticut cattle was driven to Valley Forge under the direc-

23. Quoted in Ward, *The War of the Revolution*, II, 546.
24. Quoted in Stuart, *Life of Jonathan Trumbull*, p. 367.

tion of Trumbull and Champion. These provisions, along with emergency shipments from New York, New Jersey, Maryland, and Virginia, were the crucial element in maintaining the American Army through spring, when the reorganization of the Commissariat made possible regular provisioning of Washington's troops. Bitter though the experience of the American troops at Valley Forge was, the army nevertheless survived its trial of hunger and cold, and in the spring of 1778 Washington was ready once again to fight in the cause of American independence.

The logistical problems of the American Army were, however, far from over. Indeed, by 1780 Trumbull and Connecticut were again called upon to rescue Washington's famished troops. While the winter at Valley Forge is often portrayed as the nadir of the American troops in the Revolutionary War, the winter of 1780 at Morristown, New Jersey, may have been an even more taxing period. The Commissary Department through the last half of 1779 went through various alterations. An attempt to establish a committee of Congress to oversee the limping operations of the Commissariat, and varying purchasing efficiency in the states, resulted in a bureaucratic tangle that brought provisioning almost to a complete halt. Washington had picked Morristown as the site of his winter encampment, as he had in the previous year, because of its accessibility from both the South and New England. Washington expected substantial supplies from the South for the winter but sought to remain near crucial Hudson Valley fortifications. Morristown selected, Washington began to move in for the winter in December 1779.

From the beginning, the Morristown sojourn was a disaster. Little preparation had been made to shelter the troops before their arrival, and the poorly provisioned men had to set to work to build log huts. The enterprise was made more complicated by the weather. The winter of 1778–1779 at Morristown had been a relatively mild one; that of 1779–1780 was terrible. By the time the troops arrived in camp there was already two feet of snow on the ground. On January 3, 1780, when the huts were little more than half completed, the worst blizzard of the century hit the area. As bitter, cold winds lashed the camp, drifts mounted to six feet. In desperate straits once again, Washington wrote Trumbull from Morristown on January 8, 1780:

> The army has been near three months on a short allowance of bread; within a fortnight past almost perishing. They have been sometimes without bread, sometimes without meat; at no time with much of either, and often without both. They have borne their distress . . . with as much fortitude as human nature is capable of; but . . . the soldiery have in several instances plundered the neighboring inhabitants . . . Without an immediate remedy this evil would soon become intolerable . . . We are reduced to this alternative, either to let the army disband or . . . to have recourse to a military impress. . . . Our situation is more than serious, it is alarming. I doubt not your Excellency will view it in the same light, and that the Legislature of the State of Connecticut will give a fresh proof of their wisdom and zeal for the common cause, by their exertions upon the present occasion.[25]

Trumbull's response to Washington's emergency was just as energetic as that during the Valley Forge crisis. The rider who brought the above letter to Trumbull arrived in Lebanon in the early afternoon. The governor made provision for the man to rest for the evening. The next morning Trumbull gave the rider a message for Washington, detailing the exact quantity of provisions that would be forthcoming from Connecticut and specifying the day and the hour that the foodstuffs would arrive in camp. Despite the difficulty of purchasing provisions from Connecticut farmers who were disgruntled with Continental paper and in the face of frozen roads and icy winds, the provisions, as Trumbull had promised, arrived on time to feed the starving troops.

Connecticut's support of Washington's forces during the Revolutionary War was not restricted to provisions; the state in addition made significant contributions of gunpowder, weapons, and troops. America entered the Revolutionary War with few facilities for the production of gunpowder. While some ninety

---

25. George Washington to Jonathan Trumbull, January 8, 1780, Trumbull Papers, *Massachusetts Historical Society Collections*, pp. 152–153.

percent of the powder used by American troops in the first two and a half years of the war came from Europe and imported powder remained important, some states, including Connecticut, made an effort to produce gunpowder themselves. Under the leadership of Trumbull and the General Assembly, Connecticut offered a bounty on the production of powder in the first year of the war. Soon mills were operating in East Hartford, Windham, New Haven, Stratford, Glastonbury, and Salisbury. Though the state's production was limited by insufficient supplies of saltpeter and sulphur, Connecticut was able to provide gunpowder to the American forces at Ticonderoga (1775), Cambridge (1775), Fishkill (1781), and Horseneck (1781). The bulk of the state-produced gunpowder, however, was dispatched to those Connecticut towns—Wallingford, Durham, Stratford, New Haven, Groton, Norwich, and New London—that were apprehensive of British attacks from either New York or the sea.

Connecticut made an even more significant contribution to the Patriot cause with its guns than with its gunpowder. The state was fortunate in 1775 in having a number of skilled craftsmen who had already distinguished themselves in the field of gunmaking. These craftsmen were induced to increase their production by a state bounty of five shillings per gun. Hence gunmakers, especially in Mansfield, Windham, and Goshen, labored energetically to produce sufficient guns so that Connecticut men sent to the Continental forces were generally adequately armed.

The production of cannon at the Salisbury foundry, taken over by the state at the beginning of the war when the Tory owner fled to Britain, was as important as the efforts of Connecticut's gunsmiths. Cannon went to General Schuyler in the Northern Department in the spring of 1777. More generally, however, cannon, grape shot, and round shot from Salisbury were sent to fortify Connecticut coastal areas such as Norwalk, New Haven, Greenwich, and New London. If these areas had not been protected by the products of Salisbury, it is likely that Connecticut would have felt more keenly than she did the lash of the British sword.

While Connecticut was laboring to provide the American forces with provisions, powder, and weapons, Governor Trumbull was constantly being called upon for troops by Washington and the Continental Congress. While proclamations were sufficient in the opening years of the war to bring forth Connecticut sons for state and Continental service, by 1777 Trumbull and the General Assembly had to resort to bounties to insure that the state would have sufficient manpower for militia and national service. On the whole, Connecticut's manpower contribution was impressive. With a total population of 200,000, the state had almost 40,000 of her sons in military service of some sort. Connecticut troops were at most of the significant engagements of the Revolutionary War, especially those in the North—the northern campaign (1775–1776), Boston (1775–1776), Long Island (1776), White Plains (1776), Trenton (1776), Saratoga (1777), Germantown (1777), Stony Point (1779), and Yorktown (1781).

The military charge of Governor Trumbull and the Council of Safety also included supervision over the state's small but potent fleet. During the Revolutionary War Connecticut floated a total of thirteen vessels, including brigantines, ships, sloops, schooners, and row galleys. Trumbull and the Council of Safety had direct control of the vessels: orders were issued in Lebanon to raise crews, to assign officers, and to provide for arms and provisions.

Although the Connecticut naval operation was perhaps not the most polished and sophisticated, the state's fleet won honors during the Revolutionary War. The *Oliver Cromwell,* largest of the state's vessels, was a full-rigged ship that took nine enemy prizes between 1777 and 1779, the most valuable of which was the brig *Honour* carrying a cargo worth £10,000. The *Defence,* another full-rigged Connecticut ship, was even more successful. She took thirteen British ships, including three troop transports, before she was broken on a reef trying to limp back to New London in 1779. Nor did the Connecticut vessels confine their attacks to merchantmen and transports. The *Trumbull,* a 36-gun frigate of 700 tons that was built in Connecticut and later sailed for the Continental Navy, fought a three-hour battle with the

British man-of-war *Watt* and more than held her own. All in all, the Connecticut fleet was responsible for capturing over forty enemy vessels and thus rendered significant service to the Continental cause.

In many ways an even more formidable naval weapon was the privateering activity of state vessels. Connecticut merchant-shipowners, finding their ships and crews idled by the disruption of normal trading patterns and by an increasingly stringent British blockade, were not sorry to see the passage of national and state legislation to legalize privateering. In the fall of 1775 and the spring of 1776, Congress established provisions for both itself and the states to commission privateers. The Connecticut General Assembly in May 1776 authorized Governor Trumbull to issue commissions "for Private Ships of War." Connecticuters were eager to combine their patriotic and acquisitive impulses, and as a result between 200 and 300 privateers sailed during the Revolutionary War from ports such as New London, New Haven, Wethersfield, Hartford, Saybrook, and East Haddam.

While the especially tight British blockade of New England kept Connecticut privateering at a minimum during 1776 and 1777, the shift of British military interest southward in 1778 signaled the flowering of state privateering activity. The high tide came in the period 1779–1780, with New London serving as the state's favorite privateering port. Although the signing of commissions for privateers was another of the endless tasks for which Trumbull was responsible during the Revolutionary War, at least the governor had the pleasure with his Council of Safety of enjoying the record of Connecticut's privateers. They were able to take as prizes over 500 British merchantmen, a blow that encouraged British merchants to regard George III's continued prosecution of the Revolutionary War with less than elation.

Using its men, its arms, and its ships, Connecticut clearly made a major contribution to the achievement of American independence. While other states dragged their heels in their support of the Patriot cause, Connecticut worked tirelessly to establish American nationhood. The aging governor perhaps best expressed Connecticut's appreciation of the stakes involved in

the Revolutionary War when he wrote to the president of the
Continental Congress in October 1783:

> That superintendg [*sic*] of Wisdom which governs human Affairs
> has bro't to a happy Termination our arduous Contest, It has bro't
> these United States to be named among the Nations of the Earth, as
> a Free, indepedendent & Sovereign People. . . . Suffer me to
> congratulate you, on this great Event—an Event . . . undoubtedly
> in the Work of Heaven and as such claims our utmost Gratitude &
> Love to the supreme Disposer of all Events.[26]

26. Jonathan Trumbull to Henry Laurens, October 5, 1783, Jonathan Trumbull, Sr., Papers, Box 4.

4

1783–1850:
Conservatism and Then Some

$\mathcal{F}$ ROM the end of the Revolutionary War in 1783 to the middle of the nineteenth century the United States bristled with change. The youthful nation exerted itself in foreign affairs via the War of 1812, the Monroe Doctrine, and the Mexican War; in the process it strengthened its image abroad and extended its boundaries to the Pacific. New lands were penetrated, explored, mapped, and finally settled by pioneer farmers hungry for rich harvests from virgin lands. Political life was convulsed by the birth and death of a score of parties, and national dialogue included acrimonious debate over suffrage, slavery, women's rights, temperance, the tariff, internal improvements, the rights of labor versus capital, and banking systems. Traditional economic patterns were impacted by exciting innovations in commerce, transportation, and manufacturing. Yet Connecticut, while not oblivious or even uninvolved in these transformations, remained true to its essentially conservative character between 1783 and 1850 and followed a path entirely appropriate for the "Land of Steady Habits."

The Revolutionary era brought little change to Connecticut society. While the easterners who swept to power in 1766 wished to repudiate the soft position of western Connecticut leadership regarding the controversy with the mother country, they had no intention of disturbing Connecticut's political or religious patterns. As would occur often in the future, Connecticut's former political "outs," once in office, proved far less recalcitrant than they had been when not in office. The easterners led by Jonathan Trumbull guided Connecticut through the pre-Revolutionary and war years ever respectful of Puritan concepts of rule by a political elite and religious worship supervised by the established Congregational Church.

During the 1780s Connecticut's conservative Standing Order—dedicated to the development of a national government with sufficient financial and military strength to preserve order and stability—took on and turned back a challenge from farmers in the northeastern and northwestern sections of the state. The strains of the war had produced serious internal division in Connecticut between merchants and farmers. The state's merchants did not fare badly during the Revolutionary War. Although hurt by a state trade embargo and Britain's blockade of New England, merchants were able to adjust by exploiting various economic routes. Some state merchants were able to carry on a lucrative trade with French and Danish possessions in the Caribbean by securing special permits from Trumbull and the Committee of Safety or by simply ignoring the state embargo. A number of merchants became involved in privateering, others had profitable dealings with state and national commissary agents, and a few threw both honor and patriotism to the winds and traded with the British and the Tories on Long Island.

Farmers found their wartime situation much less encouraging. While some large producers did enjoy increased demand for their crops by the state militia and the Continental Army, most of Connecticut's small farmers in the northern part of the state passed the war years in acute economic distress. They did not produce enough of a surplus to become involved in provisioning the military, and they were squeezed by steadily rising prices of manufactured goods. Disturbed by Connecticut's inability during the war to establish consistent price regulations, the agrarians complained about the "great pests of society," the merchants who were able to turn wartime scarcity to their own benefit.

At the same time, small farmers were bitter about Connecticut's approach to wartime taxation. They asserted that they had been forced to bear the greatest burden of new taxes (which were based on real property) while merchants, most of whose assets were liquid, had not generally been so affected. Although the Connecticut General Assembly had effected a revision of taxation during the war so that business profits as well as real estate were evaluated as taxable, small farmers never ceased to complain that they were bearing too large a portion of the increased taxes.

Thus embittered, Connecticut's small farmers were extremely sensitive in the 1780s to national political centralization that they believed would bring with it additional financial burdens. These farmers challenged Connecticut's nationalist-oriented Standing Order at a convention at Middletown in September 1783; they left no doubt that they intended to agitate against the Connecticut political establishment in order to prevent any state support for a stronger central government. Although they were defeated in their attempt to unseat the state's conservative-nationalist leadership in 1784, the agrarians constituted the principal opposition in Connecticut to the ratification of the United States Constitution in 1788. But they were no match for the state's Standing Order: Connecticut was a bulwark of strength in both the drafting and the ratification of the constitution.

The Connecticut General Assembly dispatched Oliver Ellsworth, William Samuel Johnson, and Roger Sherman as its delegates to the Constitutional Convention in Philadelphia. Ellsworth, a Princeton graduate who had studied theology and then the law, had been a member of the Continental Congress; after, ratification was one of Connecticut's first two United States senators; and later served as chief justice of the United States. Johnson was a Yale graduate, an Anglican who sat out the Revolution, and the President of Columbia College from 1787 to 1800. Sherman, born in Massachusetts, was a self-made man who after coming to Connecticut succeeded as a merchant, lawyer, and public official—serving as a judge of the County Court and the State Superior Court; as a member of the Continental Congress; and as the first mayor of New Haven. He is particularly noted in American history as the only person to sign the Association of 1774, the Declaration of Independence, the Articles of Confederation, and the Constitution. At the Constitutional Convention he was instrumental in the development of the so-called "Connecticut Compromise" by which the large and small states resolved their dispute regarding representation by the establishment of the House of Representatives, in which representation would be based on population, and the Senate, in which each state would have equal representation.

When the work of the convention was completed and the Constitution sent to the states for ratification, Connecticut's Standing Order waged a tireless campaign on behalf of the new framework of government. Beating back the opposition of the agrarians, the state's nationalist-conservatives, led by Ellsworth, Sherman, Noah Webster, Governor Samuel Huntington, and Lieutenant Governor Oliver Wolcott and aided by the Congregational clergy and the press, won an overwhelming victory for the Constitution by a vote of 128 to 40 at Connecticut's ratifying convention in Hartford on January 9, 1788. Connecticut thus became the fifth state to ratify the Constitution.

After the adoption of the Constitution and the subsequent formation of political parties, Connecticut manifested its essential conservatism by ardent support of the Federalist Party. Connecticut's leading lights—large farmers, successful businessmen, members of the Congregational clergy, officeholders, and newspaper editors—saw in the Federalist Party at the national level the same conservatism and respect for authority that they valued at home, and they managed to maintain the state as a Federalist stronghold until 1817. Connecticut's Federalists set up a system that left little hope for electoral success by the opposition, the small farmers and non-Congregationalists who supported the Jeffersonian Democratic-Republicans.

A principal device used by Connecticut's Federalists to maintain their control of the state was an elaborate process to select members of the Council, the upper house of the General

Assembly and the most conservative organ of Connecticut's government.

> Each voter was permitted to list the names of twenty persons whom he favored for the Council. In the October assembly meeting, these votes were counted, and the top twenty, on a state-wide basis, were declared nominated. At the ensuing April election, about six months later, each voter could vote for any twelve of the list of twenty. However, in listing the names of the twenty Council nominees (members of the Council were called "assistants") the current assistants or ex-assistants were listed first, regardless of how many votes they had received in the original balloting. Since voting started on the names at the head of the list, it can be seen that the system was stacked against any newcomer breaking into the highly-prized sanctum of the Council chambers. It would require considerable independence, even courage, to cast one's vote for a name far down on the list, and apparently few ever did.[1]

This restrictive system was made even more so by the passage in 1801 of the "Stand-up Law," which required that nominations of assistants at town meetings be made by standing up or a show of hands. Such a procedure made it likely that only a voter of real independence and strong character would dare risk the wrath of the local Federalist and Congregational establishment by standing up and nominating a detested Republican to the Council.

The Federalists were also aided in their retention of political power in Connecticut by Republican foreign policy. When Jefferson established an embargo on American commerce in 1807 in response to the British practice of impressment, Connecticut suffered economic devastation. The Federalist *Connecticut Courant* declared that the embargo had resulted in "[a] great reduction of the prices of the produce of our farms, a total stagnation of trade, vast distress among merchants, the depriving of bread for seamen who are dependent on the sea for livelihood. . . ."[2] Such assertions carried great political weight:

1. David M. Roth and Freeman Meyer, *From Revolution to Constitution: Connecticut 1763 to 1818* (Chester: The Pequot Press, 1975), pp. 51–52.

2. Quoted in Roth and Meyer, *From Revolution to Constitution*, pp. 57–58.

the number of Republicans in the lower house of the General Assembly fell to sixty-one in 1808 and forty-five in 1809. In 1812, when Madison fell before the pressure of the War Hawks and resigned himself to war against Great Britain, the Federalists, who had strong commercial ties to England and favored England in her clash with Napoleonic France, denounced the war in no uncertain terms and reduced the strength of the Republicans in the Assembly to thirty-six.

Although some 1,800 Connecticuters served in the American armed forces during the War of 1812, the state's Federalist governor and Assembly effected little cooperation with the Madison administration's war effort and even refused to allow the Connecticut Militia to leave the state. As the American Army suffered humiliation after humiliation, the state's Federalist press kept up its denunciation. The *Courant* declared the War of 1812

> an unnecessary war;—a war which might have been avoided without the sacrifice of natural rights, or national honour;—which, having been undertaken without the necessary preparation, has been . . . productive of little besides disaster and disgrace.[3]

Connecticut's ire over the War of 1812 was hardly diminished by two British attacks on the state in 1814. In April over two hundred British sailors and marines landed at Pettipaug Point (Essex) and proceeded systematically to destroy some twenty ships, causing losses estimated at $200,000. Connecticut felt the lash of the British sword once again the following August when an enemy fleet appeared off the coast of Stonington. Prevented from landing for two days, the British vented their frustration by pumping sixty tons of metal into Stonington. Since the British landing was prevented and the townspeople were able to withstand the bombardment with little damage, Stonington's citizens have ever since taken great delight in the lines of Philip Freneau on the Battle of Stonington:

> It cost the king ten thousand pounds
> To have a dash at Stonington.[4]

3. Quoted in Roth and Meyer, *From Revolution to Constitution*, p. 59.
4. Quoted in Van Dusen, *Connecticut*, p. 185.

But the episodes at Pettipaug Point and Stonington, along with Connecticut's long-felt disgust at "Mr. Madison's War," led the state's Federalists along a path that would prove fatal for continued Federalist control of Connecticut. They joined with representatives from other New England states at the Hartford Convention of 1814–1815. The assembled Federalists passed a number of resolutions, among them provisions for amendments to the United States Constitution requiring a two-thirds vote in Congress for a declaration of war and declaring that presidents could not be elected from the same state two terms in succession. While Connecticut's Federalists were none too guardedly taking swipes at Virginia's Republican dynasty and the War of 1812, the war was being concluded under circumstances that thrilled the nation. News of Andrew Jackson's victory at New Orleans, along with notice that the Treaty of Ghent did not reduce America's territory, left the impression that the nation had forced Britain to the peace table. Such an impression was undoubtedly good for the young nation's psyche, but it left Connecticut's Federalists in a terribly vulnerable political position.

The state's Republicans lost no time in exploiting the soft spot. A Republican pamphleteer characterized the Hartford Convention as "the foulest stain on our escutcheon," [5] and another Republican posed the question:

> What federalist can hereafter reflect on the events of the year 1814, and not feel ashamed of his party! What federalist can hereafter read the history of that year, and tell his children—"I acted with the party which favored and fed our country's enemy: I was one of that number that discouraged the government and preached rebellion! [6]

While the report of the Hartford Convention did in fact hint that secession might be a course of action for New England to consider, it was a bit much for the Connecticut Republicans to label the efforts at the Convention "rebellion." Nevertheless, Connecticut's Republicans were able to accuse the state's Federalists of unpatriotic activity and to translate their accusation into electoral gains. By the end of 1815 the Republicans had increased their seats in the General Assembly to 57.

5. Quoted in Roth and Meyer, *From Revolution to Constitution*, p. 63.
6. Quoted in Roth and Meyer, *From Revolution to Constitution*, p. 63.

The issue that ultimately enabled Connecticut's Republicans to topple the Federalists from power was disestablishment of the Congregational Church. Connecticut's established church, long a Federalist stronghold, occupied a unique position in the state: everyone—regardless of his religious preference—was taxed to support it. A predictable result was the retardation of the growth of other churches; any dissenter would be forced to contribute to both his own church and the Establishment's. Another result was that non-Congregationalists, particularly Baptists and Methodists, supported the Republican Party because the Federalists were such ardent advocates of the Congregational establishment. A break came for the Republicans in 1815 when the Episcopalians—traditional adherents of the Federalist Party—failed to receive funds they thought due them from the Federalist-dominated General Assembly. The Episcopalians promptly deserted Federalist ranks and associated themselves with an electoral effort that in 1817 defeated the Federalists for control of both the governorship and the lower house of the General Assembly. The long Federalist reign was over.

The Republican victory sparked the achievement of a long-sought Republican goal—the calling of a state convention to frame a new constitution for Connecticut. Unlike most of her sister states, Connecticut did not at the time of independence evolve a new state constitution but retained the Charter of 1662 based on the Fundamental Orders of 1639 as the framework of government. While Federalists were quite satisfied with this arrangement, Republicans for decades had maintained that the state's government needed overhauling along more liberal lines. With their control of the governorship and both houses of the General Assembly after the election of 1818, the Republicans called successfully for a state constitutional convention.

The Constitution of 1818 that emerged from the convention and was subsequently ratified by the state's voters achieved the Republican aim of disestablishment of the Congregational Church. The denomination that had been established and sustained in Connecticut by Thomas Hooker and his followers was to be reduced to one among several competing Christian sects. Connecticut henceforth would have separation of church and state and equality before the law of all Christian denominations.[7] In addition the Constitution of 1818—which would serve Connecticut until 1965—provided for liberalized suffrage requirements, strengthened prerogatives of the governor, gave greater independence to the judiciary, and established annual elections and legislative sessions. Finally, the constitution provided that each existing town would have two representatives in the House of Representatives, the lower house of the General Assembly, while new towns established after its adoption would have but one.

Just as the easterners had effected a political revolution in Connecticut in 1766, the Republicans had done likewise in 1817–1818. Federalist control of the state had been smashed, and the career of the Congregational Church as the state's established church was terminated. At this point, the Republicans—fresh from their recent triumphs—might have been expected to initiate additional liberal measures and thus lead Connecticut beyond the deadening retention of the status quo that had been the *raison d'etre* of the Federalist Party in the state. No such thing occurred.

For over a decade Republican Governors Oliver Wolcott, Jr., and Gideon Tomlinson advocated aid to agriculture, the stimulation of industry, new taxes for the building of roads and canals, opening the Connecticut River to navigation as far as the northern border of Vermont, the improvement of prisons with special attention to facilities for juvenile offenders, and increased taxation for the support of education. To these pleas for action and advance the Republican-dominated General Assembly generally turned a deaf ear. There were some legislative advances, to be sure—the end of imprisonment for debt for women; a simplification of land purchases by aliens; a redistricting of the state's Senate districts; and a revision of the tax structure to place a heavier burden on the wealthy and to include items such as stocks and bonds as taxable assets. But on the whole the Republican Assembly members distinguished themselves as thoroughgoing fiscal conservatives and ignored the pleas of their pro-

7. Connecticut's Jews were not granted the right of public worship until 1843.

gressive governors for an enlightened legislative program.

Indeed, in some areas the Republican Assembly retreated into reactionary postures. A reform of the poor laws in 1820 that placed greater responsibility on the towns resulted in decreased aid for the poor and the infirm. Support of education did badly as well. Since 1795 Connecticut's common schools had been supported in part by monies Connecticut had received from land sales. In 1820 the Assembly decided to cut yearly appropriations for education and let the School Fund serve as nearly the sole state support for education. The towns, ever loath to raise taxes themselves, failed to supplement the School Fund adequately so that the common school system noticeably deteriorated.

Thus, like the Federalists before them, the Republicans directed Connecticut public life with a marked commitment to the state's traditional conservatism. A comparable conservatism was maintained in the 1830s and 1840s by the successors to the Federalists and the Republicans, the Jacksonian Democrats and the Whigs.

Connecticut's Democrats, encouraged by the election of Andrew Jackson as president in 1828, emerged in the late 1820s and early 1830s and included newcomers to politics as well as the most liberal elements in the Republican Party. The Democrats, who elected four governors in the 1830s and 1840s, had an elaborately liberal program at their birth that included resolutions for an unrestricted franchise, the accountability of state officials, specific terms of office for judges, and shifts in taxes to remove some burdens from laboring classes. Once in office, the Democrats did enact a number of forward-looking measures, including ones that provided for altering restrictions on liquor sales; ending the exemption of clergy from poll taxes; abolishing traditional prohibitions on recreation during public fast days; abolishing imprisonment for debt; and simplifying divorce procedures. Yet the state's Democrats, although capable of securing office, were never able to stir the electorate so as to achieve the broad suffrage and humanitarian reforms that the Jacksonian movement achieved in other states.

As for the Whigs, they were hardly inclined in the direction

CONNECTICUT

A photographer's essay by Georgiana B. Silk

Photographs in Sequence

Long Island Sound.
Lighthouse Museum, Stonington.
Greenfield Hill Congregational Church, Fairfield.
Yale University.
Old State House, Hartford.
Boats on the Connecticut River off Essex.
"Thistles" (small boats) racing on Long Island Sound.
Lighthouse at Mystic Seaport.
Wetlands, Old Lyme.
Dairy farm at North Stonington.
Houses in Waterbury.
B. F. Clyde's cider mill, Old Mystic.
Mark Twain house, Hartford.
Girl with polo pony at Fairfield County Hunt Club, Westport.
Square-rigged ships, Mystic Seaport.

of liberalism. Founded in the 1830s by old Federalists and conservative Republicans (who for a time were National Republicans), the Whigs stood foursquare for conservatism and economic retrenchment whenever possible. The essence of the Whig philosophy was indicated by Whig Governor William W. Ellsworth in a speech in the 1830s: ''The time has come when experiments [by the Democrats] upon our dearest interests are no longer to be tolerated; and when experience, that great and unerring teacher in human affairs, is to resume her influence, and put to silence visionary politicians.''[8] Although Whigs were responsible for the establishment of a State Board of Commissioners for the Public Schools, which under the leadership of Henry Barnard improved public education, the party on the whole spent much of its career slashing away at the qualified liberalism of the state's Democrats.

Connecticut's drift through the decades between 1783 and 1850 holding fast to its traditional political conservatism was the result of a number of factors. The Congregational Church, even though disestablished in 1818, influenced greatly the approach to life of a good portion of the Connecticut population. While there had been discernible anticlerical sentiment in the years before disestablishment, it had to do more with worldly than with specifically religious matters. People's lives still revolved around the ways of the church:

> Well into the nineteenth century the first family exercise of the morning was Bible reading followed by prayer, and the ideal of Sabbath observance remained unaltered, in theory at least, until Civil War times. Only slight modifications crept into the law, one in 1818 permitting mail transportation on Sunday, and another in 1833 removing restrictions against labor and recreation on Fast Days. With these exceptions the law surrounded holy days with rigid constraint, prohibiting work, or play, or travel save to and from the meeting house.[9]

More important than the maintenance of the practices of Con-

8. Quoted in Jarvis Means Morse, *A Neglected Period of Connecticut's History, 1818–1850* (New Haven: Yale University Press, 1933), p. 305.

9. Morse, *A Neglected Period*, p. 121.

gregationalism was the fact that Connecticut's nineteenth-century Congregationalists, like their Puritan ancestors, held a view of life that placed very little emphasis upon progress. It thus follows that Connecticut's Congregationalists would not experience in the first half of the nineteenth century a burning desire for change but would be quite content with a political system that fostered stability and placidity. And finally, although Congregationalism's primacy was threatened in the decades between 1783 and 1850 by increasing numbers of Espiscopalians, Methodists, Baptists, Universalists, and eventually Roman Catholics, the Congregational Church in 1850 was still the dominant religious institution in Connecticut.

Still another factor that contributed to Connecticut's continuing conservatism in the first half of the nineteenth century was the political dominance of the state's small towns and rural areas. The Constitution of 1818 in providing for two seats in the House of Representatives for all of Connecticut's existing communities had been gravely unfair at best to the state's urban areas. In 1820 New Haven, with 7,000 people, had the same two representatives as the town of Union, which possessed but 725 souls. By 1850, the situation had become preposterous. Connecticut's small towns—those with less than three thousand inhabitants—comprised only fifty-five percent of the total population but controlled sixty-five percent of the seats in the House of Representatives.

Moreover, life in Connecticut's rural communities hardly produced a person who was inclined toward political innovation. Like all those engaged in agriculture, Connecticut's farmers lived tight, demanding lives centered on those chores that constitute the essence of life in an agricultural setting.

[The New England farmer]. . . . was responsible for the acres he tilled—for his grains, his root crops, his flax and hops, and his orchard. He bred, milked, and pastured his cows. He found grazing for the sheep, sheared them in late spring or early summer, and kept them in warm sheds in winter. The fowl he usually left to his wife, but the care of the swine, the oxen, and the horses was his. Planting, cultivating, fertilizing, and harvesting took days of hard labor. In winter when he could not work in the fields he built and repaired fences, kept his harness in order, husked, threshed, flailed, and winnowed grain, bottled cider, repaired the house, shed, and barns, and shoveled and ploughed snow on paths and roads, cut wood endlessly. . . .[10]

This sturdy farmer's life was much more challenging than most because he toiled on thin, stony, almost unyielding soil. Such unremitting toil in essentially bleak surroundings bred a person who went about his daily and yearly chores with the same absence of originality with which he charged his representatives in the General Assembly to hold the line against innovation and change.

A Connecticut farmer had generally paid dearly for the hard land that he made his own. A young man often went heavily into debt for the land that was requisite for respectability and standing in an agricultural community. Working for years— indeed a lifetime—to pay off his obligations produced the highest regard for both land and money. Consequently, Connecticut's rural population, which dominated the General Assembly, was quite predictably averse to dropping landholding as a suffrage requirement and to spending money for anything but the most basic government necessities. Although Connecticut's rural electorate changed its party allegiance a number of times between 1783 and 1850, through all political transformations it acted as a firm brake on government that even hinted at departing from established, traditional patterns.

The third factor that reinforced the state's conservatism between 1783 and 1850 was also linked to the condition of rural, agricultural Connecticut. The state's adherence to the *status quo* in these decades was strengthened by a massive migration from Connecticut that began in the years before the French and Indian War and peaked in the period from the 1780s to the 1840s. While the population of Connecticut was over 250,000 in the early 1800s, it has been estimated that almost three times that number had left for ostensibly greener pastures. What drove

10. Catherine Fennelly, *Life in an Old New England Country Village* (New York: Thomas Y. Crowell Company, 1969), p. 26.

thousands of Connecticuters from home and fireside is not difficult to discern.

Connecticut's supply of fertile land was insufficient to satisfy the demands of an astounding population explosion. Large families in early Connecticut appear to have been socially encouraged and economically demanded, and young men and women were induced to marry early and meet their conjugal responsibilities with more than ordinary attention. "A seventy-five-year-old grandfather with a head for arithmetic could count fifty or sixty grandchildren, and his dividend in great-grandchildren easily totaled three or four hundred." [11] Such a throng simply could not be integrated economically into a society in which there was a shortage of fertile land. Moreover, there were undoubtedly those—especially between 1790 and 1820—who could not bear the stifling political and religious pressures of Federalism and Congregationalism and who chose precarious travel and homesteading to the ideological confinement that existed at home. In addition, temporary phenomena such as the harshness of the weather in 1816, when there was frost in every month, drove thousands of Connecticut's Yankees to the road. Of the situation in 1816–1817, Samuel Goodrich wrote:

> I remember the tide of emigration through Connecticut, on its way to the West during the summer of 1817. Thousands feared or felt that New England was destined, henceforth, to become a part of the frigid zone. . . . A sort of stampede took place from cold, desolate, worn-out New England. . . . Some persons went in covered wagons—frequently a family consisting of father, mother, and nine small children, with one at the breast—some on foot and some crowded together under the cover, with kettles, gridirons, feather-beds, crockery, and the family Bible. . . .[12]

For whatever reason, Connecticut's sons and daughters left their homeland in amazing numbers destined for north, south, and especially west.

Before and after the French and Indian War, Connecticuters

11. Lee, *The Yankees of Connecticut*, p. 262.
12. Quoted in Lee, *The Yankees of Connecticut*, pp. 261–262.

were attracted by the Berkshire country in western Massachusetts. Enterprising pioneers from Canaan, Colchester, Danbury, Hartford, Litchfield, Lebanon, Lyme, Middletown, Ridgefield, Stonington, West Hartford, and Wethersfield helped to settle Berkshire county towns such as Alford, Becket, Egremont, Great Barrington, Hancock, Hinsdale, Lee, Lenox, Otis, Pittsfield, West Stockbridge, Washington, and Windsor. Largely of orthodox Congregational stock, these migrants from Connecticut no sooner seeded their land, built their homes, and hacked out their roads than they sent back home for a Yale-trained minister to preside over their churches. Indeed, nearly three quarters of the pastors in western Massachusetts by 1800 were from Yale.

With the settlement of western Massachusetts, the seemingly endless stream of emigrants from Connecticut fixed their eyes on the area between New York and New Hampshire which was to be Vermont but for decades was a source of bitter contention among New York, New Hampshire, and Massachusetts. Connecticuters played by far the most important role in the evolution of the state of Vermont. The area east of the Green Mountains was settled primarily by migrants from such eastern Connecticut towns as Lebanon, Hebron, Mansfield, Coventry, and Canterbury. These eastern Connecticuters generally were traditional Congregationalists and set up communities in Vermont that were models of Puritan propriety. Not so west of the Green Mountains. That region was settled by western Connecticuters (from towns such as Canaan, Cornwall, Litchfield, Milford and Salisbury), among whom were "the discontented, the religious deviates, the rustic individualists, the impatient, and the unpopular." [13] But more important than the differences between the eastern and western Connecticuters in Vermont was that when Vermont declared its independence in 1777 and drew up a constitution, the Connecticut influence on the document was profound. Such features of the Vermont constitution as those making the town the basis for representation in the legislature and demanding membership in a Protestant church as a

13. Lee, *The Yankees of Connecticut*, p. 264.

requirement for members of the legislature had their origins in Connecticut practice.

Eighteenth-century Connecticuters did not only go northward. Another major Connecticut population thrust was westward into New York. After the Revolution, Connecticuters from every corner of the state migrated by the thousands into western New York from Binghamton to Buffalo. When Timothy Dwight later toured the area, he wrote: "It is questionable whether mankind has ever seen so large a tract changed so suddenly from wilderness into a well-inhabited, and well-cultivated country. . . . The mass of the population forms . . . a most important accession to the State of New York; continually increasing both in numbers and value." [14]

Even more Connecticuters went farther west to Ohio. In 1786 Connecticut gave up its claim to that portion of Pennsylvania for which the founders of the Susquehannah Company had hungered in return for a congressional grant of the Western Reserve, a tract extending halfway across Ohio that included over three million acres. A portion of the Reserve—the so-called Fire Lands—was set aside as compensation to residents of Fairfield, New Haven, Norwalk, Danbury, and New London who had suffered losses at the hands of the British during the Revolution. The rest of the Reserve was sold on August 5, 1795, for $1,200,000 to a land company, after which the General Assembly set aside the money as a permanent endowment fund for education. Connecticut residents as well as former Connecticuters who had settled in western Massachusetts, Vermont, or New York flocked to Ohio, where by 1800 there were settlements in over a third of the townships of the Reserve. Perhaps the most often remembered of these Ohio-bound Connecticuters was Moses Cleaveland of Canterbury who laid the foundations of the settlement on Lake Erie that grew into the city of Cleveland.

Connecticut's migrants continued to swarm westward. A number of Connecticut families settled in LaGrange and LaPorte counties in Indiana. The Collins brothers of Litchfield went to Illinois, where in 1817 they founded Collinsville near St. Louis;

14. Quoted in Lee, *The Yankees of Connecticut*, p. 270.

Walter L. Newberry of Windsor went to Illinois too, and bequeathed much of his real estate fortune to found the great Chicago research library that bears his name. Connecticuters journeyed to Michigan and there made contributions like those of Isaac Crary, who helped to pattern the Michigan school system. Nelson Dewey, Wisconsin's first governor, was a Connecticut native son, and in Minnesota Connecticut migrants contributed to the evolution of such communities as New Haven, Hartford, and Winsted. Moses Austin of Durham tried Philadelphia, Virginia, and Missouri before his death; his son Stephen went on to Texas and became a prominent state-builder. From Torrington came John Brown, who slashed his way into American history by the "Pottawatomie Massacre" in Kansas in 1856 and by his abortive raid on the federal arsenal at Harper's Ferry, Virginia, in 1859. By 1860 almost three thousand Connecticuters had reached the end of the line—California. Especially remembered in California's history are Stephen J. Field of Haddam, who wrote the legislation creating the state's judiciary system, and Collis P. Huntington of Harwinton, who helped shape a vital link in the first transcontinental railroad—the Central Pacific.

There is, of course, much grandeur in this tale of Connecticut's sons and daughters populating various parts of the nation—and in the process exhibiting the rare courage that enables a person to leave the safe and the known to face the new and the challenging. But it spelled stark tragedy for Connecticut. While all points of the compass benefited from the drive and ambition of these Connecticut pioneers, Connecticut itself lost generations of men and women who might—if they had stayed at home—have served as a vitalizing influence in a state stricken with a blind adherence to the *status quo*.[15] Such a conclusion was not lost on conservative Connecticuters such as Timothy Dwight, who in thinking about this mass emigration concluded that ancient Rome was peaceful because it "sent [its] restless

15. The degree to which Connecticut's emigrants made their marks in their new homes was borne out by the remarkable fact that in 1831 one third of the United States Senate and one fourth of the House of Representatives had been born in Connecticut.

spirits abroad in [its] armies. Connecticut derives the same blessings to a considerable extent from her emigrations.'' [16]

A final factor in explaining Connecticut's continuing conservatism from 1783 to 1850 was that its emigrants were not replaced by any great numbers of European immigrants who might have acted as a balancing force to the state's dominant rural agrarians. While there were a goodly number of Irish living in the Wooster Square neighborhood of New Haven by the late 1840s, neighborhoods of this sort were rare in Connecticut before 1850. Until the era of the Civil War Connecticut had relatively few foreign-born residents and was pretty much as Henry Adams had described it as being in 1800: "a part of New England rather than of the United States.'' [17]

Influenced by rural political domination, the continuing strength of the Congregational Church, the impact of mass emigration, and the absence in any great numbers of the foreign-born, Connecticut between 1783 and 1850 thus followed its traditional conservative course.

16. Quoted in Roth and Meyer, *From Revolution to Constitution*, p. 81.
17. Quoted in Morse, *A Neglected Period in Connecticut's History*, p. 287.

5

1850–1865: Connecticut and the Ordeal of the Union

$\mathcal{OS}$OME events produce repercussions as unavoidable as the rush of a runaway locomotive barreling down a steep incline. In the Revolutionary era there was such an event. The Boston Tea Party of December 1773 set off a chain reaction that led inexorably to the military confrontation at Lexington and Concord in April 1775. The Tea Party drove an enraged King and Parliament to the punitive Coercive Acts of June 1774, to which the American Whigs responded with a tough line (at the First Continental Congress of September–October 1774) that included the decision to arm if necessary to protect beleaguered Boston. It was an American store of arms—as well as Sam Adams and Hancock—that the British set out to seize on their fateful march into the Massachusetts countryside. The result—with British determination to put a brake on the Bay Colony's recalcitrance and comparable Massachusetts determination to stand fast for American "rights"—was the beginning of the Revolutionary War.

There are similar chain reactions in later American history. The Mexican War of 1846–1848 was in many ways a lark for the United States, not unlike the experience in 1898 in the war against Spain. But from the earlier war stemmed a series of events that advanced American sectional disunity until the

123

North–South issue erupted at Fort Sumter in April 1861. The Mexican War reignited the dreaded question of expansion of slavery into the territories. That issue tortured the nation through the Compromise of 1850, the Kansas–Nebraska Act of 1854, the rise of the Republican Party at mid-decade, and the Dred Scott decision of 1857, finally bringing the election of Abraham Lincoln in November 1860 and the resultant beginnings of southern secession in December 1860, and ultimately the outbreak of war. The ordeal of the Union from the end of the Mexican War through the sectional disputes of the 1850s and the tragic years of 1861 to 1865 involved not only Connecticut's inevitable participation in sectional disharmony but, equally important, the state's response to the issues of the Civil War era with predictable faithfulness to its historic traditions and values.

An appreciation of Connecticut's sense of reverence toward the concept of the American Union is central to an understanding of the state during the era of the Civil War. The Puritan Congregationalists who supported the Patriot cause during the Revolution and who stood for ratification of the United States Constitution in the late 1780s conceived of the United States as a vehicle for the realization of America as the Wilderness Zion free of the Old World's corrupting influences. On the basis of such a conviction, the American Union took on a significance that transcended mere political arrangement: it was a divinely ordained instrument for the fulfillment of God's will. As the nation expanded and prospered in the first half of the nineteenth century despite sectional wranglings and periodic economic fluctuations, it appeared more and more to the Connecticut Yankee that his Union was a sacred trust to which he owed devotion as much as allegiance. Thus, by the time the concept and reality of the American Union were assaulted by rebels' shells at Sumter in 1861, the Connecticuter was as ready as anyone north of Mason's and Dixon's line to express devotion to the national cause by joining the Union Army, which Stephen Crane thirty years later would beautifully describe as "the vast blue demonstration."

The Connecticuter's devotion to the Union was hardly surprising given his traditional conservative political orientation. An obvious and pervasive respect for authority was basic to the conservative credo that had dominated Connecticut since the days of Hooker. The seventeenth-century Puritan Congregational fathers had drilled into their charges the conviction that society's leaders were to receive the obedience owed to God's "Chosen." Despite the relative secularization of Connecticut society in subsequent centuries, the Connecticuter was still periodically preached to by his Congregational clergymen on the respect owed to one's elders, to one's parents, and to one's political and ecclesiastical shepherds. The Connecticuter, immersed in an atmosphere permeated by such respect, could hardly ignore the necessity of respect for the ultimate symbols of earthly authority—the Constitution and the Union—as well as the appropriateness of designating the secessionist South as the exponent of disorder and anarchy.

Through the years from Sumter to Appomattox, Connecticut's leading clerical and political leaders thundered forth on the sanctity of the Union and the righteousness of the Union cause. Supreme among Connecticut's defenders of the Union was Horace Bushnell (1802–1876), the state's most distinguished nineteenth-century Congregational clergyman and theologian. Bushnell, in works such as *Views of Christian Nurture* (1847), *God in Christ* (1849), and *Vicarious Sacrifice* (1866), liberalized Congregational thought by repudiating the Calvinist conception of the depravity of children and had a profound influence upon the religious education of young people by sparking the Sunday School movement.

During the Civil War Bushnell, in his sixties and frail, gave testimony to his passionate devotion to American nationalism by preaching the inseparability of civil government and the Union. Since civil government was for Bushnell divinely ordained, it followed that secession was not only treason but a violation of the laws of God. By 1863, when he was tortured by Union defeats and the apparent growing strength of Democratic advocates of "peace at any price," Bushnell proclaimed that the sanctity of the Union cause justified a suspension of civil rights and civil liberties—or, as Bushnell put it, a "temporary waiving of the Constitution itself to save the Constitution and the nation.'' [1]

Another outspoken proponent of Connecticut's strong Unionist posture was William Wolcott Ellsworth. He was the son of jurist Oliver Ellsworth of Windsor, who had served Connecticut and the nation in the Revolutionary and early national periods as a member of Trumbull's Council of Safety, a Connecticut delegate to the Continental Congress, a member of the Connecticut delegation to the Constitutional Convention, a United States senator, and the second chief justice of the United States. The younger Ellsworth, himself a lawyer, spoke in Litchfield County in January 1862 in ringing defense of the Union:

> Consider the physical and natural relations of this country, which like ligaments bind these states indissolubly together, as well may the human body be separated and expect vitality and health. Can the hands say to the feet, ''I have no need of thee'' or the head to the heart, ''I have no need of thee?'' No more can this Union be divided, and our free government continued. [2]

If Connecticut thought in the Civil War era was decisively Unionist, sentiment in the state was also noticeably hostile to the institution of slavery. Connecticut had assumed a significant role in the antislavery thrust evident in America during and after the Revolution. By 1790 slavery had generally been abolished north of the Mason–Dixon Line, and every state but Georgia and South Carolina had enacted legislation against the slave trade. In Connecticut as well, the Revolutionary era brought advances against slavery. During the Revolutionary War many Connecticut blacks secured their freedom in exchange for military service; the record indicates that Connecticut's blacks received the same pay as whites and were given the opportunity to serve as soldiers and sailors rather than as laborers or servants. Of greater significance, in 1784 the Connecticut General Assembly enacted legislation providing that

---

1. Quoted in John Niven, *Connecticut for the Union: The Role of the State in the Civil War* (New Haven, Connecticut: Yale University Press, 1965), p. 275.
2. Quoted in Niven, *Connecticut for the Union*, p. 273.

every black born after March 1, 1784, would be free at age twenty-five, and in 1788 and 1790 legislation was passed to end the traffic in slaves in the state. By the time slavery ended in Connecticut in 1848, there were only twenty blacks still in servitude.

In the decades before the Civil War Connecticut had a number of antislavery and abolition societies whose members were actively engaged in routing fugitive slaves to Canada through the Underground Railroad. Slaves on the run from southern masters and northern hunters were protected in hiding places in communities such as Deep River, Hartford, Killingly, Middletown, and Willimantic.

Connecticuters provided additional evidence of their antislavery disposition in the *Amistad* case. The *Amistad* was a Spanish slave ship found drifting off Montauk Point in August 1839. After the vessel had sailed from Havana, the slaves had taken over the vessel and ordered the Cuban owners to set a course for Africa. The Cubans, hoping to land the ship in slave territory, accidentally sailed into Long Island Sound, where the vessel was boarded by the crew of the U.S.S. *Washington*. When the vessel was subsequently landed in Connecticut, there took place a complicated series of legal maneuvers during which the Cubans and the Spanish government sought the return of the vessel and its human cargo to their owners while the Africans sued for their freedom. A committee of Connecticut and New York antislavery people came to the defense of the Africans, providing them with such distinguished lawyers as Roger Sherman Baldwin, Theodore Sedgwick, and Seth P. Staples. The defense, which eventually came to include the aging John Quincy Adams, finally won the day when the United States Supreme Court upheld a Connecticut judicial decision that the Africans were to be free. Thirty-five of the African survivors of the *Amistad*—sixteen had died of cruel treatment before the mutiny—were returned to Africa and freedom.

Connecticut retained its antislavery posture as the North–South controversy heated up in the 1850s and exploded into warfare in 1861. Connecticut nullified the Fugitive Slave Act of 1850; supported the "free-soilers" in Kansas following the passage of the Kansas–Nebraska Act of 1854; and embraced the antislavery Republican Party by the mid-1850s. It had also produced Harriet Beecher Stowe. Born in Litchfield in 1811, Harriet Beecher in 1836 married Professor Calvin Ellis Stowe, an authority on biblical literature at Lane Theological Seminary in Cincinnati. Her distaste for slavery was nurtured by the antislavery atmosphere at the Lane Seminary as well as by a trip to a Kentucky plantation where she saw the reality of slave life. The most significant product of her experience was *Uncle Tom's Cabin, or Life Among the Lowly,* published in 1852. Within a year the book had sold 300,000 copies; within several years sales totaled three million and a generation of northerners was strengthened in its rejection of the South's "peculiar institution."

By the second year of the war, opinion in Connecticut—save for that of the Peace Democrats or Copperheads—strongly favored a legal death blow to slavery by means of emancipation. The *Hartford Courant* ran the following jingle on February 25, 1862, calling on Lincoln to free the slaves:

> Dread no future. Let the word
> Like the voice of fate be heard;
> Free the slave, the work is done!
> *Freedom's battle fought and won.*
>
> In the place of Contraband
> Let the name of freedom stand
> Up and act! and while you may
> Sweep a nation's curse away.
>
> Shake the horrid nightmare off
> Ere the world begins to scoff
> Take your station in the van
> Be a hero—and a MAN! [3]

In August of 1862 Connecticut's Civil War governor, William A. Buckingham, led a state delegation to Washington to

3. Quoted in Niven, *Connecticut for the Union,* p. 280.

present an emancipation petition to President Lincoln. When
Lincoln did in fact act on emancipation—by his preliminary
proclamation on September 26, 1862, just four days after the
Battle of Antietam—Buckingham wrote the President that the
emancipation policy had "my cordial approval and shall have
my unconditional support." [4]

Connecticut's obvious distaste for the institution of slavery
had both ideological and economic roots. In the late eighteenth
century Connecticuters shared with a great many Americans—
northerners and southerners—the realization that slavery hardly
squared with the natural-rights philosophy spelled out in the
Declaration of Independence. By the nineteenth century, aware
more than most Americans of the importance of farmland in
the West, Connecticuters were loath to see sites for settlement
swallowed up by plantation masters and their gangs of slaves.
Speaking in Connecticut during the campaign of 1860, Lincoln
revealed his awareness of the importance of western lands to
the Connecticut mentality when he said in Meriden: "The new
territories are the newly-made bed to which our children are to
go, and it lies with the nation to say whether they shall have
snakes mixed up with them or not." [5]

Yet Connecticut's adoption of an antislavery posture between the Revolution and the Civil War did not carry with it
any modification of the state's belief in white supremacy that
was operative in the colonial period. By the first decades of
the nineteenth century, when the state had some 8,000 blacks,
most of whom were free, Connecticut blacks were far from enjoying the rights and opportunities that most Connecticuters
took for granted. Of the situation in his boyhood town of
Farmington, the abolitionist John Hooker wrote: "The black
man seemed to have no rights as a man. He was often kindly
regarded by humane people, but such a thing as his having
rights of a man were hardly thought of." [6] Of the black's

4. Quoted in Niven, *Connecticut for the Union*, p. 282.
5. Quoted in Niven, *Connecticut for the Union*, p. 4.
6. Quoted in Janice Law Trecker, *Preachers, Rebels, and Traders: Connecticut
1818 to 1865* (Chester: The Pequot Press, 1975), p. 28.

plight in early nineteenth-century Connecticut, one scholar has written:

> The supposed mental and moral weakness of black people were the excuse for depriving them of educational opportunities, including vocational training, and for denying them equal access to employment, public accomodations, and transportation facilities. While exceptional blacks were successful as contractors and builders, waiters, barbers, farmers, or small businessmen, the majority found themselves without skills and without opportunities.[7]

The absence of educational opportunity was the condition of the nineteenth-century Connecticut black that was most discouraging and most likely to limit black progress. It seems to have been the practice either to bar blacks from schools or to isolate them if they did attend. It was reported that in Windsor in the 1820s "there were one or two Negro boys who attended schools, and sat apart from the other scholars, in the southeast corner of the house." [8] When efforts were made to establish educational institutions specifically for blacks, Connecticut community reaction was hostile. In New Haven in the early 1830s Simeon Jocelyn, a white philanthropist, encouraged the establishment of a college for blacks that would offer academic and vocational training. New Haveners would have no part of the idea, claiming that Yale and the town's female seminaries would be "damaged" by the existence of a "black college."

A more famous example of community resentment halting plans for black education took place in the town of Canterbury in northeastern Connecticut in the 1830s. Prudence Crandall, born of Quaker descent in Hopkinton, Rhode Island, in 1803, taught in Plainfield before opening a school for girls in Canterbury. When Miss Crandall accepted a black girl and the townspeople withdrew their white children from the school, the Quaker schoolmistress decided to keep a school exclusively for black girls. Canterbury's citizens were so enraged at her intentions that they succeeded in getting the Connecticut General

---

7. Trecker, *Preachers, Rebels, and Traders*, pp. 29–30.
8. Quoted in Trecker, *Preachers, Rebels, and Traders*, p. 30.

Assembly to enact legislation in 1833 that prohibited the establishment of private schools for blacks without community approval. Under the "Black Law," Miss Crandall was arrested, imprisoned, and convicted after two trials. Although the State Court of Errors overturned the conviction on grounds of insufficient evidence, Prudence Crandall's school had no future. Residents of Canterbury, who had harassed the school by poisoning the well and other acts of vandalism, delivered the *coup de grace* on September 9, 1834, when they smashed the school's windows. With no prospect of protection from such vicious acts, Prudence Crandall ended her experiment.

Connecticut's antislavery and pro-Union postures of the 1850s and 1860s did not mark any increase in general receptivity to Connecticut's blacks. During the Civil War the treatment accorded the state's black regiments was discouraging to the black soldiers. Lieutenant Colonel David Torrance of the state's black Twenty-ninth Regiment concluded: "The poor rights of a soldier were denied them, Their actions were narrowly watched and the slightest faults . . . commented upon." [9] In 1865 the voters of Connecticut firmly rejected an amendment to the state constitution that would have given Connecticut black men the vote. They did not receive the franchise until the state and the nation ratified the Fifteenth Amendment to the Constitution of the United States in 1869. But even with the vote, Connecticut's blacks found themselves in the late nineteenth and early twentieth centuries in a society that accorded them few opportunities for educational, economic, or social progress.

Thus during the era of the Civil War Connecticuters generally functioned on the basis of pro-Union, antislavery, and antiblack sentiments. The antiblack attitude manifested itself in a blunt racism that was unfortunately characteristic of nineteenth-century America; Connecticut's pro-Union and antislavery postures contributed to the state's emergence as a Unionist stronghold during the war years.

One manifestation of Connecticut's Unionist posture was its

9. Quoted in Trecker, *Preachers, Rebels, and Traders*, p. 43.

consistent support of the Republican cause. The Republican Party, completely unrelated to the Jeffersonian Republican Party of fifty years earlier, was an outgrowth of northern indignation at the passage of the Kansas–Nebraska Act in May 1854. The Kansas–Nebraska legislation was the brainchild of Senator Stephen Douglas of Illinois, a bouncy five-footer who had no end of financial and political goals and sought to achieve most of them via the Kansas–Nebraska bill. As a major holder of western lands and Chicago real estate, Douglas hoped to see a much-discussed transcontinental railroad take the proposed central route (from St. Louis up the Kansas and Arkansas rivers, across the Great Salt Lake, and by the California Trail to San Francisco) because such a route would be closer to Chicago than the other proposed routes—the northern, the thirty-fifth parallel, and the southern. Organization and settlement of the Kansas territory, through which a central transcontinental railroad would run, was accordingly essential. Douglas also hoped that the Kansas–Nebraska legislation might strengthen his chances for the presidency by making him as popular among southern Democrats as he already was among northern Democrats. The bill provided that the question of slavery in Kansas and Nebraska would be decided on the basis of the operation of popular sovereignty—a process by which residents of the territories would have the opportunity to vote slavery in or out. Popular sovereignty was especially pleasing to Southerners in the case of Nebraska because it lay north of the 36° 30′ line—north of which slavery was prohibited by the Missouri Compromise of 1820.

The Kansas–Nebraska Act did not carry Douglas into the White House. While the legislation did for a time make the Illinois senator the darling of the South, a far more crucial result of the measure was a surge of anger among antislavery Northerners at the prospect that the long-accepted 36° 30′ northern boundary for slavery might be breached by slaves in Nebraska. With the Democratic Party in the hands of southerners or prosouthern northern politicians, the Whig Party on the fence on the slavery issue, and the Free-Soil Party weak and ineffective, antislavery northerners had no place to go politically to express their anger at the passage of the Kansas–Nebraska Act. The result was the birth in 1854 of the Republican Party as a vehicle to force an end to the expansion of slavery. The new party quickly swallowed up antislavery Democrats, Whigs, and Free-Soilers and gained astounding momentum in the northern states.

In Connecticut the Republican Party was launched in a series of meetings in February and March 1856. The two principal movers of Republican organization in the state were Joseph R. Hawley and Gideon Welles, both major figures in nineteenth-century Connecticut politics.

Hawley (1826–1905) was a Hartford lawyer who by the 1850s revealed strong antislavery inclinations. He was associated with the Free-Soil Party in the early 1850s and in mid-decade became a pillar of the new Republican Party. He fought hard for Republican candidate John C. Frémont in the 1856 presidential campaign and in 1857 became the editor of the Republican-oriented *Hartford Evening Press*. During the Civil War Hawley rose to the rank of General and was commended for "meritorious conduct" in engagements at Bull Run (1861) and at Olustee, Florida (1864). Although Hawley became editor of the *Hartford Courant* after the war, he drew most satisfaction from a distinguished political career during which he served as governor of Connecticut and a member of both houses of Congress.

Gideon Welles (1802–1878) started and ended his political career as a Democrat and in the interim served as a Republican Secretary of the Navy under Presidents Lincoln and Johnson (1861–1869). During the first phase of that career Welles was a Jacksonian Democrat who served in the Connecticut General Assembly, as state comptroller, and in the federal system as postmaster of Hartford and head of the Bureau of Provisions and Clothing for the Navy. As a Democrat in the General Assembly Welles was a staunch opponent of imprisonment for debt, property and religious qualifications for voting, religious tests for witnesses in court, and grants of special privilege by the Assembly. He left the Democratic Party in the 1850s because of its pro-Southern and proslavery postures and became a leading light in the Connecticut Republican Party.

After his appointment as Secretary of the Navy in 1861,

Welles reorganized his department and built a navy more than adequate for Union war needs. He ran the Union Navy with independence and courage, refusing to bow to senators who wished naval yards built in their states, shipowners who wished to unload inappropriate vessels on the navy, or naval officers who sought promotions through political pressure. He handled orders to officers and the formulation of tactical directives closely and intelligently, but perhaps his greatest contribution to Union naval success was his willingness to back innovations such as ironclads, heavy ordnance, improved steam machinery, and armored cruisers. The essence of the man was captured by an associate: "There was nothing decorative about him; there was no noise in the street when he went along; but he understood his duty, and did it efficiently, continually, and unvaryingly." [10]

For all his achievements as a Republican Secretary of the Navy, Welles broke with the party and returned to the Democratic fold in 1868. During the war he had loyally supported the Lincoln administration even though as a strict constructionist of the Constitution (of the Jackson school) he was displeased by measures such as the suspension of habeas corpus, the arrest of Copperhead Clement Vallandigham, and the suppression of the *Chicago Times*. But his patience with the Republicans ended when the Radicals in the party took command after the election of 1866, imposed a harsh Reconstruction policy on the South, and undertook the impeachment of Johnson.

During the mid-1850s Connecticuters with an antislavery disposition responded with enthusiasm in both state and national elections to the Republican Party led by Hawley and Welles. At the national level, Connecticuters gave Frémont the nod over Democratic candidate James Buchanan in the presidential election of 1856 by a sizable plurality (42,715–34,995), and in the presidential election of 1860 Connecticuters gave Lincoln a landslide victory in the state. At the state level, the Republicans

10. C. A. Dana, *Recollection of the Civil War,* quoted in Howard K. Beale, "Gideon Welles," in Allen Johnson and Dumas Malone, eds., *Dictionary of American Biography,* 20 volumes (New York: Charles Scribner's Sons, 1943), 19:632.

enjoyed success in the gubernatorial elections of 1856 and 1857, as they effected a coalition with the Know-Nothing Party (an anti-Catholic party that rose and died quickly in the 1850s). In the gubernatorial election of 1858 the Republicans had enough support on their own in the state to elect a governor—William A. Buckingham.

In a sense Buckingham's election was as significant for Connecticut as had been the election as governor and deputy governor of Pitkin and Trumbull in 1766, which assured that Connecticut would be in Patriot hands as the Anglo-American controversy deepened in the late 1760s and 1770s. With Buckingham's election in 1858, and his repeated re-election through the election of 1865, Connecticut would have a strong Unionist in command as sectional controversy erupted into civil war.

Buckingham (1804–1875) was born in the eastern Connecticut community of Norwich, a town not far from Lebanon, the home of Jonathan Trumbull. Buckingham worked on his father's farm as a boy and was immersed in the deeply held Congregational beliefs of his parents. Although apprenticed to a surveyor, Buckingham chose not to enter that profession but instead associated himself with his uncle's dry goods store in Norwich. Buckingham then went into business for himself, for twenty years ran the largest dry goods store in Norwich, and subsequently made heavy investments in the successful Haywood Rubber Company of Colchester. By the time of his first election as governor, Buckingham was a wealthy man. After his governorship, Buckingham served as a United States senator from 1869 until his death on February 5, 1875. In the Senate he was known as a conscientious and hardworking member of the committees on commerce and on Indian affairs. One of his senatorial colleagues said of him: "While the powers of his intellect were upon a high plane, yet were I called upon to define the impression that remains strongest with me, I should say it was that of incomparable rectitude and dignity." [11] But Buckingham's place in Connecticut and American history is based

11. John J. Ingalls, quoted in "William Alfred Buckingham," in *Dictionary of American Biography*, 3:229.

primarily on his effectiveness as Connecticut's governor during the Civil War.

In some respects Buckingham's challenge as governor was not unlike Lincoln's as president. Just as Lincoln was confronted with a northern constituency that contained pro-southern and "peace-at-any-price" advocates, so Buckingham found himself during the war challenged by a good many constituents who were not convinced that either the preservation of the Union or the termination of slavery justified the horrors of internecine war.

There were a number of Connecticuters—mostly Democrats—who despite Unionist strength in the state would not accept the thesis that the South had been responsible for the war; they maintained that the war had been caused by a justifiable resort to arms by southerners who were about to be deprived of their fair claims to the West by Black (that is, abolitionist) Republicans. These Peace Democrats demanded that the South be allowed to leave the Union in peace or that the Union be reconstructed on the basis of a northern guarantee to the South that slavery would forever be undisturbed south of 36° 30'. The Peace Democrats thundered against the battlefield butchery to which Lincoln had committed the nation and demanded an end to the carnage.

The leader of the Peace Democrats in Connecticut was Thomas Hart Seymour, a Hartford lawyer. Seymour was in many respects a far more impressive figure than was Buckingham. Buckingham had a common-school education while Seymour was a highly educated jurist; Buckingham was something of a parochial Yankee, his travels limited to occasional trips to New York City, Boston, Worcester, and Saratoga, while Seymour had served in the Mexican War and had been an American diplomat for six years in Russia. Even in governmental service Seymour was the more distinguished of the two, having been a congressman in his twenties and governor of Connecticut from 1850 to 1853 while Buckingham was devoting his attention to business.

Defeated for the governorship by Buckingham in the state election of 1860, Seymour emerged during the war years as

Connecticut's most memorable opponent of Lincoln's policy of re-establishing the Union by the force of arms. Seymour and his cohorts hammered away at incompetent generals, war profiteers, and alleged unconstitutional acts by Lincoln and regularly insisted that the war would take thousands of lives, cost billions of dollars, and still result in a deadlock that would insure the success of the Confederacy. Spelling out his position in July 1862, Seymour wrote: "The monstrous fallacy of the present day, that the Union can be re-established by destroying any part of the South is one which will burst with the shells that are thrown into defenseless cities . . . a spectacle for the reproach or the comiseration [*sic*] of the civilized world." [12]

In the gubernatorial election of 1863, Seymour and the state's other Peace Democrats hoped to capitalize on war weariness, a succession of Union military disasters, and Connecticut's reservations regarding the Conscription Act of 1863. Seymour declared that as governor he would not enforce conscription and damned Lincoln for his suspension of the writ of habeas corpus for anyone seeking to avoid the draft; and he accused the Buckingham Administration of unthinking adherence to Lincoln's policies and mismanagement.

Pushed to the wall by Seymour and threatened by low morale among northerners, Buckingham and his fellow Republicans pulled out all the stops to keep Connecticut firmly in the Unionist column. Troops in Connecticut's regiments were given special leave to come home and, it was hoped, cast their ballots for Buckingham. Federal appointees were mobilized for the campaign and a host of national Republican figures was brought into the state to speak at Buckingham rallies. But most important of all, Buckingham and the entire state Republican ticket aimed their shots at Seymour, pointing out that as governor he would be a menace to the continuation of the state's war effort. Although the campaign was long and ferocious, in the end Buckingham was able to carry the election by calling successfully on Connecticut's antislavery, pro-Union majority.

The state election of 1863 was the high-water mark for Con-

---

12. Quoted in Niven, *Connecticut for the Union*, p. 304.

necticut's Peace Democrats. By the elections of 1864, with Gettysburg and Vicksburg history and Grant in command, both
Buckingham and Lincoln were victors. There was little suspense
in the 1865 election, too. Sherman was slashing through South
Carolina after perfecting his scorched-earth policy in Georgia,
and Grant was hounding Lee into submission. Finally, on the
morning of election day—April 3, 1865—news arrived that
Grant had captured Richmond. No furloughed soldiers' votes
were needed as Buckingham swept to an easy win over his
Democratic opponent.

Buckingham's tenure in office during the war years was of
critical importance to the state's war effort. Like Jonathan
Trumbull during the Revolutionary War, he was the heart and
soul of Connecticut's mobilization. On that dark, rain-whipped
Friday of April 12, 1861, when Connecticut heard the news that
Sumter had been attacked, the state—like most of the Union—
was pitifully unprepared for war.

> [T]he militia had been a laughing stock for thirty years; the militia
> laws, as then constituted, could not be enforced; arsenals were in
> disrepair, equipment obsolete. In the entire state there were but
> 1,020 army muskets of Mexican War vintage, and 2,000 percussion
> muskets, heavy, unreliable, practically useless as weapons.
> Ammunition was also in short supply; only 50,000 ball cartridges
> had been purchased since December 1860. Thirty pieces of artillery,
> all smooth-bore napoleons, were owned by the state, but there were
> no caissons, harnesses, or baggage wagons.[13]

What Connecticut did have on that black Friday were a firm
resolve to stand for the Union and a governor who was absolutely determined that the state's Unionist convictions be trans-
lated into Union victory. With Buckingham overseeing the
state's war effort, Connecticut made a major contribution to the
Union victory.

> No war governor was more indefatigable than he in visiting
> Connecticut soldiers at training camps in the state or in actual
> theaters of operations. He was always the chief speaker at war
> meetings in the cities and large towns . . . and he made it a point

13. Niven, *Connecticut for the Union*, p. 47.

to answer personally all direct inquiries from Connecticut soldiers in the field. . . . Constantly shuttling between the two Connecticut capitals of Hartford and New Haven and the three national centers of Boston, New York, and Washington, he put in a twelve-hour day, seven-day week schedule during the war years. With not a quarter of the staff personnel enjoyed by Governors Andrew of Massachusetts, Morgan of New York, or Curtin of Pennsylvania, Buckingham was able to cope with the constant pressures of and multiplying complexities of raising, equipping, and caring for an army of some 50,000 men.[14]

After Sumter, Union sentiment blazed forth. Ministers preaching from Elijah thundered for war; bands blared martial tunes; war meetings were called around the state; banks opened their vaults to offer money for the state's immediate military expenditures; and young and not-so-young Connecticuters— farmers, factory workers, clerks, merchants, and lawyers—left fields, factories, offices, stores, and—most important—homes, to wear Union blue. Within three days the first regiment of Connecticut volunteers was formed; within three weeks Connecticut had mustered six full regiments. By the time Appomattox came, Connecticut had given to the Union Army over 50,000 men who made up thirty regiments of infantry, one of cavalry, two of heavy artillery and three battalions of light artillery. To the Union Navy the state provided 250 officers and 2,500 men.

The dedication and patriotism of these Connecticuters carried them to almost every theater of the war. The state's troops won their red badges of courage at Cedar Mountain, Port Royal, Roanoke Island, New Bern, Port Hudson, Fort Fisher, Vicksburg, Fort Henry, Fort Donelson, and Island Number Ten and along the bloodstained path cut by the Army of the Potomac as it traded blows with Lee's Army of Northern Virginia in the decisive period between Antietam and Appomattox.

At Antietam in September 1862 the 14th Connecticut was advancing through a field of ripening corn toward a sunken road (to be known thereafter in American military history as ''bloody

14. Niven, *Connecticut for the Union*, p. 72.

lane'') when it was pinned down by a wall of fire. The men of the 14th held their position for two hours, hugging the ground while they loaded, capped, and fired their rifles at the cloud of smoke yards ahead that marked the Confederate position. The 11th Connecticut traded fire at point-blank range with Confederate gunners across Antietam Creek long enough to permit the 51st New York and the 51st Pennsylvania to charge across the Stone Bridge and rout a Confederate brigade. But no state unit had a more blistering time at Antietam than the 16th Connecticut. As it gave support to an artillery battery under attack, the 16th was hit by a flank attack by men from A. P. Hill's division. Before it broke and fled, the 16th was cut to pieces while its regimental officers gave confusing orders that nobody understood. Of the 940 men who had been with the 16th at the start of the fire-fight, only 200 were left alive to retreat to cover.

Almost as devastating to the Connecticut troops at Antietam as the deaths of their comrades was the treatment available for the wounded. One Connecticut soldier described the situation:

> In a room 12 feet by 20 feet a bloody table stood and around it five surgeons. A wounded man was laid on the table and it took but a few seconds for them to decide what to do and but a few minutes to do it. The amputated limbs were thrown out of the window. In forty-eight hours there were as many as two cart loads of amputated legs, arms, and hands in the pile.[15]

In December 1862 the Union blue—including the troops from Connecticut—paid dearly for the determination of Ambrose E. Burnside, the handsome West Pointer whom Lincoln had placed in command of the Army of the Potomac in November. Whatever military competence Burnside possessed was not evident at the battle of Fredericksburg, where Burnside massed his army of 113,000 to attack Lee's force of 75,000 well dug in on Mayre's Heights. Six times Burnside sent his Union infantry across open ground toward a stone wall at the foot of Mayre's Heights. Six times Confederate artillery and infantry fire behind the stone wall mowed down the advancing Yankees. At the end of the senseless attacks the Union had lost almost 13,000 men to only

---

15. Quotation cited in Niven, *Connecticut for the Union*, p. 223.

5,000 casualties for the Confederacy. The 14th Connecticut was in the first wave, but it paid a terrible price for the honor, suffering losses of twenty-five percent. The 27th Connecticut was in the second wave—and left a third of its strength dead and dying on the slopes of Mayre's Heights.

After Fredericksburg, Burnside was replaced by General Joseph Hooker. For a time things looked up for the Connecticut troops in the Army of the Potomac. Rations improved, mountains of supplies that had been gathering dust in Washington were distributed to the men, and paymasters appeared to hand out as much as six months' back pay to the Connecticut regiments. But when Hooker had the opportunity at Chancellorsville in May 1863 to go against Lee, he did no better than McClellan or Burnside. Hooker worked out a neat battle plan that called for a double envelopment of Lee's army. When the Confederates stopped the Union thrusts, however, Hooker apparently ran out of ideas and ordered his men to reform defensively. Lee, ever pleased by Union tactical paralysis, then sent 25,000 of his men under Stonewall Jackson along a circuitous route to hit the Union right flank. When Jackson attacked at dusk on May 2, 1863, the troops of the 17th Connecticut, square in the path of Jackson's drive, were lounging, playing cards, or cooking supper. Then the woods came alive with bugle calls and a rush of rabbits and foxes driven from the forest ahead of the advancing Rebels. The men of the 17th grabbed their rifles and fired at point-blank range as the enemy burst upon them. While the 17th fell back toward Chancellorsville, valuable time was gained for Hooker to set up a new defense line. On the next day—May 3, 1863—the 14th Connecticut was hit at its front and right flank, losing over 30 of its depleted strength of 219. After two such days of pounding, Hooker retreated across the Rappahannock.

Such successive poundings at the hands of Lee and the Confederates took their toll on the morale of the Connecticut troops. One Connecticut sergeant wrote after Chancellorsville:

Oh, it seemed dreadful to think that with all the advantages we had and everything in our favor, we should be whipped,—whipped so easy too, by a party of men, even dirtier and worse looking than we were, with not half the fighting qualities or discipline that the army of the Potomac possessed.[16]

But the tide was soon to change. Following Chancellorsville Lee moved north into Pennsylvania, hoping by a victory on northern soil to weaken Union morale, encourage the northern Peace Democrats to come down harder against the war, and possibly gain European recognition of the Confederacy. When Lee and the Army of Northern Virginia met the Army of the Potomac in Pennsylvania, the Union troops had still another commander—General George Gordon Meade, a tough, steady man with the ability to make sound decisions in fluid tactical situations. The two armies, following a parallel course northward, finally met on July 1–3, 1863, in the formerly quiet little town of Gettysburg. For the first two days of the battle the two armies maneuvered for position, with Meade's forces winding up on Cemetery Hill and Lee's men three quarters of a mile away at Seminary Ridge. In the afternoon of the third day came the most important hours of the most important battle of the Civil War. About one o'clock some 172 Confederate guns opened fire at Cemetery Hill. When the firing stopped, three Confederate divisions, 15,000 strong, advanced over open ground from Seminary Ridge to break through the Union center.

Among the Union units atop Cemetery Hill were three Connecticut regiments—the 14th, the 17th, and the 27th—and the 14th found itself at the Union left, directly in the path of the Confederate charge under Pickett, Pettigrew, and Trimble. Sergeant Edward Wade of the Connecticut 14th has left us a description of the titanic clash:

> About 3 o'clock the enemy's fire died away, and we could see in the distance about a quarter of a mile, extending across the plain, and coming towards us, two rebel lines of battle, preceded by a line of skirmishers, and a third line in the rear. The spectacle was magnificent. On they came, with colors flying, and bayonets shining in the sunlight. . . . When the enemy had advanced their first line to within two hundred yards our fire spread almost simultaneously along the whole line. The enemy's first line was broken and the

16. Quoted in Van Dusen, *Connecticut*, p. 231.

second line came on in the same good style as the first did. They
fired into us, but they could not stand the raking fire we gave them,
and so they too fell back . . . Detached portions of their lines then
rallied, and for a while maintained their ground, but being cut down
by our terribly destructive fire, they commenced falling back. By
this time the 14th was all excitement. They remembered Antietam,
and Fredericksburg, and Chancellorsville, and over the wall they
went, nothing could stop them, and soon they were fighting hand to
hand with the rebels. We captured 6 battle flags and forty prisoners,
and over one hundred prisoners came in and surrendered to us
afterwards, including 2 Colonels, 3 Lieut. Colonels, majors and any
number of line officers.[17]

Although the cream of the Army of Northern Virginia was
decimated on the bloody slopes of Cemetery Hill, the Confederacy was far from finished. The Confederate dream did not
die until, with Grant as General in Chief of the Armies of the
United States and Meade in command of the Army of the Potomac, a series of hammerlike blows were struck at Lee between the spring of 1864 and the spring of 1865. But Grant's
blows at Lee were delivered at terrible cost to the Union blue,
including the regiments from Connecticut. At the Battle of the
Wilderness (May 4–5, 1864) Lee caught Grant in the same
dense forest where Jackson had attacked Hooker at Chancellorsville. Grant took the challenge and fought his way out, but not
before the Union lost 17,000 men in two days and the 14th Connecticut left 100 of its comrades behind. Following the Wilderness came Spotsylvania (May 8–12, 1864) where the 14th Connecticut fought desperately at the "Bloody Angle" and held off
a vicious Confederate counterattack. Pushing on relentlessly,
Grant next attacked at Cold Harbor (June 3, 1864), where in
two hours the Union lost 12,000 men, the 14th Connecticut lost
20, and the Second Connecticut Artillery took the heaviest
losses in a single engagement of any Connecticut regiment in
the war—75 killed and 184 wounded. There then followed
Grant's nine-month seige of Petersburg, about which a soldier
of the 14th Connecticut wrote: "If there was one thing more
than another that became indelibly impressed upon the men's

17. Quoted in Van Dusen, *Connecticut,* pp. 231–232.

minds of the Fourteenth . . . it was plodding through this ever-lasting Virginia mud.'' [18] And finally, agonizingly, in April 1865 it was all over. Lee abandoned Petersburg and Richmond, found himself squeezed between Grant and Sheridan without rations, and finally requested an ''interview'' with Grant. When Grant went to accept Lee's surrender, he was escorted by the First Regiment Connecticut Volunteer Infantry. Connecticuters had thus done their duty for the Stars and Stripes, but the cost was high. Of almost 55,000 Connecticut men in the Union Army and Navy, over 20,000 became casualties.

It was not only the state's soldiers and sailors who gave testimony to their dedication to the Union during the Civil War. The inadequate war-making apparatus of the federal government made it necessary for Connecticut's civilian population to join the war effort in support of the men in service. Urged on by Governor Buckingham, Connecticut's towns and cities formed voluntary societies to render a variety of services to the military, and Buckingham appointed state agents in New York City and Washington to supervise Connecticut services for the state's troops.

Communities collected blankets, clothing, medical supplies, and food for the men at the front. While these supplies were delivered to army units throughout the war, often shipped free of charge by the Hartford and New Haven Steamboat Company and insured without premiums by Hartford's insurance companies, special efforts were made for the soldiers' comfort on holidays. Every Thanksgiving and Christmas during the war tons of food were sent to the troops in the field. For the Christmas comfort of the state troops on the Carolina coast in 1863, Bridgeport alone sent 471 barrels, 181 boxes, 20 half-barrels, 4 kegs, 1 firkin, and 1 bale of food and clothing.

When special needs of the troops were evident, Connecticuters responded with special dispatch. During the winter of 1863–1864 the United States Sanitary Commission and the Army Medical Corps issued a frantic call for fresh vegetables to stem an outbreak of scurvy in the Union Army. Towns all over

18. Quoted in Van Dusen, *Connecticut*, p. 233.

the state threw themselves into a major effort and collected 700 barrels of vegetables to be shipped free of charge to Washington, where the Navy Department assumed responsibility for transportation and distribution to the troops.

Connecticut's voluntary aid societies also concerned themselves with the care of needy soldiers' families. Even when a Connecticut soldier was receiving both state and federal payments, the financial situation was hard for the family at home pressed by wartime inflation. When a soldier was incapacitated, captured, or killed, all pay stopped and the family was the recipient of no insurance or pension. What happened under such situations was grimly reported by the *Hartford Courant* in December 1864, when it told of a soldier's widow and two children found in a Hartford tenement destitute and hungry. During the winter of 1864–1865 it was estimated that seventy percent of the charity cases in Connecticut were soldiers' families. Voluntary societies did what they could for these victims of the war, distributing food and clothing collected at fairs, mass meetings, and benefits for soldiers' families.

Another focus of the war effort of the state's civilian population was care of the Connecticut troops who were wounded or ill from malaria, dysentery, typhoid, pneumonia, and typhus. Even before the Union Army was overwhelmed with casualties from Antietam through Petersburg, there were never adequate facilities to deal with the wounded. Battlefield medical facilities were primitive and overcrowded. The army hospitals that were developed around Washington could not handle the swelling tide of Union wounded. To fill the breach, civilian volunteers from the state as well as relatives of the wounded frequently went to care for incapacitated soldiers in makeshift hospitals near the front or in the hospitals around Washington. Harriet Hawley, wife of General Joseph Hawley, wrote of her experience in the spring of 1865 at Wilmington in helping to care for thousands of Union troops recently freed from Confederate prisoner-of-war camps:

> You know that over nine thousand of our prisoners were delivered to us here; and no human tongue or pen can describe the horrible

condition which they were in. Starving to death, covered with vermin, with no clothing but the filthy rags they had worn during their whole imprisonment—a period of from five to twenty months; cramped by long sitting in one position, so that they could not straighten their limbs; their feet rotted off! o God! I cannot even now endure to speak of it.

Of course they brought the jail fever with them—it could not be otherwise; yet they must be fed, and cleansed, and clothed, and cared for. There are no special hospital accomodations here worth mentioning. There were not doctors enough and those here overworked themselves, and caught the fever and died. Buildings of all sorts were converted into temporary hospitals, and the nurses (enlisted men) fell sick at the rate of fifty a day.[19]

At home, scores of Connecticut women volunteered for service at Knight Hospital, a United States Army hospital in New Haven that Governor Buckingham enlarged during the war. Daughters of the best New Haven families put in long hours to comfort those troops who would carry the scars of war long after Appomattox.

The state's manufacturing genius also made enormous amounts of materiel available to the war effort.

Connecticut was a major producer of arms. It has been said that Colt's Armory alone produced enough rifles to equip the entire Army of the Potomac and enough revolvers to outfit every Union soldier. Other major companies such as the Winchester Arms Company and Christian Sharps' Rifle Company very early in the war were each producing about 1,000 rifles a month. Smaller companies sprang up around the state and by the period 1863–1865 were turning out impressive numbers of weapons. By February 1864 the Norwich Arms Company was manufacturing each week some 1,200 muskets, several hundred breech-loading Kentucky rifles and carbines, and 3,000 bayonets. The Connecticut Arms Company of Norfolk was producing 1,400 muskets a month by 1863, and by the end of the war the Eagle Arms Company of Mansfield was manufacturing 300 rifles and 400 bayonets a day. The Ames Iron Works of Falls Village manufactured 5,600-pound wrought-iron rifles capable of firing

19. Quoted in Trecker, *Preachers, Rebels, and Traders,* p. 91.

a 56-pound projectile five miles, and the Collins Company of Collinsville, the world's largest producer of axes and edged tools, diversified its operation to turn out sabers and bayonets. Hartford County was the center of the state's ammunition industry, which included both a number of small shops that manufactured powder and cartridges and the 125-building complex of the Hazard Powder Company of Enfield that produced twelve tons of powder a day.

Moreover, Connecticut's manufactures for the military were not restricted to arms and ammunition. Textile and clothing manufacturers produced uniforms, and factories in the Naugatuck Valley manufactured millions of brass uniform buttons. The Union Army's needs for rubber blankets, ponchos, and boots were met by state firms such as the Haywood Rubber Company of Colchester, the Goodyear Rubber Company of Naugatuck, and the Candee Rubber Company of New Haven. New Britain led in the Connecticut production of saddles and horse-drawn transport equipment, and New Haven carriage companies converted from producing fine carriages for Southern planters to the manufacture of wagons for the United States Army.

6

1865–1914:
The Fruits of "Progress"

My earliest memory pictures the dirt road and the horse-drawn
street sprinkler slowly moving up toward our house, stirring up
clouds of brown dust as the artificial rain descended from
innumerable holes in the curved brass pipe at the rear of the
wooden tank. Whip and reins in one hand, the driver, perched
high on his narrow seat, had the other hand free to wave at little
boys, barking dogs, and friendly neighbors as the chariot slowly
laid a wet swath up one side of the broad street. . . . In those
days our street was used only by horses and horse-drawn vehicles.
. . . The cows went out to pasture and returned daily down the
elm-shaded street.[1]

$\mathcal{T}$HIS serene picture of Norwich in the 1890s, probably
duplicated in a score of Connecticut towns, leaves the impression of a tranquil society with simple pleasures. Yet the historical evidence indicates that such a scene was a reflection more
of a way of life that was passing than of one that was being
reinforced and strengthened. Economic expansion, immigration, and urbanization made the Connecticut of 1914 far more
complex than it had been in 1865.

1. Gerard E. Jensen, quoted in Andersen, *From Yankee to American*, p. 79.

One of the most significant features of Connecticut society in the post-Civil War period was a tremendous growth in the manufacturing industries of the state. The number of manufacturing establishments increased from 5,128 in 1870 to over 9,000 in 1900, and the gross product of Connecticut's manufactures more than doubled from $161 million in 1870 to over $350 million by 1900.

By 1900 Danbury's hat factories were producing hats and allied products worth more than $7 million; Connecticut's production of typewriters was valued at three fourths of a million dollars; the gross product of electrical supplies manufactured in Bridgeport and Hartford was over $3 million; the state's bellmakers were turning out more than two thirds of the bells produced in the nation; Connecticut's machine tool industry and associated foundry work were grossing $20 million; and the state's hardware industries, centered in New Britain, were turning out products worth more than $25 million a year. Connecticut's textile industry, with cotton mills in Norwich, Thompson, Putnam, Plainfield, and Killingly; woolen mills in Rockville, Stafford Springs, and Broad Brook; the Cheney Silk Mills in Manchester; and the American Thread Company in Willimantic, ranked sixth in the nation with an annual output of $50 million. By 1904, exclusive of government establishments, Connecticut's firearms industry was producing four fifths of the ammunition and over one quarter of the total value of firearms manufactured in the United States.

Connecticut's boom in manufacturing in the decades after the Civil War was of course related to the general industrial thrust of America between Appomattox and World War I. At the same time, the state was uniquely prepared to participate in the industrial advances of the era. Its manufacturing expertise, evident before and during the Civil War, provided Connecticut with a firm manufacturing base from which to move ahead. The development and maturation of the New York, New Haven, and Hartford rail line and its linkage with national trunk lines enabled Connecticut to market her products throughout the nation. Connecticut's manufacturing burst was also facilitated by its enormous capital resources. The state's

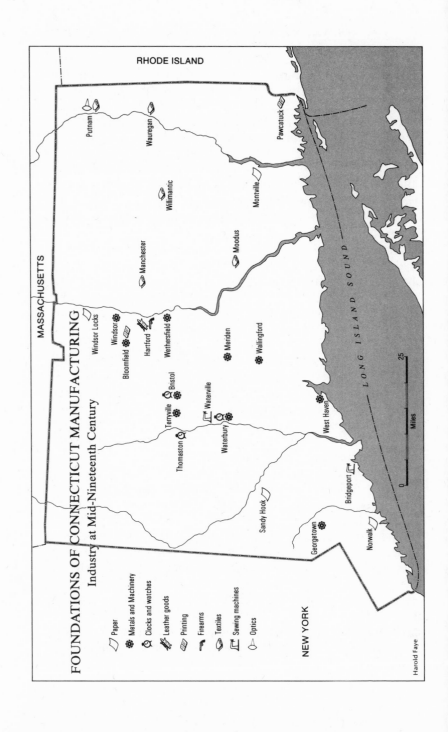

FOUNDATIONS OF CONNECTICUT MANUFACTURING
Industry at Mid-Nineteenth Century

RHODE ISLAND

MASSACHUSETTS

NEW YORK

LONG ISLAND SOUND

Putnam
Wauregan
Pawcatuck
Willimantic
Montville
Manchester
Moodus
Windsor Locks
Windsor
Bloomfield
Hartford
Wethersfield
Meriden
Wallingford
Bristol
Terryville
Waterville
Thomaston
Waterbury
West Haven
Sandy Hook
Bridgeport
Georgetown
Norwalk

Paper
Metals and Machinery
Clocks and watches
Leather goods
Printing
Firearms
Textiles
Sewing machines
Optics

0   25
Miles

Harold Faye

grand list increased by $40 million and its bank deposits jumped by $10 million during the Civil War. The assets of Connecticut's insurance companies rose from $117 million in 1875 to almost $215 million in 1900. Finally, the state's industrial progress was supported by the construction and factory work undertaken by a stream of immigrants who were attracted to Connecticut between 1865 and 1914.

Connecticut's late-eighteenth- and early-nineteenth-century political conservatism and lack of economic opportunity not only drove away the state's native sons and daughters but made Connecticut a less than attractive homeland for newcomers. In 1850 there were only 38,518 foreign-born in Connecticut, about ten percent of the state's population. But with the tremendous increase in immigration to the United States between the Civil War and World War I and Connecticut's expanding manufacturing opportunities, the state reaped more than its share of arriving immigrants.

In 1870 native-born Americans composed seventy-five percent of Connecticut's population; by World War I the immigrant influx had reduced the native-born figure to only thirty-five percent. Except for Rhode Island and Massachusetts, Connecticut had come to have a larger proportion of foreign stock in its population than did any other state. While Connecticut had foreign-born—and native-born of foreign or mixed parentage—residents by 1930 from Armenia (1,458); Austria (17,176); Czechoslovakia (32,491); Denmark (7,529); England (63,328); Finland (2,974); France (8,174); Germany (76,281); Greece (6,523); Hungary (23,175); Lithuania (30,690); Norway (3,896); Portugal (4,701); Rumania (2,646); Russia (59,536); Scotland (22,727); Spain (1,567); Sweden (41,374); Switzerland (4,769); and Yugoslavia (2,005), the largest groups were the Italians, Irish, Poles, and French Canadians.

The Italians, the largest group of foreign ancestry in twentieth-century Connecticut, came to the state in a rush between 1900 and the First World War. The number of Italians in the state in 1860 was 61; in 1870 about 100; and at the turn of the century almost 20,000. Northern Italians seeking higher wages and better jobs and southern Italians escaping from crushing peasant poverty immigrated to Connecticut by the thousands, and by 1930 the number of Connecticuters of Italian birth or ancestry was 227,262. Italians in Connecticut went into unskilled labor, skilled factory work, the wholesale and retail food businesses, and the building trades and became an undisputed majority among barbers, cobblers, tailors, and musicians. The Italians congregated in Hartford and especially in New Haven. Outside of New Haven, according to a speech by former President William Howard Taft in 1921, they transformed waste lands "into productive gardens, magnificent vineyards, fields, and orchards rich in fruits and vegetables, which supply the city, thereby releasing it from the burden of importation from Long Island and from the markets of New York, and creating in itself a new source of wealth beyond the fondest expectations of anyone." [2]

The Irish, the second-largest immigrant group in twentieth-century Connecticut, began arriving in the state in the early nineteenth century and came in increasing numbers after the potato-crop failures of the 1840s. What the resulting famine meant for the Irish was described by Elihu Burritt, the New Britain scholar and reformer, who visited Ireland in 1847:

> As we continued our walk along this filthy land, half-naked women and children would come out of their cabins, apparently in the last stage of the fever to beg for food "for the honour of God." As they stood upon the wet ground, we could almost see it smoke beneath their bare feet, burning with fever. We entered the grave-yard, in the midst of which was a small watch-house. This miserable shed has served as a grave where the dying could bury themselves. It was seven feet long and six in breadth. It was already walled round on the outside with an embankment of graves half way to the eves. . . . And into this noiseless sepulchre living men, women, and children went down to die; to pillow upon the rotted straw, the grave cloths vacated by the preceding victims, and festering with their fever. [3]

2. Quoted in Samuel Koenig, *Immigrant Settlements in Connecticut: Their Growth and Characteristics* (Hartford: Connecticut State Department of Education, 1938), p. 28.

3. Quoted in Trecker, *Preachers, Rebels, and Traders,* p. 89.

Although they eventually recovered from the potato blight, the Irish were plagued by grinding poverty and callous British rule and thus continued to leave their homeland for America. As of 1930 there were in Connecticut over 150,000 persons of Irish ancestry. The first Irish in Connecticut worked as weavers or spinners or secured unskilled and semiskilled jobs building the state's railroads and canals. By the last half of the nineteenth century the Irish predominated among police and firemen, mailmen, trolley and bus drivers, and railroad conductors.

Minute peasant holdings, low wages for farm workers, and political instability caused by the 1905 Revolution motivated the Russian-dominated Poles to migrate to America, especially between 1900 and World War I. There were 133,813 persons of Polish ancestry in Connecticut by 1930. The Poles in Connecticut concentrated in the four counties of Middlesex, New London, Tolland, and Hartford and came to make up a significant proportion of the population in communities such as Meriden, Middletown, New Britain, and Norwich. While a great many Poles went into factory work, more Poles went into farming than did representatives of any other immigrant group.

French Canadians first began to come to Connecticut in the nineteenth century, escaping from the bare livelihood that many achieved by farming and lumbering in Quebec. In Connecticut the French Canadians located especially in the northeastern part of the state, where they became prominent in textile factories. In 1930 there were 98,296 French Canadians in Connecticut.

A major result of the quickening of industrialization and immigration was the transformation of Connecticut from a rural to an urban state. In 1890 the population of towns with less than 2,500 inhabitants was 123,097, while that of the urban areas was 623,161. By 1910 the rural population was down to less than 115,000 and the urban population was near one million. New Haven and Bridgeport were the first Connecticut cities to reach a population of 100,000; Hartford and Waterbury had populations in the period over 50,000; and Ansonia, Danbury, Meriden, Middletown, Naugatuck, New Britain, New London, Norwich, Stamford, Torrington, and Willimantic had populations between 10,000 and 50,000.

The results of the forces operative in Connecticut between 1865 and 1914 were diverse. Economic expansion and urbanization undermined the Currier and Ives farm scene as the principal habitat of the Connecticuter. By the turn of the century, although Connecticut still had its colonial-rooted villages and hamlets, mushrooming cities with streets lined by ever expanding stores and banks and crowded with electric trolley cars roofed by overhead wires were as common. The state's wealth was evident in the increase of plush residences—in New Haven along Hillhouse and Whitney avenues and Prospect and Orange streets; in Hartford along Asylum, Farmington, and Wethersfield avenues; and in Bridgeport, where P. T. Barnum built a lavish estate overlooking the sea.

Business expansion, immigration, and urbanization brought more than enterprising city scenes and opulent townhouses. Within the expanding cities, close by the factories, came the inevitable urban slums. Connecticut urbanization brought with it the same terrible living conditions that characterized the workers' neighborhoods in most expanding American cities of the era. Whether in Hartford, New Haven, or other urban centers, the steadily increasing number of working-class city dwellers, especially the foreign-born, were milked by landlords who consigned them to dark, filthy tenements.[4] Sanitary conditions were primitive, with families using common facilities. As bathtubs were a luxury of the affluent, the urban poor had to resort to commercial bathhouses for their infrequent ablutions. Lacking adequate light, air, and fresh food, the massed-together city dwellers fell prey to smallpox, cholera, typhus, tuberculosis, and diphtheria. A survey by the United States Bureau of Labor in 1905 disclosed that housing conditions in Hartford were worse than those of any other city of its size investigated. Such conditions understandably fed demoralization and a rising crime rate, especially among the young.

4. Not all of the immigrants in Connecticut settled in urban areas. In addition to the Italian truck farms near New Haven, immigrants from Germany, Ireland, Russia, Sweden, England, Austria, Canada, and Hungary took over farmlands which were vacated by Connecticuters. By 1920 more than one third of Connecticut's farmers were foreign-born, and only in the northwest and southeast sections of the state were farmers predominantly native-born.

Another unpleasant result of the period was growing disharmony between capital and labor. While workingmen in the state were beneficiaries of the increasing number of jobs available in manufacturing-oriented Connecticut, workers of the era had difficult times, particularly as a result of the depressions that followed the Panics of 1873 and 1893.

The depression of the 1870s was triggered by a sharp panic in May 1873 on the Vienna Bourse, during which European investors unloaded their substantial holdings in American securities. That summer the dumping of American securities in Europe had an inevitable result in America—prices on the New York Stock Exchange tumbled and by September heavy American investors in the market saw their capital wiped out. With a prevalent psychology of fear, American business came to a standstill.

Out of the business paralysis grew widespread unemployment. The Pennsylvania Bureau of Labor Statistics estimated that one third of the nation's working force were without jobs. Reports of unemployment, each more serious than the last, crowded into the headlines. Twenty-five thousand were laid off in Philadelphia, twenty thousand in Newark, eighteen thousand in Troy, three thousand in Lynn. The situation became critical even for those workers who managed to retain their jobs, for although prices were rapidly declining, wages were falling at an even faster rate. In order to sustain their families, workingmen were forced into constantly increasing debt.

As unemployment and indebtedness increased among workingmen, a new social type, the tramp, appeared. Groups of men, usually factory or farmhands looking unsuccessfully for a livelihood, drifted into gang life and spent their energies in aimless wandering, drinking, and stealing. State after state—New Hampshire, Rhode Island, Massachusetts, Maine, Pennsylvania, New Jersey, and Illinois—reacted to this "tramp" menace by erecting strict vagrancy laws.

If the unorganized, individualistic violence of the tramps brought fear to Americans, seemingly well-planned outrages of organized workingmen were the opening scenes in a spectacle depicting the decline of American society. Few states entirely escaped bitter industrial warfare. In Pennsylvania the "Molly Maguires" became a household phrase until the Philadelphia and Reading Railroad, working with Pinkerton detectives, instituted a drive that resulted in twenty-four convictions and ten executions. The climax of the industrial violence came in July 1877 when a general strike against the Baltimore and Ohio Railroad spread to other lines. Massive rioting took place in Maryland, Pennsylvania, Illinois, West Virginia, and Missouri, and before order was restored state and federal troops had to be called into action.

Connecticut, as a major industrial state, participated in the hard times following the crash of 1873. Banks were forced out of business, bankruptcies multiplied, and imposing enterprises such as the Sprague Textile Mills shut down. Workingmen were especially hard hit, as unemployment soared and wages fell five to twenty percent between 1873 and 1875. The bleak conditions of the workers, although not leading to the massive rioting that took place in other states, did bring on serious capital–labor confrontations in Connecticut.

One such confrontation occurred when employees at the Ponemah Cotton Mill in Taftville struck on April 1, 1875. The immediate causes of the strike were heavy pay cuts and the mill's attempt to break a union which had been organized. But underlying the labor unrest at the Taftville mill was the conviction of the workers that the company sought to gain back all wages paid out ($8 to $9 for a sixty-seven-hour week) through high rents for company-provided housing and through exorbitant prices at the company-operated store. One worker asserted that he and his daughter, working full time from February to April, received only four dollars in cash payment for the period. Although the State Commissioner of Labor, who investigated the Taftville situation, concluded that the company policy was "calculated to make the operatives completely dependent upon their employers," [5] the response of the General Assembly was to enact a strict tramp law, apparently aimed at workers—such as those at Taftville—who became drifters after their strikes were broken by the companies' employment of less recalcitrant employees.

5. Quoted in Harold J. Bingham, *History of Connecticut*, 4 volumes (New York: Lewis Historical Publishing Company, 1962), 2:682.

Similar hard times for Connecticut's workingmen came as a result of the Panic of 1893. That national decline began in May with the spectacular failure of the National Cordage Company. The market collapsed almost immediately. Banks began to call in their loans; businesses, finding credit unavailable, failed daily. The crash was so swift and so devastating that before the year was out some five hundred banks and sixteen thousand businesses had declared themselves insolvent. Unemployment became alarmingly high. The winter of 1894 saw over two and a half million men stumbling through America vainly seeking jobs. Country roads and city streetcorners were filled with knots of hungry, beaten men who saw nothing in the future but a continuation of their present misery.

In Connecticut the most difficult period of the business slump lasted from the summer of 1893 to the fall of 1894. Connecticut's cutlery, firearms, machine-building, carriage-making, and silver industries operated at less than seventy percent of capacity. Employees were discharged or had their hours cut and in over fifty percent of the state's manufacturing establishments workers labored at reduced wages. Even after business revived in the mid-1890s, a number of employers refused to restore workers' wages to pre-panic levels.

But more than hard times following the Panics of 1873 and 1893 made life difficult for the Connecticut workingman. Through much of the time between the Civil War and World War I Connecticut workers were plagued by a series of distressing practices common to the business enterprise of the time. Workers were angered by the refusal of employers to pay wages on a weekly basis, and employees of scores of firms had to submit to the practice of withholding the first month's pay. Workers in the cotton and woolen industries in the Quinebaug and Shetucket valleys had a particularly tough time. Both job opportunities and wage levels were depressed by widespread employment—at pitiful wages—of women and children, and workers throughout the textile industry were reduced to near bondage by the indebtedness to company stores and company landlords.

Hard times after the panics and the prevalence of difficult working conditions drove Connecticut workers by the thousands to unionize—in the early and mid-1880s in the Knights of Labor and, after the decline of the Knights in the late 1880s, in the evolving American Federation of Labor. While unionization proved a comfort and boon to the workingman, the existence of unions militantly pressing for workers' advances was hardly regarded with approval by the employers of the period.

For, while we have discussed at length the difficulties of workers in Connecticut between 1865 and 1914, the fact is that employers of the era lived lives not without stress and pressures. A great many businessmen did incredibly well. But for every businessman whose company succeeded, there were many more who saw their enterprises crumble and collapse. The highly competitive economic environment that prevailed in the United States in the late nineteenth and early twentieth centuries offered few men a second chance; businessmen knew full well that their competition was always on the prowl, anxious to exploit any soft spot. Thus, when employers resorted to money-saving practices that distressed workers, the motivation behind such practices was rarely simply rapacious profit-seeking but rather the necessity of keeping operating costs at an absolute minimum.

The stage was thus set for confrontation when workers resorted to unionization. Workers distressed by long hours, low pay, and humbling conditions of employment pressed hard for redress of very real grievances. Employers, struggling for survival in an age of ruthless competition, believed that any increase in overhead might well prove disastrous. The predictable result was growing disharmony between capital and labor manifested by decades of strikes—25 in 1881; 144 in 1886; 126 in 1901.

Along with urban slums and growing disharmony between capital and labor, there was a third negative factor during the period—a growing resentment on the part of native Connecticuters toward the growing numbers of foreign-born in the state. Focusing on urban blight and continuing industrial confrontations, longtime residents of the state began to wonder what had happened to the serene, placid land that once was Connecticut. Native Connecticuters pondered responsibility for disease-infested urban slums and unrelenting warfare between workers and employers. Not surprisingly, the Connecticuter discovered that wherever he saw problems, he saw hordes of foreigners. When he looked to the expanding urban centers, he saw that immigrants "surround our . . . [cities] . . . in colonies like a Roman wall." When he looked to the industrial scene, he saw foreign-looking men with strange names at the forefront of increasingly militant labor unions. From such experiences the Connecticuter, like J. Moss Ives, a former member of the General Assembly from Danbury, was moved to ask: "Will old New England, her standards of living, her ideals, her customs, and her laws survive the constantly increasing influx of alien blood?" [6]

This nativist reaction to Connecticut's immigrants was not, however, directed at all immigrants. There was relatively little resentment toward those who came from northern and western Europe and were Protestant.

> The northern and western Europeans . . . had an easier time [in Connecticut] than the rest. Except for the matter of language, these people were not unlike the rest of the state's population—they had the same religion, education, and values. With the industrial revolution going full tilt in Connecticut, these people, except in times of depression when all workers had a hard time, could readily find jobs, support themselves and their families, send their children to church and school, and become a part of the community in which they settled.[7]

Quite another situation prevailed when it came to immigrants from eastern and southern Europe. In comparison to those from northern and western Europe, these immigrants were generally less educated, had customs and values very different from those of native Connecticuters, tended to huddle together in a highly visible fashion in urban, ethnic ghettos, and, perhaps most damaging of all as far as the Connecticuter was concerned, were mostly Catholics and Jews. While the Connecticuter was not terribly exercised in his reaction to the Jews—perhaps because their numbers were not terribly large—the Puritan Yankee was

---

6. Quotations cited in Herbert F. Janick, Jr., *A Diverse People: Connecticut 1914 to the Present* (Chester: The Pequot Press, 1975), p. 2, p. 1.

7. Andersen, *From Yankee to American*, p. 10.

horrified at the prospect of large-scale Catholic immigration into Connecticut.

From its beginnings in the seventeenth century, Connecticut had been militantly anti-Catholic. Connecticut's Puritans, reared in the anti-Catholicism of the Reformation period, regarded the Catholic Church as nothing less than the devil's instrument. Connecticut's anti-Catholicism had been reinforced during the colonial period when the principal international adversary of the American colonies had been Catholic France. Although French contributions to the American victory during the Revolutionary War had softened the attitude of some Connecticuters, the reaction to waves of Catholic immigrants in the nineteenth and twentieth centuries indicates that anti-Catholicism was still very much a part of the Puritan Yankee mentality.

Connecticut's reaction to Irish Catholic immigrants in the nineteenth century demonstrated the vitality of the state's anti-Catholicism. In the 1850s, when Irish Catholics came to the state in great numbers, Connecticut experienced a nativist movement of substantial strength. Connecticuters were particularly afraid that the Irish would form some sort of political bloc that would dominate state politics. The *Hartford Courant* spoke out in 1856:

> Here is a mass of ignorant foreigners, marched to the polls in a body, under the guidance of a band of priests who, in turn, are mere puppets in the hands of their bishops, who in turn, *have all sworn allegiance to a foreign power!* Yet we call this a Republic! [8]

Such editorials struck a responsive chord; during the 1850s Connecticut contributed its backing to the Know-Nothing Party. The constitution of the Connecticut Know-Nothings clearly indicated the thrust of the party:

> [The party's] object shall be to resist the insidious policy of the Church of Rome, and all other foreign influences against the institutions of our country, by placing in all offices in the gift of the people, whether by election or appointment, none but native-born Protestant citizens. [9]

8. Quoted in Trecker, *Preachers, Rebels, and Traders*, p. 55.
9. Quoted in Van Dusen, *Connecticut*, p. 221.

The Know-Nothings in the 1850s constituted considerably more than a lunatic fringe in Connecticut politics. The state had a Know-Nothing governor from 1855 to 1857 in the person of William T. Minor. As governor, Minor proposed a longer residence period before naturalization for aliens as well as the disbanding of militia units composed of foreign-born [Irish] persons. During the period of Minor's governorship the General Assembly demonstrated its nativist leanings by legislation that struck at the Roman Catholic system of property-holding by bishops; prohibited the state courts from naturalizing aliens; and revised the state constitution, with popular approval, to require that the vote be limited to those men who could read Connecticut's constitution and laws. Yet for all their strength in the mid-1850s, the Know-Nothings within three years had been swallowed up by the emerging Republican Party as the issues of slavery and union dominated the state political scene. The nativism that was at the heart of the Know-Nothing thrust, however, did not disappear from Connecticut.

In the 1890s, when the Catholic population of Connecticut soared because of immigration, Connecticut proved fertile ground for another anti-Catholic political organization—the American Protective Association, formed in Iowa in 1887 to deny political office to Catholics. The APA grew slowly but steadily in the Midwest until the Panic of 1893. As the depression of the 1890s deepened and competition for jobs became more intense, the APA emerged in Connecticut. By 1894 there were APA chapters in Hartford, New Haven, Meriden, New Britain, Waterbury, Bridgeport, Danbury, Ansonia, Winsted, and Greenwich, and it was estimated that the organization had almost 25,000 members in the state.

In Connecticut the APA published materials warning of the peril of the Roman Catholic Church and entered politics by seeking control of local Republican Party caucuses. The APA, supported mostly by Yankees and by some first- and second-generation Protestant immigrants from northern and western Europe, succeeded in taking control of local Republican organizations in urban areas such as Bridgeport, New Britain, and Greenwich. The organization did not draw much support from

Connecticut's rural areas, where there were relatively few Catholics to serve as objects of fear. But the APA died in Connecticut almost as suddenly as it had emerged. By the fall of 1896 the APA in Connecticut was a thing of the past. The organization was undercut by the return of prosperity and by an unwillingness on the part of Connecticut's Republicans to cast aside the entire Catholic vote by visible alliance with the nativist APA. Still, the hostility of the state's Yankees to Catholic newcomers remained a potent force in Connecticut affairs for decades to come.

Thus the fruits of Connecticut's "progress" between 1865 and 1914 were not altogether sweet. While economic expansion brought remarkable affluence for some, immigration created an exciting and ultimately enriching ethnic diversity, and urbanization produced cities alive with energy and activity; forces at work in the period also brought urban slums, turbulent employer–employee disputes, and intense friction between native-born Protestants and Catholic newcomers. Perhaps the negative results of "progress" might have been rendered less severe and less socially disruptive by the existence in the state of creative and energetic political leadership. Such leadership, however, was not generally visible in Connecticut in the decades between the Civil War and World War I.

The most basic feature of political life in the period was continuation of the essential conservatism that had characterized Connecticut since its founding in the seventeenth century. A small number of reform-minded Republicans deserted President Taft in 1912 to support the political return of Theodore Roosevelt. Urban Democrats, generally of immigrant stock, from the 1880s onward pressed for legislation to control corporations, to improve the lot of the workingman, and to increase popular participation in government. But Connecticut's leading Republicans and Democrats were Yankees who were probusiness, anti-labor, and generally unwilling to support any alteration of the state's or the nation's political procedures. They were particularly unwilling if proposed alterations such as the open primary, woman suffrage, the initiative, the referendum, the recall, and the popular election of United States senators might decrease party control and increase citizens' involvement in governmental decision making.

The probusiness posture of the state's political leadership was evident in the treatment accorded to Connecticut's insurance companies and railroads. The General Assembly, the executive branch, and the state courts were all remarkably solicitous of the insurance companies in the last quarter of the nineteenth century. While the declared assets of the insurance companies were almost doubling, the General Assembly year after year reduced the taxes the companies paid to the state. The insurance companies' contribution to the state's tax receipts went from twenty-five percent in 1879 to eight percent in 1885 and stood at ten percent by the turn of the century. The influence of insurance firms on the executive branch was all too evident in 1887 when Governor Phineas C. Lounsbury stated to the General Assembly: "[T]here is little doubt that our insurance companies as a rule are managed by upright and capable men. There is no doubt that all new legislation touching these companies should be begun with caution and adopted only after the most patient and thorough consideration." [10] John W. Stedman, reform-minded editor of the *Norwich Advertiser* who became the State Commissioner of Insurance in the mid-1870s, found out the posture of the state courts toward Connecticut insurance companies when he mounted a campaign against the corrupt American National Life and Trust Company. Stedman held that the "guaranteed capital" of the company was "rubbish which would not, in the pockets of the subscribers, have produced one cent of income." [11] Stedman charged, among other things that the company had identified as assets stocks and bonds without value and real estate with greatly inflated value. The Court of Probate of the District of New Haven denied Stedman's petition that the company be ordered to cease operations.

While the state's insurance companies were receiving such gentle treatment, Connecticut's railroads had an equally beneficial relationship with the General Assembly. In the process of

10. Quoted in Bingham, *History of Connecticut,* 2:648.
11. Quoted in Bingham, *History of Connecticut,* 2:644.

expansion and consolidation, the railroads mishandled funds, misrepresented facts, and milked towns along proposed new routes for financial assistance. One rail company was able to collect some $6 million from the towns along a projected line from Willimantic to New Haven, but it wound up deep in debt with an uncompleted line. The members of the General Assembly, enjoying railroad passes and champagne suppers at the railroad's expense, sat very still for all of this, leaving the railroads pretty much free to do as they wished.

That the Connecticut political establishment was antilabor was also beyond dispute. I would suspect that most of the state's leading politicians would probably have applauded William Graham Sumner's performance before a committee of the U.S. House of Representatives. Sumner was a professor of social science at Yale from 1872 to 1909. A brilliant scholar and magnificent teacher, he was the leading nineteenth-century exponent of *laissez faire,* the position that government should intervene as little as possible in economic affairs. Sumner's acceptance of *laissez faire* was conditioned by his adherence to Social Darwinism, the theory that social phenomena are subject to natural laws in the same manner as physical phenomena. Social Darwinism contended that the life of man is surrounded and limited by the physical law of the survival of the fittest and man must function within an environment unfettered by human attempts to influence the natural laws of social development. Sumner went on to oppose trade unions, social legislation, government regulation, and anything else that attempted to impede "natural" development.

In the late 1870s, Sumner gave testimony to the Select Committee on Depression in Labor and Business, a committee of the House of Representatives formed to investigate the causes of and possible cures for the depression triggered by the Panic of 1873. In an exchange with Congressman William Whitney Rice of Massachusetts, Sumner made clear an aversion to aid for workingmen, a position entirely in tune with the views of political leaders in the state in which he taught:

> Mr. Rice: What is the effect of machinery on those laborers
>   whom for the time being it turns out of employment?
> Mr. Sumner: For the time being they suffer, of course, a loss of

income and a loss of comfort. There are plenty of
people in the United States today whose fathers were
displaced from their labor in some of the old
countries by the introduction of machinery, and who
suffered very great poverty, and who were forced to
emigrate to this country by the pressure of necessity,
poverty, and famine. When they came to this country
they entered on a new soil and a new system of
industry, and their children today may look back on
the temporary distress through which their parents
went as a great family blessing.

Mr. Rice: But the fathers had to suffer from it?

Mr. Sumner: They had to suffer from it.

Mr. Rice: Is there any way to help it?

Mr. Sumner: Not at all. There is no way on this earth to help it.
The only way is to meet it bravely, go ahead, make
the best of circumstances; and if you cannot go on in
the way you were going, try another way, and still
another, until you work yourself out as an
individual.[12]

Rice, who knew personally of extensive unemployment in Pennsylvania among iron and coal workers, then asked Sumner about the possibility of the government helping the unemployed to migrate to the West. Sumner responded:

I do not think that that is a proper thing for the government to do,
and I do not see any practical way whatever for the government to
do it. These persons in Pennsylvania have been in the receipt of
very good wages indeed during the ten years before the panic. They
are not paupers; or, if they are, it must be entirely their own fault.
Neither are they a helpless class of people, so unintelligent as not to
be able to take care of themselves. There is no such class of persons
in this country that I know of. The true course for them,
unquestionably, is to get on the land, and if there be need of
executive or administrative care in carrying out the movement, that
seems a matter for the undertaking of private societies.[13]

12. Select Committee on Depression in Labor and Business, House of Representatives, "Causes of the General Depression in Labor and Business," *Miscellaneous Document 29*, 45th Cong., 3d Sess., 1879, p. 183.

13. "Causes of the General Depression in Labor and Business," p. 202.

More direct evidence of the antilabor posture of Connecticut's leaders was discernible during the harsh times that American workingmen experienced following the Panic of 1893. Groups of the unemployed, called "industrial armies," set out for Washington to demand public relief projects. In 1894 seventeen such "armies" took the roads to Washington. The most famous of these left Massillon, Ohio, on Easter Sunday under the leadership of Jacob S. Coxey, but its fate was exactly the same as that of other petitioning groups. The effort brought the men nothing but hunger, cold, blistered feet, and a policeman's club upon reaching the nation's capital. The government, startled and frightened by these hordes of shabby men, reacted with force.

In Connecticut a Coxey-type march was led by George Sweetland, an unemployed male nurse who resided in Bristol. "Sweetland's Army" marched from Bristol to New York—via Hartford, New Britain, Meriden, and New Haven—where Sweetland was promptly arrested for parading without a license. When Sweetland reached New York he had with him a pitifully small contingent of sixty-nine men, but of far more significance than the size of the group was the disgust that the effort produced in Connecticut's leading politicians and in newspaper editors who generally reflected the conservatism of the state political establishment. Senator Hawley, the former Union general, thundered that the armies of men led by such as Sweetland and Coxey contained "the bacteria and bacilli of anarchy," [14] and for his denunciation of the "armies" Hawley was deluged with letters of commendation from fellow Connecticuters. The editor of the *New Haven Sunday Register* joined the chorus of condemnation:

> Let us stick to Jefferson here in Connecticut no matter what states join the rabble of Coxey's following, for after all Coxey is but the full fruitage of the Populist idea that the business of the government is to support the people. The democratic idea is that it is the business of the people to support the government. [15]

14. Quoted in Frederick M. Heath, "Politics and Steady Habits: Issues and Elections in Connecticut, 1894–1914" (Ph.D. dissertation, Columbia University, 1965), p. 20.

15. Quoted in Heath, "Politics and Steady Habits," p. 20.

Another episode of the 1890s that brought out the antilabor views of the Connecticut establishment was the Pullman strike of 1894. Wage cutting by the Pullman Palace Car Company provoked a strike by the American Railway Union, led by Eugene V. Debs. In the course of the strike some Pullman cars were overturned and rail traffic from Chicago to the West Coast was paralyzed. The strike was crushed by President Grover Cleveland's attorney general, Richard Olney, who utilized federal troops on the legal grounds that the strikers were interfering with the transit of the United States mail. A number of the leaders of the union, including Debs, were sentenced to six months in jail for defying a federal court injunction to terminate the strike.

In Connecticut leading politicians and editors were ardent supporters of the tough line taken by the Cleveland Administration. The *Hartford Courant* declared: "No American worth his salt knows or cares anything just now, in this matter, about any politics, save the politics of patriotism. As soon as the embers of sedition are trampled out, we shall be republicans and democrats again, but until then we are members of one party—the American party." [16] The *New Haven Sunday Register* expressed the hope that some of the strikers would be shot down. The behavior of the American Railway Union also drew the ire of one of Connecticut's leading political figures of the day— United States Senator Orville Hitchcock Platt. Born in Washington, Connecticut, in 1827 and a lawyer for many years, Platt was, on the basis of his distinguished work in the Senate from 1879 to 1905, the closest thing Connecticut had to a national political figure in the late nineteenth and early twentieth centuries. He was mentioned several times as a prospect for the Republican vice-presidential nomination. In the Senate, Platt was known for his work in the framing of patent laws; the formation and passage of an international copyright law (1891); and, after the Spanish–American War, his vigorous imperialistic views, reflected in part by the Platt Amendment of 1901 that made Cuba a virtual protectorate of the United States. On mat-

16. Quoted in Heath, "Politics and Steady Habits," p. 22.

ters pertaining to business and labor, Platt was an unqualified proponent of business interests—supporting high tariffs, opposing regulation of industry, and damning "radical" reformers such as Benjamin R. Tillman and William Jennings Bryan. At the time of the Pullman strike, Platt, although a highly partisan Republican, had nothing but praise for Cleveland and Olney in putting down the "insurrection" of Debs and his cohorts.

By far the most definitive indication of the fundamental conservatism of Connecticut's political establishment came during the presidential campaign of 1896. That campaign, the closest thing to a class war ever seen in national politics, pitted conservative Republican William McKinley of Ohio against "the boy orator of the Platte," thirty-six-year-old William Jennings Bryan of Nebraska. Bryan's candidacy was a product of such agrarian ills in the 1880s and 1890s as falling farm prices, deflation (the currency in circulation for each American was only $22.67 in 1890),[17] high railroad charges, high prices of manufactured goods, high interest rates, and natural disasters such as droughts and invasions of grasshoppers and the cotton-boll weevil. These conditions drove thousands of farmers into growing indebtedness, many into bankruptcy. In 1892 they also spawned the Populist Party, which demanded the free and un-limited coinage of silver as a device to increase the currency in circulation; government ownership of the telephone, the telegraph, and the railroads; popular election of United States senators; a graduated income tax; an eight-hour day for workers; the secret ballot; the initiative; and the referendum. The Populist candidate for president was General James B. Weaver of Iowa, a veteran of the Greenback Party—a political movement of the 1870s that sought an increase in available currency through the retention of Civil War-issued paper currency. In 1892 Weaver rolled up over a million popular votes and carried four states: Colorado, Idaho, Nevada, and Kansas.[18]

17. By comparison, the currency in circulation for each person was $27.35 in 1900; $51.36 in 1920; $59.40 in 1940; and $177.48 in 1960.

18. Kansas was the home of one of the most unrestrained of the Populist leaders—Mary Elizabeth ("Mary Yellin") Lease, who advised farmers to raise "less corn and more hell." Conservative Connecticut would have been delighted at the response of the

Between 1892 and 1896 thousands of Americans, especially southern and western Democrats, were converted to the new Populist inflationary demand of the unlimited coinage of silver at the ratio of sixteen ounces of silver to one of gold. Many were influenced by a pamphlet, *Coin's Financial School*, written in 1894 by William J. Harvey. In the pamphlet, Harvey declared:

> Hard times are with us; the country is distracted; very few things are marketable at a price above the cost of production; tens of thousands are out of employment; the jails, penitentiaries, workhouses . . . are full . . . hungered and half-starved men are banding into armies and marching toward Washington; the cry of distress is heard on every hand . . . riots and strikes prevail throughout the land. . . .[19]

Harvey's analysis of the nation's ills was that

> adherence to the gold standard only deepened the depression. He explained that the country's prosperity or want depended upon money's abundance or money scarcity, and ever since silver money was abolished [in 1873], the circulation of currency had not been sufficient for the economy. . . . There was not enough money . . . to keep the economy going. To remedy this situation . . . [Harvey] suggested that silver should be used as well as gold; thus credit would multiply, money would circulate, prices would rise and the debtor [i.e., the farmer] would no longer be at a disadvantage.[20]

Among those converted to the cause of silver was William Jennings Bryan, a former lawyer who had been elected to Congress in 1890 and 1892 and subsequently edited the *Omaha World-Herald*. Bryan, handsome and possessed of a great voice, took to the stump for silver in the months before the Democratic convention at Chicago in the summer of 1896. At

---

New York Evening Post to Lease's characterization of the American government as "of Wall Street, by Wall Street, and for Wall Street": "We don't want any more states until we can civilize Kansas."

19. Quoted in Stefan Lorant, *The Presidency: A Pictorial History of Presidential Elections from Washington to Truman* (New York: The Macmillan Company, 1952), p. 427.

20. Lorant, *The Presidency*, p. 427.

the convention—stocked with Silver Democrats—Bryan won the presidential nomination following his "Cross of Gold" speech. Before 15,000 people, his booming voice reaching the far corners of the great hall, Bryan declared:

> You come to us and tell us that the great cities are in favor of the gold standard. We reply that the great cities rest upon our broad and fertile prairies. Burn down your cities and leave our farms, and your cities will spring up again as if by magic; but destroy our farms and grass will grow in the streets of every city in the country. . . .
>
> Having behind us the producing masses of the nation and the world, supported by the commercial interests, the laboring interests and the toilers everywhere, we will answer their demand for a gold standard by saying to them: You shall not press down upon the brow of labor this crown of thorns, you shall not crucify mankind upon a cross of gold.[21]

After his nomination on the fifth ballot, Bryan went on to mount a campaign that covered 18,000 miles, took him into twenty-seven states, and included 600 speeches—36 in one day. Speaking for the farmers of the West and the South, Bryan pounded away at the railroads, the trusts, the industrialists, and most of all the financiers, the creditors who were reaping the rewards of deflation by being paid back in dollars that had greater purchasing power than those originally lent.

In Connecticut the reaction of the state's leading Democrats to Bryan and silver was comparable to that of a vegetarian served a slab of uncooked beef. The party's leadership—Yankee bankers, businessmen, editors, and professionals—took the stand that

> the honest payment of public debts, and the preservation of the public faith and credit, require that the gold standard of money, as a measure of value, shall be maintained.
>
> While we favor the most liberal use of silver consistent with the enforcement of a gold standard, we are unalterably opposed to the free coinage of silver, deeming it a device for the debasement of our currency, and to the compulsory purchase of silver by the Government. Under existing circumstances to pay public debts in

21. Quoted in Lorant, *The Presidency,* p. 438.

silver coin is repudiation; to repay private debts in silver coin is to rob the wage-earner; and to provide for the free coinage of silver means the destruction of legitimate business, and great suffering among the laboring classes.[22]

Subscribing to such a position and fearing that silver at 16 to 1 would convert their wealth into fifty-cent dollars, most of Connecticut's leading Democrats left the party: the state party chairman and secretary, twelve of the twenty-four members of the state central committee, a national committeeman, two former governors, two former congressmen, four of the five candidates for state office in the election of 1894, and leading Democrats in the General Assembly. When election day came, many of the state's leading Democrats either sat at home, voted for McKinley, or voted the ticket of the National Democratic Party, an organization of Gold Democrats that was formed at Indianapolis after Bryan's victory at Chicago.

If the reaction of the state's leading Democrats to Bryan was negative, the response of the Connecticut Republican leadership was even stronger. They branded Bryan a "revolutionary" or a "lunatic," advised the middle class that a Bryan victory would endanger its property, cautioned the state's farmers that Bryan in the White House would strengthen western farmers already providing tough competition for Connecticut's agrarians, and went about raising money for the McKinley campaign. The state's voters got the message. Of some 175,000 votes cast for president in the state in 1896, Bryan received only about 55,000 (mostly from urban workers). McKinley's winning percentage was a thumping 63.24, a landslide by anyone's reckoning. "The Land of Steady Habits" wanted no part of wild-eyed reformers—even ones with magnificent voices.

There is more significance to the campaign of 1896 in Connecticut than the fact that the state's political establishment revealed its basic conservatism in its repudiation of Bryan and silver. The Bryan campaign of 1896 wrecked the Connecticut Democratic Party and left it a shambles for a generation. The prominent Democrats who denied the party their votes, influ-

22. Quoted in Heath, "Politics and Steady Habits," p. 63.

ence, and financial support in 1896 because of Bryan and silver generally wound up as Republicans. The result was that Connecticut Republicans—led by Yankee businessmen, lawyers, professionals, and newspaper people—were in charge from 1896 until the 1930s.

Despite the fact that there was little difference between the leading Democrats and Republicans in the state, Republican domination after 1896 was significant for Connecticut in two respects. One-party rule at any time and in any society tends to breed irresponsibility, and between 1896 and the 1930s Connecticut Republicans ran the state with little or no concern for much else than their own political futures and the happiness of the business interests that dominated the party. In addition, while there was little difference between Democratic and Republican leaders during most of the years from 1865 to 1914, there was a crucial difference between the constituencies of the two parties.

The rank and file of the Republican Party consisted of rural farmers and small-town businessmen who, because of the representation aspects of the Constitution of 1818, were grossly overrepresented in the General Assembly. These men, very much wedded to the *status quo,* gave no thought to legislative programs that would confront problems created by industrialization, urbanization, and large-scale immigration.

On the other hand, the rank and file of the Democratic Party consisted of urban workers of immigrant stock. These new urban Democrats were the only significant group in the state motivated to do anything about the regulation of business and industry and the enactment of social and labor legislation. They had been at the forefront of a thrust in the General Assembly in the 1880s and 1890s that enacted legislation providing for the regulation of child labor, the worker's right to join unions, the prohibition of employers' blacklists, the establishment of a State Board of Mediation and Arbitration, and the establishment of free public employment bureaus. I do not think that such legislation was very important, for I am certain that the state political establishment may have allowed these laws to pass only as a means of cooling union militancy in Connecticut and made certain after the laws were enacted that they were enforced with a clear absence of enthusiasm or energy. But passage of such legislation did reveal the pressure of urban Democrats and did indicate that Connecticut—at least in the statute books—could move off political dead center if pushed.

An even clearer reflection of the reform inclinations of urban Democrats came during the governorship of Simeon Baldwin from 1911 to 1915. Baldwin, the only Democratic governor in Connecticut between the Bryan disaster and the 1930s, was a distinguished Yale professor and jurist. One of those prominent Democrats who did not jump ship in 1896, he won the governorship in 1910 because the Republicans fell to internal feuding and won again in 1912 when the Republicans were at odds because of the Taft-Roosevelt division in the party. The Baldwin governorship brought some significant legislation—a corrupt practices act, the establishment of a public utilities commission, and a workmen's compensation measure that held employers liable for industrial accidents. These measures were enacted in good part because of the clout of urban Democrats— Irishmen such as Thomas J. Spellacy; Russian Jews such as Herman Kopplemann; and Italians such as Tony Zazzara. These men stuck with the Democratic Party in 1896 not because of any enthusiasm for Bryan and silver or because they thought Bryan might win, but because they realized that the prominent-Yankee exodus from the party would open up positions of party leadership for them. Urban Democrats by 1911 to 1915 had become the lieutenants and captains—if not the colonels and generals— of the Democratic Party and were committed to a Connecticut government that would confront the problems of the era.

Thus the Republican domination from 1896 onward meant that Connecticut's urban Democrats, with their inclination toward reform, were doomed to wander the political wilderness of the "outs" for decades; and that the Republicans—probusiness, antilabor, and anti-immigrant—would continue to guide Connecticut along a course devoid of any impetus toward political reform or innovation.

7

1914–1929:
Yankee-Republican Domination

WHAT might the world be like if the principal European statesmen in the summer of 1914 had not been led by blind nationalism into decisions for war? Might the western world have survived as it was before 1914 if by some miracle World War I had been a quick affair, with one side or the other able to press a definitive attack that brought immediate victory and peace? Such speculations fade before reality. The decisions for war were made and any possibility of a quick, socially and morally painless victory was wiped out as British and French troops stopped the initial German thrust at the Battle of the Marne in September 1914. After the stalemate at the Marne, the nature of World War I on the Western Front was determined by the inability of either side to overcome the defensive trinity of the machine gun, barbed wire, and the trenches that ran from the North Sea to Switzerland. Each side tried to achieve a breakthrough—tried so hard that a generation of young men was slaughtered or maimed at places like Verdun, the Somme, and Ypres. Finally, when the Germans knew they had to counteract the British–French naval blockade or lose the war, the submarine was turned loose, neutral shipping was blown out of the seas, and the United States entered the war in April 1917. American involvement was a major factor in ending the conflict at the eleventh hour, on the eleventh day, of the eleventh month in the year 1918. But it was too late to save the Europe that had been. The Europe that had believed in progress, hope, and humanity before the war became a land cursed by despair and agony, a land that by the early 1930s was bedeviled by Fascism and Communism.

Nor did the United States escape the repercussions of World War I. American losses, compared to those of the European combatants, were not great. Of the 1,390,000 Americans who saw combat, 49,000 were killed in action or died of wounds; 230,000 more were wounded; and 57,000 died of disease, many from the influenza epidemic that ravaged military camps in America and France in the fall of 1918. Moreover, the war sparked a roaring prosperity in the United States that, except for a brief postwar slackening, continued and expanded through the 1920s. But America lost more than it gained. The America of 1914 was an idealistic land committed to continued progressive advance under the leadership of Woodrow Wilson. Americans were delighted in 1914 at their good fortune in being separated by the Atlantic from war-ridden Europe; reelected Wilson over Charles Evans Hughes in 1916 largely on the basis of the Democratic slogan "He kept us out of war"; and did go to war in April 1917 only reluctantly, dedicated to the selfless cause of "fighting a war to end all wars." Then something went wrong. The idealistic and humane Wilson permitted a vicious propaganda campaign against Germany that fed an explosion of national hate and war hysteria; promised America and the world "a peace without victory" and delivered the Versailles Treaty, which left Germany economically and territorially devastated; and lay bedridden after a stroke while the nation turned on radicals and ethnics during the Red Scare of 1919–1920. When the dust had settled in the 1920s, America had repudiated Wilsonian internationalism and idealism by rejecting the Versailles Treaty and the League of Nations and had accepted domestic "normalcy"—which meant conservative Republicanism as expressed by Warren Harding and his "Ohio gang"; Calvin Coolidge, the taciturn mediocrity; and Herbert Hoover, who although bright and talented was paralyzed when the bubble of prosperity burst in 1929.

Connecticut tended to reflect the American experience of the period. The state generally enjoyed prosperity during World War I and the 1920s. At the beginning of World War I it was mired in an economic slump that dated back to 1913. Figures indicate that many of the state's factories were operating only three to four days a week, and a survey in 1914 revealed that thousands of workers in Hartford were either out of work entirely or on short hours. But all this changed much for the better as war orders started coming in.

By early 1915 Connecticut's major firearms and munitions firms—Remington Arms and Ammunition and Remington Union Metallic of Bridgeport; Winchester Repeating Arms of New Haven; Colt's Patent Firearms of Hartford; and Marlin-Rockwell of New Haven—increased production to meet British and French war contracts. In the spring of 1915 Remington publicized a program to add 500 new employees a week until it had a total work force of 10,000. By the late summer of 1915 Winchester had constructed almost forty new buildings or additions. What expanded production meant in terms of profits was indicated by the experience of the Colt firm in 1915. Colt stock stood at 200 in 1914 and at 950 by the end of the following year. Although Colt greatly increased its dividends to its stockholders and paid its salaried workers a bonus of twelve-and-a-half percent every three months, by the end of 1915 the firm was reported to have on hand a cash surplus of $5 million. Once the United States entered the war in 1917, the Connecticut firearms industry turned to supplying America's armed forces.

With the end of hostilities in November 1918, Connecticut arms manufacturers had compiled a truly astounding record of productivity. Winchester produced more than 450,000 Enfield rifles. Remington manufactured almost fifty percent of the small-arms cartridges used by the American forces, and along with Winchester turned out some 2,000,000 bayonets—the scabbards for which were made by the Jewell Belting Company of Hartford. Trench knives were made by Landers, Frary and Clark of New Britain. Over 250 155-mm. guns had been manufactured by 1919 by Bullard Engineering Company of Bridgeport. Fuse castings were made by Waterbury Brass Goods; trench-mortar fuses by the Ansonia Manufacturing Company in Ansonia and the Russell and Irwin Manufacturing Company of New Britain; and hand grenades by the Bassick Company of Bridgeport and P. and F. Corbin of New Britain. Colt's was known not only for the production of the Colt .45 official service pistol but for the production of new weapons developed by a Colt employee, John M. Browning. The government demand was so great for the Browning water-cooled machine gun, the light Browning automatic rifle, and the Browning aircraft gun that Colt's had to share the production of these weapons for the duration of the war—in return for a royalty plan—with Marlin–Rockwell and Winchester. By the end of the war Marlin–Rockwell had manufactured 16,000 Browning automatic rifles and Winchester almost 30,000.

Not all defense production centered on arms. Danbury's hat factories produced carloads of hats for the military and Cheney Brothers of Manchester made silk for parachutes. The Russell Manufacturing Company of Middletown made some 1,500,000 woven articles for the military—machine-gun and cartridge belts; pistol holsters; haversacks; canteen covers; and braid for goggles and gas masks. Four fifths of Connecticut's industries were producing goods for military use.

Connecticut's defense production brought boom times not only to manufacturers but to the state as a whole. During the era of World War I the Connecticuter's bank account and number of purchases grew—if goods could be had in the face of wartime scarcity. And, except for a slump from the end of the war until 1922, the state's productivity and prosperity continued during the 1920s. By the summer of 1923 employment and factory output had climbed back to peak wartime levels. Utilizing its skilled work force, experienced managers, and relatively new factories (some $32 million went into factory construction and expansion from 1914 to 1918), Connecticut was distinguished in the 1920s for the production of specialty parts for the aviation, automotive, and electrical power industries. Bridgeport became a leader in the automotive and electrical industries, with factories turning out products such as electric cable, fractional horsepower motors, fans, sun lamps, light sockets, brake linings, gear shifts, and tire valves. The state's leadership in the aviation industry came from Hartford in the mid-1920s:

> In 1925 a Hartford machine shop, Pratt and Whitney Company, began to manufacture air-cooled airplane engines. Sizable orders from the navy and commercial airlines for these Wasp engines encouraged Frederick Rentschler and his associates to develop the more powerful Hornet engine, capable of producing 525 horsepower. In ten years Pratt and Whitney grew from twenty-five to over two thousand employees and occupied a modern plant on a six hundred acre site in East Hartford. The company became the nucleus of United Aircraft which brought to the state Hamilton Standard Propellers from Pittsburgh and Chance-Vought, developer of the navy "Corsair" fighter plane from Long Island. Sikorsky Aircraft of Stratford, specialists in multi-engine and amphibious airplanes, joined United in 1939.[1]

There were, unfortunately, some soft spots in Connecticut's generally strong economic situation. Perhaps the most obvious was the declining condition of the eastern Connecticut textile industry. The South, able to offer favorable tax breaks, a work force satisfied with relatively low wages, and an abundance of raw materials, drew off a number of textile plants. As a result, from 1919 to 1929 the state lost fourteen of forty-seven cotton mills and a third of the mills' work force. The value of finished goods went from $101 million dollars to $40 million.

But the textile industry was the exception rather than the rule, and a good many Connecticuters geared themselves for the enjoyment of those pleasures that a generally prosperous economy made possible. They flocked to the movies to see lightly clad Theda Bara and dynamic Rudolph Valentino locked in amorous embraces with their respective lovers and huddled around their radios to enjoy the "Cowboy Philosopher" Will Rogers and "Amos 'n' Andy." The focus of Connecticuters was not on Harding, Coolidge, or Hoover, but on

1. Janick, *A Diverse People*, p. 22.

the truly important of the era—the nation's sports heroes. Knute Rockne's Notre Dame teams brought an aura of professionalism to college football, and the Irish backfield of the "Four Horsemen" blazed new records each Saturday afternoon in the fall. Ty Cobb dominated baseball until a thin-legged young man from a Baltimore boys' home, George Herman Ruth, disdained the single and started hitting balls out of the park. Babe Ruth began his four-bagger spree in 1915 and in the course of the next twenty-two years chalked up a total of 714 home runs. Tennis was dominated by William T. "Big Bill" Tilden and Helen Wills. In boxing Jack Dempsey was the heavyweight champion, holding the title from 1919 to 1926 when he was outboxed by a slender ex-Marine, Gene Tunney. But even the sports heroes were forgotten when young Charles A. Lindbergh touched down his "Spirit of St. Louis" at Le Bourget airdrome on May 21, 1927, completing the first solo transatlantic flight from New York to Paris in 33 hours, 39 minutes.

Like the rest of the nation, Connecticuters overcame their disdain for the motor car—first looked on as a toy of the rich—especially as Henry Ford reduced the price of the Model T from $825 in 1908 to $260 by 1925. Between 1915 and 1920 the number of automobiles in the state went from 40,000 to 120,000 and the number of trucks from 7,000 to 24,000. While livery stables, carriage and wagon factories, harness makers, grain stores, and other enterprises that lived on horse transport were hard hit, gas stations sprang up along main routes, "gifte shoppes" appeared to appeal to weekend joyriders, and country inns burgeoned to accommodate the vacationing family. Most important, the automobile gave Connecticuters a physical mobility that previously had not been dreamed of.

Another attempted change in the average way of life was less successful. Nobody in Connecticut—save the membership of the Connecticut Temperance Union and the Connecticut Dry Alliance—took prohibition very seriously. Before the Eighteenth Amendment became law in 1920 Connecticuters made known their opposition to the "noble experiment." In 1918 former governor Simeon Baldwin held the Eighteenth Amendment to be "contrary to the fundamental principles of our constitution," and the *Hartford Courant* characterized it as a "highly dangerous invasion of the rights of the individual states." [2] With such views expressed, local, state, and federal prohibition officials never had a prayer. In 1921 New Haven alone had over 400 speakeasies—almost all of which, it appears, were regularly visited by members of the Yale student body. A Yale faculty member living on campus in the 1920s recalled that he "expected to be and was usually awakened during the night by noisy students coming home." [3] But college students had no monopoly on skirting prohibition. From governors to bootblacks, Connecticuters got as much alcohol as they wanted from state moonshiners and New York City gangsters. Otherwise law-abiding citizens were arrested—an average of 489 per year between 1924 and 1929; bootleggers were "rubbed out" in grand Chicago style; and thirsty Connecticuters died from poisonous liquor. But Connecticut's lust for the bottle went on nevertheless.

Thus Connecticuters in the war years and the 1920s lived a life marked by affluence, amusements, and diversions. They might have seemed exuberantly content with the present and at least wildly optimistic about the future, but they were not. During the years of World War I and the 1920s Connecticut was a troubled land that experienced an enlargement of the rift between native-born and foreign-born or ethnic that had appeared in the late nineteenth and early twentieth centuries.

On the eve of World War I, the Connecticut Yankee saw his civilization and its mores under assault by the ethnic. The Yankee identified the ethnic as the determining factor in bringing about urban slums and crime and industrial altercations and violence. The Yankee's fear of the ethnic was, if possible, intensified during the era of World War I and the subsequent Red Scare.

Perhaps because he had for so long been surrounded by the

2. Quoted in Van Dusen, *Connecticut,* p. 282.
3. Quoted in Janick, *A Diverse People,* p. 20.

foreign-born, World War I with its confrontations with the dreaded "Hun" was a truly traumatic experience for the Connecticut Yankee. He reacted to the threat to America as though the Germans occupied Massachusetts and were but one good forced march away. The person who most clearly reflected the Yankee's fears during World War I was the state's governor, Marcus Holcomb, who previously had been a judge of the state superior court. Holcomb, who concluded that American intervention was inevitable once the Germans announced unrestricted submarine warfare in January 1917, immediately set out to mobilize Connecticut for war.

An early step, with the cooperation of the General Assembly, was the formation in March 1917 of a Home Guard to protect Connecticut. The response of Connecticuters was astounding:

> Eager citizens bombarded the State Capitol with offers to help. Letters poured in from Civil War veterans, elderly businessmen, and high school students. One individual donated a thirty-two-foot power boat, five saddle horses, and a fleet of automobiles supplied with chauffeurs for the use of the state. Another offered to turn his estate into a wireless station. It took just three months to organize, uniform, and arm ten thousand men between seventeen and sixty years of age. During the war that followed these troops clad in distinctive blue coats staged weekend manuevers and stood guard over railroads, factories, and bridges.[4]

But the establishment of the Home Guard was only the beginning of frenetic Holcomb-led Connecticut war activity. Shortly after the American declaration of war on April 3, 1917, Holcomb set up a State Council of Defense—dominated by Republican businessmen of Puritan Yankee ancestry—to oversee all war programs in Connecticut. The Council of Defense in turn organized committees to deal with functions such as manpower and food procurement. Soon Connecticut produced a torrent of war-related programs. Four Liberty Loan drives were sponsored in which Connecticut raised more than any other state, $437 million; youngsters were signed up to work on farms; hundreds of thousands of Connecticuters were enrolled in

4. Janick, *A Diverse People,* p. 9.

the Hoover food conservation plan and pledged to abstain from meat on Tuesdays and wheat on Wednesdays; and speakers, posters, and films were dispatched around the state to whip up appropriate hate for the "Prussian Menace."

Nothing was left unsaid in the Connecticut establishment's war frenzy. The president of Trinity College advised a group of Protestant laymen to "pray for the slaughter of the Germans." Holcomb ordered Connecticut troops to take "damn few prisoners." Particular attention was given to those who did not seem to show appropriate enthusiasm for the war. Addressing a "War Convention" in Hartford in January 1918, Holcomb told the audience: "Don't let any disloyal person show his head in your community," and the governor directed the First Regiment of the Home Guard "to squeeze some of the yellow out of the state of Connecticut." Those who spoke out against the war or who failed to join the unrestrained war effort found themselves subject to intense condemnation and even to prosecution under the Federal Espionage Act.[5]

Perhaps the most telling feature of the Connecticut war program was a concerted attempt to "Americanize" the foreign-born or second-generation ethnic. Long distrustful of the ethnic generally and now suspicious of his loyalty to Connecticut and to the nation, the Yankee force-fed aliens with American values and mores. The State Council of Defense set up an Americanization Committee to make patriotic citizens of aliens through education. What subsequently took place was much like events in other states and on the national scene under the direction of George Creel and the Committee on Public Information. After the war, Frank Cobb, editor of the *New York World*, described the "Americanization" process: "Government conscripted public opinion as they conscripted men and money and materials. Having conscripted it, they dealt with it as they dealt with other raw recruits. They mobilized it. They put it in charge of drill sergeants. They goose-stepped it. They taught it to stand at attention and salute." [6] Moreover, the end of the war brought no

5. Quotations cited in Janick, *A Diverse People*, p. 11.

6. Quoted in Robert K. Murray, *Red Scare: A Study in National Hysteria, 1919–1920* (New York: McGraw-Hill Book Company, 1964), p. 12.

decline in the Americanization of the alien in Connecticut. If anything, it saw an intensification of the Yankee fear that the alien had not been sufficiently Americanized.

The causes of Yankee postwar nervousness were many. One was the advent of substantial unemployment and resulting strikes when war orders were cancelled. Within a year after November 1918, Remington Arms cut its work force from 13,000 to 300; Bridgeport Brass sliced its work force by fifty percent. With unemployment came labor bitterness and a series of strikes. Work stoppages hit the American Graphophone Company in Bridgeport, the Underwood Typewriter Company in Hartford, the Rockville textile mills, and the United States Rubber plants in Naugatuck. Since the Yankee had for decades associated industrial warfare with the immigrant, it took little for the Connecticuter to assume that alien agitation was behind capital–labor altercations.

Yankee postwar nervousness was also increased by the atmosphere during the Red Scare. The success of the Bolsheviks in seizing power in Russia in 1917 and subsequent establishment of the Third International in May 1919 convinced many Americans that a "Red Revolution" was shortly to explode in the United States. National coal and steel strikes, a Boston police strike, bombings, radical demonstrations, and the hysterical reaction to the "Red threat" described by United States Attorney General A. Mitchell Palmer all combined to strengthen the American fear that Bolshevism was about to inundate the nation.

Finally, a series of incidents in 1919 appeared to the Yankee to indicate that ethnic radicals and Bolsheviks were girding for a takeover within the state:

> The pastor of a Greek Orthodox church in Hartford complained that half his congregation had been converted to communism. A private detective in Waterbury informed Governor Holcomb that he had investigated forty-two cases involving the distribution of inflammatory literature by radicals in the Naugatuck Valley. An assassination threat was made on United States Attorney John Crosby by a Bolshevik group called the Blue Hand Society. . . . Bolsheviks were accused of instigating two days of violence on the Yale University campus in May 1919 when a mob of five thousand

young boys and men, ostensibly seeking to avenge insults made to parading doughboys by college students, clashed with undergraduates and faculty armed with clubs and baseball bats.[7]

The labor unrest, the general hysteria of the Red Scare, and the manifestation of radicalism in the state all combined to drive the Connecticut Yankee into a condition of outright panic. Citizens of Ansonia, Waterbury, and Naugatuck requested the General Assembly to build new armories in their respective cities; the American Legion offered to establish a special unit to help the police in identifying Reds; Governor Holcomb instructed the State Guard to institute antiriot drills; and the General Assembly passed a law in May 1919 imposing a fine and imprisonment for "disloyal, scurrilous, or abusive" criticism of the government.

The major thrust of this patriotic antiradical crusade was a concerted attempt to mold the ethnic into a Yankee-pure Connecticuter. Holcomb addressed the General Assembly in January 1919 and asserted that "Americanization is a matter of self defense and self preservation, and not one merely of sentimental or charitable impulse." [8] So Americanization went on. The Americanization Bureau of the State Council of Defense stepped up its educational programs and launched an investigation of un-American activities. Connecticut schools, especially in the urban areas, reinforced their curricula in the field of American history. When FBI agents made swings through the state in November 1919 and January 1920 to round up "dangerous aliens," Connecticut officials cooperated in the enterprise, which was carried on with a flagrant unconcern for traditional American civil liberties and due process of law. These raids brought the arrest in Connecticut of 336 aliens between November 1919 and April 1920. Some fifty-nine of these aliens were deported from the United States on the flimsiest evidence of radicalism.

Although the greatest frenzy of the Red Scare was over by the summer of 1920, the decade of the 1920s saw continued manifestations of the Connecticut Yankee's fear of and desire to in-

7. Janick, *A Diverse People,* p. 14.
8. Quoted in Janick, *A Diverse People,* p. 15.

timidate the ethnic. What little support there was for prohibition in Connecticut came from rural Yankees who associated urban vice and crime with the ethnic's "penchant for alcohol." The Yankee-dominated General Assembly turned back urban ethnic attempts to soften the state's strict Sabbath laws. And, not surprisingly, the Ku Klux Klan of the 1920s, which preached anti-Catholic, anti-Jewish, antiblack, and anti-immigrant claptrap, did well among Connecticut Yankees and Protestant ethnics from northern and western Europe. By 1923 the Connecticut Klan had almost 20,000 members divided into twenty-three chapters. When Al Smith made a bid for the Democratic nomination for president in 1924, Connecticut Klansmen took to the stump in large outdoor meetings to alert the state to the menace of the urban, wet, Catholic Smith. Some 10,000 were attracted to a gigantic Klan anti-Smith meeting in South Manchester in September 1924.

His prewar panic over the alien outsiders in his midst reinforced by xenophobia during World War I and the Red Scare, the Connecticut Yankee embarked upon a concerted campaign to push and prod the ethnic into an acceptance of what the Yankee regarded as American values and mores. Yankee ability to so haze and pressure the ethnic during the process of enforced Americanization was a reflection of the Yankee's political supremacy in the state in the period. The instrument of that supremacy was the Republican Party.

During the 1920s the Connecticut Republican Party dominated the General Assembly, with a 6-to-1 margin in the State Senate and a 4-to-1 margin in the rurally overrepresented State House of Representatives. It put in office a series of Yankee governors—Marcus H. Holcomb (1915–1921), Everett J. Lake (1921–1923), Charles A. Templeton (1923–1925), Hiram Bingham (1925), and John H. Trumbull (1925–1931); elected all the state's other executive officers; and made certain that—save for one Democrat who was elected to the House of Representatives—all the members of the United States Senate and House of Representatives from Connecticut were Republicans.

This overwhelming Republican domination was the result of a number of factors. The Democrats were in sad shape in the

1920s. At the national level they had split in 1924 on the prohibition issue and the party suffered defectors in 1928—especially
in the South—with the nomination of Al Smith. The Connecticut Democratic Party was in even more pitiful straits than the
national party. There was a devastating rift between the prominent Yankees who had not left the party in 1896 over Bryan and
silver and the urban ethnics. Ethnics held sway in the cities but
could not overcome the influence of the Old Guard, the Yankees, who dominated the party at the state level and thus picked
the candidates for state office. There were charges by Democratic urban ethnics that the Old Guard maintained its influence
by dispensing patronage that the Republican leadership made
available in return for the Old Guard's promise to make things
as easy as possible for the Republicans on election day.

Another difficulty for Connecticut's Democrats in the 1920s
was that they did not have the support of all the ethnics in the
state. Many were not naturalized citizens and hence could not
vote, and a discernible percentage of ethnics who could vote did
not do so because of political apathy. Moreover, substantial
numbers of ethnics voted Republican, apparently on the basis of
the conviction that there was no better way to escape the stigma
of their non-American origins and to gain social respectability
and acceptance in Connecticut than to affiliate with the Yankee-
dominated Republican Party. I would think that this pattern of
ethnics voting Republican for purposes of "public consumption" probably took place especially among ethnic farmers in
the rural areas who sought the approval of their Yankee neighbors. In the cities a good many ethnics would have no part of
the Democratic Party because of the dominance of the Irish in
urban leadership positions. A good many Protestant ethnics
from northern and western Europe voted Republican rather than
give their votes to Irish Catholic precinct and ward leaders. The
Irish, outnumbered by the Italians in the cities in the 1920s,
kept the Italians at arm's length, preferring to keep their leadership posts and lose elections rather than see the party taken over
by Italians. On the other hand, the Italians had no love for the
Irish and presumably had no inclination to go into the trenches

to assist the Irish leadership. In any case many Italians either voted Republican or stayed at home on election day.

If the Connecticut Democratic camp in the 1920s was turbulent and divided, all was serene and placid among the state's Republicans. The party had an astute leader in J. Henry Roraback of North Canaan. A lawyer, lobbyist, and president of the state's largest utility from 1925 to 1937, Roraback was the chairman of the Republican State Central Committee from 1910 until his death in 1937. Roraback ran a very tight ship, recruiting candidates for the party; serving from his headquarters at the Allyn House, a Hartford hotel, as the directing influence behind Republican governors and members of the General Assembly; and making certain that the two blocs of voters—rural Yankee farmers and Yankee businessmen—who constituted the core of the party were content.

It took little to keep Yankee farmers in the Republican column. After all, a Yankee farmer was hardly going to bolt to the Democratic Party—the party which winked at secession in the 1860s, turned loose the "maniac" Bryan in 1896, and currently was too often under the thumb of wild-eyed Irishmen bent on meddling in people's affairs with legislation to regulate just about everything. The Yankee farmer was doing well economically, getting good prices for the perishables and dairy products he sold to the cities. But Roraback took nothing for granted. Yankee farmers were kept content with the beginnings of rural electrification, some new roads, and the opportunity to lash out via the Republican-controlled General Assembly at ethnics whenever they demonstrated Old World decadence by seeking changes such as a relaxation of the state's strict Sabbath laws. The only real concern the Yankee farmer had in the period was deciding which of his neighbors would be chosen at the Republican caucus to represent him in the General Assembly in Hartford, and that decision rarely required much soul searching:

> "[G]oing to the legislature" was no more than an honor which should be handed around. Let us say that both Henry Malbone and Fred Copeland have let it be discreetly whispered that they might be persuaded to "go." Fred is a prosperous farmer of forty-two who

reads quite a lot and has sound ideas on politics. Henry is sixty-five, and his best friends admit that he "will never set the river on fire." . . . Henry's education stopped when he was twelve, and he often says that "all this talk about more schoolin' f' th' kids ain't good common sense."

Which man, Fred or Henry, gets the nomination for representative in the Republican caucus? The election is a mere detail; the Democrats always lose. Henry is the town's choice, for it is his "turn to go." If a white citizen reaches the age of sixty-five and has not shown positive signs of being degenerate, criminal, feeble-minded, or a Democrat, the town considers that it is duty-bound to send him to . . . Hartford, for a brief term of glory.[9]

Nor did Roraback have much difficulty in keeping Yankee businessmen in the Republican ranks, for a Connecticut manufacturer or insurance company executive would rather have put his hand in the fire than to let Democratic ethnics into office. But Roraback again left nothing to chance, making sure that the business community was entirely satisfied with the Republican Party.

Roraback's governors were businessmen themselves: Everett Lake owned a Hartford lumber company; Charles A. Templeton was a Waterbury hardware merchant; John H. Trumbull was president of the Trumbull Electric Company, a director of the Connecticut Light and Power Company, and became a director of several other corporations during his tenure as governor.[10] Roraback and his hand-picked candidates presided over an era of business consolidation.[11] By 1929 large corporate structures accounted for seventy-five percent of the gross state product of

9. Clarence M. Webster, *Town Meeting Country* (New York: Duell, Sloan, and Pearce, 1945), p. 153.

10. Hiram Bingham, a Yale history professor, was not one of Roraback's businessmen-governors in the 1920s. But Bingham, as it turned out, served only one day as governor. After his election as governor in 1924, United States Senator Frank Brandegee, a Republican from New London, took his own life. Bingham then ran for and won the Senate seat but insisted on being sworn in as governor before leaving for Washington as the junior senator from Connecticut.

11. The extent of his influence was evident in 1922 when Roraback, displeased with Governor Lake, refused to allow the governor to sit on the speaker's platform at a Republican Party rally. Governor Lake wound up in the balcony.

$1.4 billion, and the Roraback machine took great pains to lighten the tax burden of Connecticut's corporations. In 1921 corporation tax dollars constituted twenty percent of the total taxes paid to the state; by 1929 corporation taxes were less than eight percent of total state tax receipts.

Dear to the hearts of the members of the Connecticut business community was the assumption that government would be economical. Under Roraback the Connecticut war debt was paid off and funds for education, mental institutions, and prisons were cut. When Governor Trumbull departed from Roraback's austerity posture in 1927 and recommended a ten-million-dollar bond issue to modernize state prisons and mental institutions, Roraback returned from a Florida vacation and punctured the proposal.

Another cardinal Roraback principle was *laissez faire*. Roraback made certain that there would be no legislation that would burden the business community. Thus the Labor Committee of the General Assembly was placed in the safe hands of antilabor Republicans. The result was predictable:

> Almost all bills dealing with laws of labor, working conditions, minimum wage, old age pensions, and health insurance were blocked. The only significant piece of labor legislation passed during the twenties, an extension in 1927 of workman's compensation to cover industrial disease, was supported by many business organizations which desired to remove this emotional question from the jurisdiction of the courts.[12]

On the issue of woman suffrage, Connecticut's Republicans under Roraback's direction took an essentially negative stand. Connecticut women had a long and demanding struggle freeing themselves from the subordinate status that they had occupied under the Puritan system. As late as the early nineteenth century unmarried women were considered to owe obedience to the male head of the household, and a married woman was not any better off:

> Her property and inheritance, unless protected by pre-nuptial agreements, became her husband's. Any wages she earned were

12. Janick, *A Diverse People*, p. 30.

legally his and were paid to him. Her children were, by law, her husband's and were under his complete control. She could not sign contracts nor institute court proceedings. Her husband was given considerable power over her person, including the right of physical chastisement, and divorce was practically impossible for her to obtain.[13]

Advances for women, however, began to come in the nineteenth century. By 1846 a married woman could collect her wages; by 1877 she could control her own property; and by 1887 she could be designated—without her husband's approval—executor of wills and administrator of estates of which she was the heir.

The drive for women's political rights in Connecticut really got under way in 1869 with the establishment of the Connecticut Women's Suffrage Association. On the eve of World War I, the organization's activities and membership were increased by the infusion of leadership from college-educated women, and by 1917 the Association had 35,000 members and a treasury of $30,000. Although Connecticut women threw themselves into various war activities during World War I, in part to convince the political establishment that they were worthy of the vote, Roraback showed no enthusiasm for women's suffrage. Fearing that 200,000 new voters would "disrupt our present conditions," Roraback urged Connecticut's congressional delegation not to support the Nineteenth Amendment and supported Governor Holcomb's intention not to call a special session of the General Assembly to ratify the amendment once it was approved by Congress on January 4, 1919. Only when the necessary thirty-six states ratified the amendment did Roraback move to enlist women for the Connecticut Republican Party.

Roraback and the Connecticut Republican Party thus provided government that proved quite acceptable to the Yankee farmers and businessmen who constituted the heart of the party in the 1920s. The Yankee was permitted—if not encouraged—to express his distaste for the urban ethnic; farmers were satisfied with electrification and some new roads; and businessmen en-

13. Trecker, *Preachers, Rebels, and Traders,* p. 3.

joyed administrations that encouraged corporate consolidation, cut corporate taxes, ignored calls for social legislation, kept government costs at a minimum, and accepted woman suffrage only after the action of Congress and other states had made it the law of the land.

Although the period of World War I and the 1920s brought prosperity and the "good life" to many residents of the state, the years from 1914 to 1929 were wasted ones for Connecticut. Yankee-Republican domination brought an unrelenting conservatism that subjected the ethnic population to a fearful hazing and did little to bring forth a natural and healthy integration of the ethnic into Connecticut society. The complete absence of wise and balanced political leadership not only fed the xenophobia of the era but also produced a climate that made the enactment of progressive legislation out of the question. And these bleak years for Connecticut were to be followed by even more trying times, for October 24, 1929—"Black Thursday"—was just around the corner.

8

1929–1945:
Liberal Interlude

$\mathscr{T}$HERE is a mysterious cycle in human affairs. To some generations much is given. Of other generations much is expected. This generation of Americans has a rendezvous with destiny.'' So said Franklin Delano Roosevelt on June 27, 1936, at Franklin Field in Philadelphia in his speech accepting a second nomination as the Democratic candidate for President of the United States. From the vantage point of the mid-1970s it is not difficult to imagine some of what Roosevelt had in mind. Certainly he was thinking of the United States response to the crushing time that followed the stock market collapse of October 1929. The Dow-Jones industrial average stood at 381 in September 1929; by July 1932 it had crashed to 41. Industrial profits after taxes, $8.3 billion in 1929, sank to a *minus* $3.4 billion in 1932. Between 1929 and 1933 farm income dropped sixty percent. Cotton that sold for an average 12.5 cents per pound from 1909 to 1914 was selling at 5.5 cents in February 1933, and the price of wheat in the same period went from 88 to 32 cents a bushel. In the cities workingmen's wages fell forty percent from 1929 to 1933, and unemployment—which ranged from 1.5 to 3 million in the pre-crash 1920s—climbed to unbelievable levels: 4 million in January 1930; 8 million by early 1931; 11.5 million by January 1932; and 15 million by March 1933.

These figures do not begin to reveal the misery experienced in America in the darkest years of the Depression. Businessmen, who in the prosperous years of the 1920s reigned as feudal princes of old, saw their enterprises and holdings wiped out; some, overcome by it all, provided the makings of a vaudeville gag about the hotel clerk who asks the registering businessman if he wants a room for sleeping or jumping. Thousands of farmers and their tenants were foreclosed off the land and made up the stream of wanderers of whom John Steinbeck wrote in *The Grapes of Wrath*. In the cities the unemployed clustered on street corners—selling apples, begging, or just delaying the time when they must return home to families and tell the now routine tale of the job not found.

As the misery spread, President Herbert Hoover—responsive to human suffering but restrained from bold action by his adherence to *laissez faire* and "rugged individualism"—issued statements that all was or soon would be well again: "Any lack of confidence in . . . the basic strength of business . . . is foolish" (November 1929); "Business and industry have turned the corner" (January 1930); and "We have passed the worst" (May 1930).[1]

Such statements were not followed by recovery, and in November 1932 the voters made it clear that they wanted a taste of the "New Deal" that Roosevelt, the Democratic candidate, referred to in the course of an aggressive nationwide campaign. He took 57.3 percent of the popular vote and 472 votes in the Electoral College. On that raw March 4, 1933, when he took the oath of office, Roosevelt in his inaugural address signaled the beginning of a new era in American government by declaring: "This nation asks for action, and action now!"[2] And action came: the Emergency Banking Act, the Economy Act, the Civilian Conservation Corps, the Federal Emergency Relief Act, the Agricultural Adjustment Act, the Tennessee Valley Authority Act, the National Industrial Recovery Act, the Glass–Steagall Banking Act, the Farm Credit Act, the

1. Quoted in Samuel Eliot Morison, *The Oxford History of the American People* (New York: Oxford University Press, 1965), p. 945.

2. Quoted in Morison, *The Oxford History of the American People*, p. 950.

Works Project Administration, the Social Security Act, and the Public Utilities Holding Company Act.

Because of the energy of Roosevelt and a Democratic Congress, the nation was put back to work, soup kitchens and the apple stands were soon gone, and those who had attempted to reconstruct America along radical lines had been pushed aside. No longer threats to American values and institutions were Louisiana's Huey Long and his "Share the Wealth" scheme; Father Charles E. Coughlin, a Detroit Roman Catholic priest who had taken to the radio to warn of a Communist takeover and to demand a Fascist-type system to control the economy; and the Communists who talked excitedly of a new Marxist America. Roosevelt and his generation of Americans had kept their "rendezvous with destiny" by effecting recovery and, more important, preserving capitalism and republican government in America by burying the maxims of *laissez faire* and radicals alike with a government that regulated business, strengthened labor, and provided the social legislation necessary for an urbanized, industrialized society.

Connecticut too in these years had a "rendezvous with destiny." Out of the misery of the Depression there came a progressive political tide such as had never been experienced in the state, a tide that enabled Connecticut not only to weather the Depression but to emerge as a far more liberal society than it had ever been before. The Depression years brought forth a vital and progressive Democratic Party that achieved scores of needed reforms; and as the Democrats enjoyed electoral success on the basis of an energetic liberalism, the state's Republicans advanced toward a liberal posture light years away from the rigid conservatism to which they had been committed for decades.

The Crash of 1929 and the resulting Depression brought terrible times to Connecticut. In the spring of 1932 the state's jobless totaled more than 150,000. Some 16,000 were unemployed in Bridgeport; 12,000 in New Haven; 14,000 in Hartford; and 11,000 in Waterbury. The ultimate dimensions of Connecticut's catastrophe in the 1930s can be seen by examining in detail the plight of Bridgeport, one of the state's most industrialized cities.

With a population of 146,000 in 1930, Bridgeport had 22,000 applying for relief despite the city's hiring of the unemployed and the efforts of the Community Chest and the Citizen's Emergency Commission. There was further deterioration by 1931, when the city had to borrow half a million dollars to fund its employment of the jobless. By 1932 Bridgeport was on the ropes. The school budget was slashed by $150,000, aliens were dropped from the relief rolls to make room for jobless citizens, and the number of operating street lights in downtown Bridgeport was cut in half. In October, the city-funded work program was replaced by handouts of food and clothing to the destitute. The end of the year saw Bridgeport $1,000,000 in debt and under seige by unemployed marchers who demanded a million dollars in aid to the poor, while a group of business and professional leaders called for an end to deficit financing and a return to municipal expenditures at the 1917 level.

Although Bridgeport's situation was duplicated in cities around the state in the early years of the Depression, Connecticut's standing order of Republicans with a business orientation did little to deal with the economic collapse but offer periodic assurances that all would soon improve. Governor John Trumbull was moved to no extraordinary efforts, apparently subscribing to the January 1930 view of *Connecticut Industry* that "[b]usiness is sound and will go forward after a short respite for planning for the future." [3] Such bland assurances were insufficient to calm an increasingly desperate electorate, and in 1930 Connecticut's voters departed from their traditional Republican habits.

Wilbur L. Cross led the state's Democrats out of their political exile in the 1930s and served as Connecticut's governor from 1931 to 1939. Born and brought up in northeast Connecticut, in the Gurleyville section of rural Mansfield, Cross became a distinguished academic at Yale—serving as a professor of English, dean of the graduate school, and editor of the *Yale Review*. But Cross was no aloof academician; he had enough political savvy to wrest the Democratic nomination for gover-

3. Quoted in Janick, *A Diverse People*, p. 48.

nor in 1930 from the Old Guard in the party, and on the campaign trail in the 1930s he proved to be a shrewd politician who understood well the necessity of putting together a strong coalition to oust the deeply entrenched Roraback Republican machine. Cross's scholarly achievements impressed intellectuals. His folksy accounts of his early years on the family farm and his whimsical rural wit assured the state's farmers that he was no wild-eyed Democratic radical. For example, in 1930 when he ran against Republican Lieutenant Governor Ernest E. Rogers, the sixty-eight-year-old Cross delighted his rural audiences by comparing Boss Roraback and Republicans in general to a group of ''settin' hens'':

> Take the eggs out from under one and throw her out of the nest and she will come back as soon as she is left alone. Put chestnut burrs into her nest in place of eggs, and she will still come back. The only way to get rid of a settin-hen is to kick her out of the coop. Likewise the Republican organization and its leader have been settin' on rotten eggs for fifteen years without hatching any chickens. The only way you can get rid of this old hen is to throw her out into the snows or cold rains of next November.[4]

The real core of support for Cross and the Democrats in the 1930s came from urban workingmen and particularly from ethnics who previously had not as a group swung behind the Connecticut Democratic Party. Among the actions Cross took to win over the urban vote was a move beyond his initial concern for states' rights in order to utilize funds that the federal government was making available to the state. In his successful campaign for re-election in 1932, Cross, a bear on the retention of ''the rights of states against federal governmental control,'' had advised Mayor Buckingham of Bridgeport not to seek Reconstruction Finance Corporation help ''unless absolutely necessary.'' [5] While Cross's concern for states' rights was undoubtedly reassuring to the most conservative of the governor's rural constituents, it was not likely to bring forth the federal

---

4. Quoted in Joseph I. Lieberman, *The Power Broker: A Biography of John M. Bailey, Modern Political Boss* (Boston: Houghton Mifflin Company, 1966), pp. 36–37.

5. Quotations cited in Janick, *A Diverse People,* p. 45.

aid that was so desperately needed in the state's urban areas. In 1932 the state's towns and cities had exhausted their limited relief funds. Indeed, from January 1932 to April 1933 employment dropped an additional fourteen percent and payrolls over thirty percent. "Hunger marchers" collected around the State Capitol in Hartford and demanded direct relief to the unemployed of $12,000,000.

With the state crisis at such staggering levels, Cross proved willing "to lay aside the unsubstantial ghost of state sovereignty" for "funds for the aged, the crippled, for humane and educational institutions, for the extension of highways." [6] In May 1933 he created the Emergency Relief Commission to seek federal assistance for Connecticut. During the next six years New Deal money flowed into Connecticut like water downhill.

At the outset Washington appropriated money to be utilized by the state for unemployment relief. In 1934 the Emergency Relief Commission spent some $15 million in federal funds plus $14 million of Connecticut funds:

> 40,000 unemployed . . . were engaged in building roads, sewers, bridges, hospitals, town halls, and airports. . . . Park Avenue in Bridgeport was widened and extended to meet the Merritt Parkway. Torrington got a sewerage treatment plant and Hartford a golf clubhouse. School playgrounds were renovated in Stamford. . . . The eastern shore area was the scene of mosquito-control experiments. Artists were hired to paint murals in Stamford and Hartford high schools. Teachers were paid to conduct summer training sessions for nursery school personnel. [7]

After 1935 the federal Works Progress Administration took a more direct role in employing the jobless. The WPA modernized state hospitals, prisons, and reformatories; worked on state college dormitories, police barracks, and the state capitol; constructed a fish-breeding pond in New Fairfield; and put artists and scholars to work on historical and artistic projects. In addition, the Civilian Conservation Corps (CCC) employed

6. Quoted in Janick, *A Diverse People*, p. 47.
7. Janick, *A Diverse People*, p. 46.

15,000 young men to work in state and national parks, and the National Youth Administration (NYA) found part-time work for high school and college students.

While unemployment relief money flowed into the state, Connecticut was also the beneficiary of other New Deal programs. The Home Owners' Loan Corporation (HOLC) provided $22,000,000 to home owners requiring mortgage refinancing assistance. The Reconstruction Finance Corporation (RFC) loaned over $20,000,000 to banks and businesses, and the Public Works Administration (PWA) made $3,500,000 available to the New Haven Railroad for new equipment and repairs.

In addition to securing vital New Deal funds for Connecticut, Cross and the New Deal sped the evolution of organized labor in Connecticut and cemented urban support for the Democrats. Such New Deal legislation as Section 7a of the National Industrial Recovery Act, which guaranteed labor the right of collective bargaining, motivated labor organizers. The Connecticut Federation of Labor drew more new members in 1934 than in any year in its history, and the formation of the CIO in 1936 drew even more members to the ranks of organized labor. Through the labor surge, the governor was more than sympathetic to the problems of the workingman.

Cross appointed Joseph Tone, Connecticut's most energetic proponent of prolabor legislation in the 1920s, as the state commissioner of labor. During the 1930s Cross and Tone were able to get General Assembly legislation eliminating sweatshops, establishing unemployment insurance, restricting the work week for women and children to forty-eight hours, and outlawing the employment of youngsters under sixteen years of age. During a number of strikes in the 1930s Cross made it clear that while he would not allow labor-inspired violence, he also would not condone management efforts to break unions.

Provided with an opening by Republican passivity in combating the Depression, Cross used his political acumen—along with New Deal aid and Roosevelt's personal charisma—to bring about a Democratic coalition that waxed stronger in each election from 1930 to 1936. In 1930 Cross had won by 5,000 votes, but he had not been able to carry any other Democrats on the state ticket to victory. In 1932 Cross increased his winning margin to 10,000 and the Democrats elected two United States congressmen, won a United States Senate seat for the first time since the 1870s, and gained control of the State Senate. In the 1934 election Cross won by 8,000 votes; Democrats swept all state offices, took four of six seats in the United States House of Representatives, and elected a second Democrat to the United States Senate. Nineteen hundred thirty-six was one loud Democratic hurrah. Cross and Roosevelt each won by 100,000 votes; the Democrats took all six Congressional seats and made major gains in both houses of the state legislature.

Cross and other urban-oriented Democrats were able to secure significant progressive legislation in the General Assembly. From 1931 to 1939 Cross encouraged the General Assembly to repeal the Eighteenth Amendment and legalize the sale of liquor; institute a building program in Connecticut's schools, penal institutions, and hospitals; reform the state banking system; establish old age pensions; strengthen the Public Utilities Commission; reorganize state government; and provide for the establishment of housing authorities in municipalities. Not all was liberal advance for Connecticut in the Cross years, however. The governor in 1935 sought a tax package from the General Assembly that would have included a retail sales tax, a tax on interest and dividends, taxes on cigarettes, and a change in existing taxes on businesses and insurance companies. The General Assembly, whose lower house was still under rural domination, responded only with some minor tax bills; the state was left with a nineteenth-century tax structure to meet the challenges of the twentieth century.

On the whole, the Cross years brought forth a revitalized Democratic Party that was able to move Connecticut along the most liberal course the state had ever followed. Connecticut overcame its states'-rights bias to secure New Deal aid, moved toward the regulation of public utilities, supported organized labor, and provided social legislation for the aged and the needy. As the Democrats achieved success with their liberal posture, Connecticut's Republicans became more forward-looking than they had ever been.

Battered during the Cross and Roosevelt years, Republicans were not inclined to accept the permanent status of a minority party. After Roraback's death in 1937, an infusion of younger, more liberal leadership moved the party to a posture that was noticeably less anti-labor and more willing to accept the role of federal and state government in planning and spending for social purposes. An indication of the revitalized and more progressive character of the Connecticut Republican Party in the post-Roraback period can be seen in the gubernatorial race of 1938.

The opening for Raymond Baldwin and the Republicans against Cross in the 1938 election came in part because Cross did not have the benefit of running on the same ticket with Roosevelt. Democrats were also burdened by the gubernatorial campaign of Jasper McLevy, the mayor of Bridgeport from 1933 to 1957. McLevy, a Socialist in name only, was—as a Democratic national committeeman from Connecticut put it—"a reasonably conservative, level-headed American citizen and an admirer of the President." [8] He became Bridgeport's mayor as a result of a protest vote against wrongdoing by the two major parties and retained his job for decades on the basis of honest, efficient government. McLevy had a field day in the 1938 gubernatorial race because Democrats and Republicans in the state had been tainted by financial scandals involving the construction of the Merritt Parkway and the misuse of city funds in Waterbury. McLevy campaigned hard, citing the scandals and promising the state the same honest government he had brought to Bridgeport. Baldwin, an experienced politician and a liberal Republican from Stratford, promised a comprehensive program including such items as more jobs in private industry and an anti-injunction bill, while other Republicans hit at Cross's age (seventy-six in 1938) and at "the prostitution of relief for political purposes." [9] McLevy

8. Quoted in Janick, *A Diverse People*, p. 53.
9. The 1938 Connecticut Republican Platform as quoted in Van Dusen, *Connecticut*, p. 312.

drew almost 170,000 votes (twenty-eight percent of the vote), hurting Cross badly, and Baldwin won by less than three thousand votes. Cross's involuntary retirement was marked by high praise and tributes from the Connecticuters he had served for eight years. The affection in which Cross was held was perhaps best expressed by the *Hartford Courant:*

> And now just a word for Governor Cross to whom we say 'Hail and Farewell!' He has been . . . a good Governor, a popular Governor, and he has wrought much for the State during these last eight years. He has brought great distinction to Connecticut by his erudition, by the fine literary qualities of his official proclamations, by the charm that his presence has lent to public occasions here and elsewhere, and by his mellowed philosophy and excellent sense of humor. The election figures indicate that if it had not been for the inroads made by Mr. McLevy he might have achieved his ambition to be the first Governor since Oliver Wolcott's day, back in 1817, to serve ten years in that office. As it is, he goes down to an honorable defeat with few personal enemies and with a multitude of friends and well-wishers.[10]

The liberalization in Connecticut in the 1930s that was sparked by the Depression, Cross, and the New Deal was continued by Raymond Baldwin. His governorship from 1939 to 1941 and from 1943 to 1946, interrupted by one term of Robert Hurley (who rode into office in the 1940 election on Roosevelt's coattails), was marked by progressive legislation.[11] Indeed, Baldwin proposed to the General Assembly considerably more liberal legislation than was enacted; but the Assembly did prohibit kickbacks, increase old-age pensions, establish an eight-hour day on state contracts, bring the Connecticut minimum-wage law in line with the Federal Fair Labor Standards Act of 1938, oppose injunctions, increase workmen's compen-

10. Quoted in Van Dusen, *Connecticut,* p. 314.

11. Hurley, commissioner of the Connecticut Department of Public Works in the Cross administration, continued the forward-looking thrust of Connecticut legislation in these years by encouraging the General Assembly to provide a new act for aid to dependent children, enact a statewide juvenile court bill, pass amendments to the state unemployment compensation and workmen's compensation acts, and approve a rural electrification bill.

sation, grant raises for and improve the retirement system of state employees, establish an interracial commission to work against discrimination, forbid discrimination for race in the merit system for state employees, and enact a comprehensive labor-relations act. While this legislation was important in the progressive evolution of Connecticut society, Baldwin is also remembered for his able and thoughtful leadership during the years of World War II.

During the war Governor Baldwin was able to encourage an energetic effort—one that had little of the blind xenophobia that had so stained the state during World War I. Connecticuters were able to draw together during World War II to make a contribution to the halt of Axis aggression. Typical of the type of unity and cohesion which prevailed was that found among the 15,000 residents of the community of Naugatuck:

> A ration board, staffed by high school teachers, doled out food coupons, gasoline cards, and fuel quotas. Teams of "Minute Men" conducted eight war bond drives. Boy Scouts collected waste paper, tin cans, metals, rubber, and cooking fat. 500 middle-aged men donned steel helmets and arm bands to direct a total of 26 air-raid tests. Auxiliary police and firemen became experts in administering first aid and extinguishing incendiary bombs. The American Legion coordinated the work of 200 airplane spotters who manned a watch-post twenty-four hours a day in all weather until 1943 when the installation of radar equipment made this vigil unnecessary. Members of a local hunting and fishing club formed the Naugatuck Rangers, a reserve unit of the State Guard. Victory gardens sprouted along highways, at the town farm, and in place of tidy front lawns. Women and girls labored in the domestic science classroom at the high school to preserve the harvest. Red Cross volunteers rounded up blood donors, ran a canteen for departing servicemen, and wrapped so many bandages that the organization was forced to move to larger quarters in the YMCA.[12]

Another characteristic of Connecticut during World War II was a booming economy much as the state had experienced during World War I. In 1939 the state had not yet recovered

12. Janick, *A Diverse People*, pp. 62–63.

from the Depression and still had substantial unemployment, but war contracts turned the situation completely around. Industrial employment jumped from 350,000 in 1939 to 550,000 in 1944, as Connecticut's specialized manufacturing facilities expanded to meet Washington's demand for materiel.

Landers, Frary, and Clark of New Britain spent $2 million on new machinery to produce commando knives, fuses, and gun mounts. The Electric Boat Company in Groton turned out three submarines in 1939, five subs in 1940, and six ships in 1941, and eventually had to recruit workers from as far away as the Midwest and Puerto Rico to keep production up to the navy's demands. The various units of United Aircraft ran at full blast during the war years. Pratt and Whitney, producer of airplane engines, went from a work force of 3,000 in 1939 to 20,000 by 1941. Sikorsky manufactured multi-engine planes and began the development of the helicopter. Hamilton Propellers raised its production during the war to sixty times that of 1938, and Chance-Vought increased its output of Corsair fighters from 72 in 1939 to over 2,500 in 1944.

The total volume of war contracts placed in the state through May 1945, when cutbacks started, was over $8,000,000,000, or more than 4 percent of the nation's total. Of the contracts, aircraft accounted for over $4,000,000,000; ordnance, nearly $2,400,000,000; ships, about $294,000,000; communications equipment, about $146,000,000; and other categories, over $1,100,000,000.[13]

To help Connecticut to fill its defense contracts, Baldwin and the State War Council did everything possible to enlist workers for the defense industries. Teachers were urged to take summer defense jobs; the state encouraged mothers to sign up for war work by establishing child care centers; special industrial training courses were set up at Yale and the University of Connecticut; and the state's job-training program graduated 30,000 people for defense work before Pearl Harbor and another 66,000 later in the war.

But all was not unity and productivity during World War II.

13. Van Dusen, *Connecticut*, p. 373.

War service and defense work hurt family life, and the state saw alarming increases in the divorce rate, the spread of venereal disease, and growing juvenile delinquency. The coming of 130,000 new workers put a strain on existing housing, hospitals, and schools, and the influx of 18,000 blacks into Connecticut from New York, the southern states, and the Caribbean challenged the state to assimilate another generation of newcomers. Postwar Connecticut would thus be taxed to meet these and even more testing problems.

9

1945–1976: Connecticut Conservatism Revisited

*T*HE decades since World War II have brought challenges for Connecticuters similar to those experienced by most Americans in the years between the surrender of the Axis powers and the era of the Bicentennial of the American Revolution. After the war the state had to grapple with the conversion of the economy to peacetime production; the reintegration of returning veterans into a swiftly changing state; a severe housing shortage occasioned by the absence of any substantial residential construction during the war years; and social instabilities linked to the weakening of traditional family-oriented life during the hectic years between Pearl Harbor and V-J Day. In the 1950s Connecticut adjusted to the strange peace of the Cold War; an economy tied to the temperature of the Cold War; an explosive expansion in education; and the rise of suburbia. And in the 1960s and 1970s the state had to respond to the expectations of new urban minorities; a discordant dialogue over the Vietnam War; adoption of nontraditional life styles by restless young people; growing aspirations of women for fulfillment in politics, business, and the professions; growing pollution of the environment; and the struggle of both state government and the cities to meet expanding needs for social services. Between 1945 and 1976 Connecticut successfully

confronted a good many of these challenges, experienced substantial growth and expansion, and enacted much progressive
legislation. But from the viewpoint of the mid-1970s it is evident that the turbulence of the last thirty years has given a new
dimension to the conservatism historically characteristic of
Connecticut.

The state's economy has generally continued to be strong
and expansive. While employment in specialized manufacturing has been at about 400,000 since 1947, service and non-
manufacturing employment has increased from 355,000 in
1947 to 832,000 in 1976. The insurance industry remains a
vital part of Connecticut's economy. As of the mid-1970s
some thirty-five insurance companies had their headquarters in
the state, and life insurance sales by Connecticut companies
rose from $5.4 billion in 1970 to $8.9 billion in 1976. Connecticut has done very well in recent years in attracting plants
and corporate offices, especially those leaving New York City.
Forty-six major corporations, twenty of them in *Fortune*'s 500,
moved their headquarters into the state from New York between
1969 and 1973. With its varied housing, including garden and
high-rise apartments as well as single homes; its quality high
school graduates; and its absence of state and local income
taxes, Connecticut has been able to convince executives that
they would be far better off locating their plants or offices
within the state rather than in Long Island, New Jersey, or New
York's Westchester County.

Tourism has become an important part of the state's economic picture. Visitors have enjoyed the Connecticut coastline
with its charming beaches; the wild scenery of the Berkshire
Hills; the gorge of the Mianus River near the New York
boundary; the well-preserved eighteenth-century homes of
Litchfield, Wethersfield, Windsor, and Lebanon; the village
and ships at Mystic Seaport; the P. T. Barnum mansion and
the Seaside Park museum in Bridgeport; the American Shakespeare Festival in Stratford; the Air Museum at Bradley Air-
port near Hartford; the United States Coast Guard Academy in
New London; Yale's impressive campus in New Haven; and

the Old State House, the Wadsworth Atheneum, the Connecticut Historical Society, and the State Capitol in Hartford.

Another source of economic strength—and pride—in Connecticut since World War II has been the continued excellence and steady growth of the state's educational facilities. Students from throughout the nation attend Connecticut preparatory schools such as Choate, Hotchkiss, Kent, Miss Porter's, The Taft School, and Pomfret. The state boasts a cluster of superior colleges and universities including Trinity in Hartford, Wesleyan in Middletown, and, of course, Yale in New Haven. Yale, with fine colleges and professional schools, an endowment of $500 million—second only to Harvard's $1 billion —and an impressive faculty, continues to provide leadership to the state and the nation. Relatively new institutions such as the University of Hartford, the University of Bridgeport, and Fairfield University have strengthened private higher education in Connecticut. In recent decades the four state colleges at Danbury, New Haven, New Britain, and Willimantic have undergone tremendous growth; thirteen two-year community colleges have been developed; and the University of Connecticut at Storrs has expanded from a poorly supported agricultural college to a multipurpose state university with an enrollment of 24,000 in 1974. Former University of Connecticut President Homer Babbidge recently said: "When I left the presidency of the University of Connecticut in 1972 after 10 years, my name was on the diplomas of more than half the graduates in the history of the institution. The exponential growth was that great." [1]

Between 1945 and 1976 many of Connecticut's cities have been transformed by urban renewal projects. Stamford began a 130-acre downtown renewal project in 1965 under the impetus of major corporations, such as Xerox, Pitney Bowes, Barnes Engineering, Olin Mathieson, Schweppes, Marx Toys, and Litton Industries, that have their headquarters in the Fairfield County city. Richard Lee, the mayor of New Haven from 1953

---

1. Quoted in Peirce, *The New England States*, p. 231.

to 1970, dedicated himself to making New Haven "a slumless city—the first in the nation." Lee brought together a Citizens Action Commission, composed of "the biggest set of muscles in New Haven," [2] to oversee the rejuvenation of the inner city and he himself took off for Washington, where by 1965 he had secured more than $110 million in urban renewal funds. Lee pushed the Oak Street project, involving the construction of an $85-million complex, and succeeded in getting the Connecticut Highway Department to build a multilane highway from the Connecticut Turnpike into downtown New Haven. Hartford's downtown transformation was encouraged by the Greater Hartford Chamber of Commerce and backed by the Travelers Insurance Company. Between 1957 and 1962 Hartford constructed Constitution Plaza, consisting of a television broadcasting facility, a 315-room hotel, and four high-rise office buildings including the distinctive glass skyscraper of the Phoenix Mutual Life Insurance Company. More recently, Hartford has added a downtown civic center and has hopes for the construction of 6,500 new housing units, 10,000 renovated units, schools, parks, and more business facilities by the mid-1980s.

Not everything has been expansion and advance in Connecticut in the years since World War II. The state in recent decades has been plagued by a series of problems that must be solved if the quality of life in Connecticut is to be maintained and improved. One is that the state's economy, with a heavy reliance on defense spending, has fluctuated wildly with the ups and downs of the Cold War. In the late 1940s unemployment stood at 100,000 until the Korean War brought not only full employment but a need for 15,000 additional workers. With the end of the war, conditions grew tight once again. The termination of military contracts resulted in unemployment of 50,000 by 1954; in 1958, unemployment stood at 112,800. Employment picked up in the 1960s because of increased government spending related to the Vietnam War and the space program. But with the winding down of the Vietnam War and

2. Quotations cited in Janick, *A Diverse People*, p. 84.

cutbacks in the space program in the late 1960s and early 1970s, Connecticut has felt another pinch. Employment in manufacturing fell from 482,940 in 1968 to 394,700 in 1972. During the 1974–1975 recession, unemployment jumped to over 125,000—over nine percent of the work force. As Connecticut has one of the highest costs of living in the nation, such unemployment bodes ill for the future—especially with current problems of high fuel and energy costs.

Another complexity of Connecticut society in recent decades has been the flight of middle-class whites to the suburbs, resulting in a concentration of minorities and the poor in deteriorating cities. The rise of suburbia was especially evident in the 1950s. While cities such as Hartford, New Haven, and Bridgeport were losing population, suburban communities were mushrooming. Bloomfield, to the north of Hartford, experienced a population jump from 5,700 in 1950 to over 13,000 in 1960; Orange, near New Haven, grew by 180 percent in the decade; and Trumbull, close to Bridgeport, expanded by more than 135 percent.

The rise of suburbia brought great problems to the expanding communities, particularly in the field of education. The rush to the suburbs took place at the same time the "baby boom" following World War II produced greatly increased numbers of school-age children. The situation in Bloomfield, where the school-age population increased from seventeen to twenty-six percent of the total in the decade, was typical:

Until 1953 the entrenched leadership of the town, composed mainly of large landowners and local businessmen, had blocked the demands of young newcomers with large families for more schools. In that year the refusal of Bloomfield's teachers to sign contracts forced the resignation of the school board. The recommendation of the new board for an accelerated building program was heatedly debated at a series of town meetings and finally approved in 1957 in a general referendum. Three years later the board voted a substantial increase in teacher's salaries. Between 1954 and 1960 a high school, a junior high, two elementary schools, and large additions to two existing elementary schools were built. The number of teachers increased in this time from 67 to 175.[3]

While communities such as Bloomfield were able to resolve their difficulties on the basis of increased services paid for by growing numbers of taxpayers, the cities from which the suburbanites fled were not so easily able to meet their unique problems. As affluent, middle-class whites were being lost to the suburbs, minorities in difficult economic straits were being gained. New Haven's black population jumped from 9,500 at the end of World War II to about 40,000, along with 5,000 Puerto Ricans, in the early 1970s. By the mid-1970s, 45,000 blacks and 20,000 Puerto Ricans made up more than half of Hartford's population.

The situation of the minorities in Connecticut's cities became especially grim in the 1960s. Urban renewal in communities like Hartford and New Haven had provided new business, office, and entertainment facilities but had failed to produce adequate inner-city housing. While the state as a whole was enjoying a stretch of prosperity, the unemployment rate for nonwhites kept at a steady eight percent—double the rate for whites. Racial imbalance in the urban school systems was increasing. Of Bridgeport's thirty-six public schools, some twenty-six were predominantly black. In New Haven some ten elementary schools and two of the four junior high schools were more than fifty percent nonwhite, and Hartford's North End district, a black enclave, had schools that were ninety-five percent black.

Pressed by a youthful generation of black militants, who pushed aside the black leadership of ministers, businessmen, politicians, and social workers who sought to work within the system and through civil rights organizations such as the NAACP and the Urban League, Connecticut cities sought in the mid-1960s to deal with racial segregation in the schools and with urban poverty. Hartford sought to implement a Harvard University Graduate School of Education plan that called

3. Janick, *A Diverse People*, p. 75.

for the construction of middle schools and high schools that would be racially balanced by transporting students by bus, and it launched the Community Renewal Team of Hartford as an antipoverty effort. New Haven proposed to achieve integration in the schools by the busing of students into the city's four junior high schools, and it set up Community Progress Incorporated, which spent $22 million in a five-year period on various projects geared to unemployment, ghetto housing, and juvenile delinquency. But the results were disappointing. A white outcry over busing forced Hartford to go ahead with a building program along traditional—and racial—lines. New Haven dropped its busing scheme after a confrontation between parents and the Board of Education, and the antipoverty programs seemed to make little dent in the depressing cycle of urban unemployment, crime, and drugs.

By the late 1960s increased black militancy, combined with the absence of substantial progress in coping with segregation in the schools and ghetto poverty, produced racial uprisings in cities across the state. Beginning in the summer of 1967 violence erupted in Bridgeport, Hartford, Middletown, New Britain, New Haven, New London, Norwalk, Stamford, and Waterbury. The most serious outbreaks took place in Hartford:

> For three consecutive summers the streets in Hartford's North End were turned into battlefields. In July and September 1967 swarms of black youths surged through the ghetto pillaging and looting. The assassination of Martin Luther King in April 1968 sent off another shock wave, as North End teenagers chanting 'You Killed Martin Luther King!' hurled bricks and stones at police and firemen. Violence reached a peak on Labor Day 1969 when mobs battled with state and city police, set fire to a public library, and damaged almost one hundred buildings. Over 500 persons were arrested during the three days of turmoil, including, for the first time, a large number of Puerto Ricans.[4]

Ghetto violence has quieted since the late 1960s, but because the conditions that produced such uprisings remain, there is no

4. Janick, *A Diverse People*, p. 95.

way of knowing how long Connecticut cities can avoid renewed strife.

In addition to the deteriorating condition of the cities and an economy too reliant upon defense spending, contemporary Connecticut has additional soft spots. Neal R. Peirce, in his excellent essay on Connecticut in *The New England States*, has put his finger on a number of issues that cry for action. Peirce points to the unfortunate strength of town government in the state at a time when "the problems of local government have outgrown the old town government structure in many areas, including education, water supply, sewage and refuse disposal, environmental protection, and the jurisdictional problems created when people live in one community and commute to work in another." [5] Peirce also identifies weaknesses in state government:

> Connecticut . . . has a poor state government budget system. The financial reporting and personnel systems have remained unchanged since the early 1950's, and the budgeting system tells little of what the state governmental agencies do, quantitatively or qualitatively. . . . The state welfare system also gets failing grades because the bureaucracy often is ineffective, clients don't get the personal contact they should, and as a result there is an unsatisfactory rate of getting people off welfare and training them for jobs.[6]

The most serious weakness in contemporary Connecticut is the incredibly antiquated tax structure under which the state functions. By fighting off an income tax for decades, Connecticuters have wound up with one of the highest tax rates in the nation—highest after Maine, Massachusetts, Vermont, New York, and Wisconsin—and one generally unrelated to fluctuations in personal income. With high property, sales, cigarette, and gasoline taxes, the tax burden in Connecticut in the last twenty years has risen over 110 percent. In addition to having a high and regressive tax system, the state is unable to offer adequate and predictable services. Connecticut, with the high-

5. Peirce, *The New England States*, p. 207.
6. Peirce, *The New England States*, p. 207.

est per capita income in the nation after Alaska and Illinois, ranked twenty-fifth in the nation in per capita expenditures for all state functions as of the early 1970s and finds itself in the mid-1970s falling deeper and deeper into a fiscal morass with state revenues insufficient to meet ever growing demands for public services.

As Connecticut celebrates the Bicentennial and moves into the last quarter of the twentieth century, it appears that the state has a demanding list of items that require attention: an economy too dependent on defense spending; deteriorating cities wracked by racial unrest; outdated local government; and ineffective state budget, welfare, and tax systems. It is unlikely that Connecticut in the very near future will gear itself to the task of tackling these issues. The electorate is noticeably cool to political figures who flirt with comprehensive governmental reform, especially in the area of taxation.

Certainly one source of contemporary Connecticut's conservatism is the affluence of many of its citizens. One result of having the third-highest per capita income in the nation is that thousands of Connecticuters, especially in prosperous Fairfield County, are very wealthy indeed and hence have little interest in political reforms likely to disturb their comfortable status quo.

But I suspect that the most important source of contemporary Connecticut's conservatism is the financial condition and social outlook of those who constitute the majority in today's Connecticut—white- and blue-collar workers who have an ethnic background, are frequently conservative Roman Catholics, and who reside in the state's suburban towns. These people, after decades of hard work and disciplined living, bought their dream homes outside of Hartford, New Haven, Bridgeport, or Waterbury. Instead of having achieved Valhalla, they find their financial condition threatened by high property taxes, mortgage and car payments, the rising expense of fuel oil and gasoline, the steadily growing cost of educating their children, recessions, and a maddening inflation. Their serenity has been jolted by wars that have brought bitter domestic divisions, restless young people who seek new modes of living, awakened women with expanded personal and vocational horizons, urban minorities whose understandable bitterness and frustration rock the cities, and national political figures who engineer one scandal after another.

These people, not surprisingly, seek most of all to be left alone. They have seen enough of social change and want no part of a political program that calls for aggressive—and probably expensive—action. Thus Connecticut conservatism, once the product of the Congregational Church and Yankee-dominated Connecticut, is now rooted in hard-working, suburban, Roman Catholic ethnics who apparently have concluded that the best government is one that is as unobtrusive and inexpensive as possible. While Connecticut government is anything but inexpensive, the consensus seems to be that were an innovation such as an income tax effected, government would go through the extra money with astounding rapidity.

These attitudes of contemporary Connecticut's ethnically varied majority are clearly understood by the leaders of state politics. In the last thirty years the principal mover in Connecticut politics was John Moran Bailey, the chairman of the state Democratic Party from 1946 until his death in 1975. Born of a well-to-do Irish-American family, Bailey was a graduate of Harvard Law School "who acted as though he wanted to hide the fact and look like a stereotyped Irish political boss." [7] Bailey started out as a Hartford precinct worker in the early 1930s; learned his politics from Hartford's Democratic boss, T. J. Spellacy; and by 1946 became the man around whom Connecticut Democratic politics revolved. Bailey took the Connecticut Democratic Party, which had fallen on hard times since the bright years of Cross and Roosevelt in the 1930s, and by exhausting labor especially among ethnics and organized labor (a sixth of the electorate in the early 1970s) turned it into a winner. Operating at Democratic state conventions at Hartford's Bushnell Auditorium, leaning against a pillar—his office—on the second floor of the State Capitol, or lunching at Parma's Restaurant—a political institution—Bailey, with a

7. Peirce, *The New England States,* p. 191.

cigar in his mouth and his spectacles pushed up on his fore-head, put together Democratic slates that were in essence eth-nic packages. In securing the election of Governors Chester Bowles (1949–1951),[8] Abraham Ribicoff (1955–1961), John Dempsey (1961–1971), and Ella Grasso (1975–), Bailey was providing progressive but fiscally cautious men and women to his ethnic supporters, who, while wanting one of their own, were not interested in panting reformers or radicals.[9]

Abraham Ribicoff, a wealthy Jewish businessman from New Britain, served in the General Assembly and the United States House of Representatives before his governorship. During the Ribicoff administration there were enacted measures to establish a state civil service commission, consolidate state services for neglected and abandoned children, abolish the outdated system of county government, effect court reform, increase state aid to schools, increase unemployment and workmen's compensation benefits, improve highway safety, and provide funding for urban renewal and public works projects during the recession of 1957–1958. But Ribicoff would have nothing to do with tax reform. Rejecting an income tax and refusing to raise other taxes, Ribicoff walked a fiscal tightrope, diverting motor vehi-cle fees from the highway fund, financing school building grants by bond issues, and effecting a moratorium on personnel and physical expansion at state institutions. Joining Bailey in early support for the presidential candidacy of John F. Kennedy, Ribicoff was rewarded in 1961 with the post of Secretary of Health, Education, and Welfare. Since 1963 Ribicoff has served

8. Bowles was the exception to the rule of cautious Connecticut Democrats in the Bailey era. Retiring from his Madison Avenue advertising agency in 1941 at age forty, Bowles then worked for the OPA in Connecticut and in Washington during World War II. Bowles was not a member of the Bailey stable, and he won the nomination and subsequently the election for governor in 1948 by herculean labors. He spent his two-year term seeking—generally in vain—General Assembly support for low-cost housing, improved mental health facilities, and government reorganization. Too liberal and energetic for his Connecticut constituents, Bowles lost the governorship in 1950 to John Davis Lodge.

9. In the 1970s, when the Democrats had almost 200,000 more registered voters than did the Republicans, Connecticut went for President Nixon over Senator McGovern in 1972 and for President Ford over Governor Carter in 1976.

in the United States Senate and captured national attention most dramatically at the Democratic National Convention in Chicago in 1968, when he attacked Mayor Richard Daley's police for using "Gestapo tactics" against antiwar protesters.

John N. Dempsey, born in Ireland and one of the Democratic Party's faithful in eastern Connecticut, took over the governorship when Ribicoff went to Washington and served until 1971. Under Dempsey Connecticut gained authorization for the University of Connecticut Medical–Dental School, a substantial increase in state aid to education, a court reorganization act, a number of consumer protection measures, increased state aid to towns for welfare programs, and the beginnings of important programs to clean up the state's air and waterways. Dempsey, who never demonstrated any enthusiasm for tax reform, decided not to run in 1970 and left the state with a $250 million deficit.

The last of the Bailey governors of Connecticut was Ella Grasso of Windsor Locks. The daughter of a baker from the Piedmont area of Italy, Grasso was educated at Chaffee and at Mt. Holyoke, where she was elected to Phi Beta Kappa, graduated magna cum laude in 1940, and earned a master's degree in economics in 1942. Before she made history in 1974 as the first woman elected governor on her own in the United States, Grasso had served in the General Assembly, as Connecticut's secretary of state, and as a two-term member of the United States House of Representatives. Although facing a budget deficit of $200 million left by her predecessor—Republican Thomas Meskill—Grasso campaigned in opposition to a state income tax. In her first year in office Ella Grasso established a new public utilities control authority, demonstrated an interest in badly needed mass transit advances in the state, and stuck to her pledge not to raise or establish new taxes. Thus, while John Bailey did a remarkable job of reviving the Connecticut Democratic Party and integrating the ethnics into state politics and society, he hardly provided the state with adventurous political leadership.[10]

---

10. In addition to his role in Connecticut, John Bailey was a major force in national Democratic Party affairs in the late 1950s and 1960s. Bailey played an important role in

As for Connecticut's Republicans, they have not been much of a political factor in recent years. The Connecticut Republican Party did enjoy a stretch of power in the late 1940s and early 1950s. The party's success grew from the momentum of the Baldwin years, the weakness of the Democratic Party in the period between Cross's defeat in 1938 and the beginnings of Bailey's successes in the mid-1950s, the reliable support of Yankee farmers and businessmen, the backing of ethnics with roots behind the Iron Curtain who were won over by Republican charges that the national Democratic Party was "soft on Communism," and the support of ethnics such as the Italians who had stuck to the Republican Party in the Cross years because of the Irish strength in the Democratic Party. Consequently, the Republicans elected Governors James L. McConaughy (1947–1948), James C. Shannon (1948–1949),[11] and John Davis Lodge (1951–1955), and these Republican administrations were responsible for substantial progressive legislation.

But the Republican Party fell on hard times in the late 1950s and 1960s. The party was torn by internal strife between liberals and conservatives, was hurt by the 1965 reapportionment of the General Assembly according to the United States Supreme Court's "one man, one vote" decision, and did not enjoy much success against Bailey's "ethnic packages" with Yankee-dominated slates that appealed primarily to the New York City bedroom communities in Fairfield County.

An opening came for the Republicans in 1970. The Democrats were surprised at Governor Dempsey's decision not to

---

John F. Kennedy's drive for the Democratic presidential nomination in 1960. In 1956 Bailey circulated among national Democratic leaders a document which maintained that a Roman Catholic could be "more of an asset than a liability on the [Democratic] national ticket" because of Catholic strength in states with large electoral votes. The document, although written by Kennedy aide Theodore Sorenson, has always been referred to as the "Bailey Memorandum" because Bailey did the job of distribution for the Kennedy camp. Subsequently, Bailey was the first Democratic state chairman outside of Massachusetts to back Kennedy for the Democratic nomination. After Kennedy's victory in 1960, he selected Bailey as the national chairman of the Democratic Party, a post Bailey held from 1961 to 1968. See Peirce, *The New England States,* pp. 192–193.

11. Shannon, the lieutenant governor under McConaughy, became governor upon McConaughy's sudden death in March 1948.

seek re-election and did not seem to get moving behind their gubernatorial candidate, Congressman Emilio Q. Daddario of Hartford. The Republicans chose a non-Yankee—Irishman Thomas J. Meskill, a congressman from New Britain. Meskill ran a "law and order" campaign that appealed to an electorate disturbed in the late 1960s by urban rioting and campus antiwar disorders. Apparently aided in his campaign by visits to Connecticut of President Richard Nixon and Vice-President Spiro Agnew, Meskill defeated Daddario—who received support from Democratic Senators Edmund S. Muskie and Edward M. Kennedy—by 125,000 votes.

As governor from 1971 to 1975, Meskill gave little indication that Connecticut's Republicans were prepared to offer leadership any more creative or innovative than that offered by the Democrats. Meskill attempted to cut the state's $250 million deficit by raising sales, cigarette, and gasoline taxes and reducing state support for education and social service and community development programs. The only noteworthy achievement of the Meskill administration was the superior effort made to clean up Connecticut's air and waterways by Dan Lufkin of Lakeville, who served as the first commissioner of the state's Department of Environmental Protection.[12]

Thus, given the nature of contemporary Connecticut society and politics, it does not appear that Connecticut in the immediate future is likely to forge ahead in confronting the unfinished items—especially tax reform—on the state agenda. That such is the case is unfortunate indeed. For Connecticut—with its thousands of acres of beautiful, unspoiled countryside; its lovely coastline dotted with picturesque lighthouses; its enchanting village greens flanked by lovingly kept colonial homes; its cities

12. As of 1976, Connecticut Republicans appeared to be heading for better days at the polls. The party had an energetic new state chairman in Frederick K. Biebel of Stratford, elected in 1975, and a proven vote-getter in United States Senator Lowell Weicker. First elected to the Senate in 1970 when the Democrats were split between antiwar minister Joseph Duffey and incumbent Thomas Dodd, who had been censured in the Senate in 1967 for the misuse of campaign funds, Weicker won again easily in 1976 after his visibility was strengthened by his active role on the Senate Watergate Committee.

rich with distinguished museums and libraries; its exceptional educational facilities; and above all with its marvelously mixed and talented population of Yankees, blacks, ethnics, and Hispanics—is, as I have discovered, a delightful land in which to live. With a political creativity to complement its physical attributes, its historic riches, and the technological expertise of its population, Connecticut could truly be the "beacon for mankind" that its Puritan fathers intended it to be.

Suggestions for Further Reading

The colonial and early state records of Connecticut have been published. See J. H. Trumbull and C. J. Hoadly, eds., *Public Records of the Colony of Connecticut,* 15 volumes (Hartford: Case, Lockwood and Brainard Company, 1850–1890), and C. J. Hoadly, L. Labaree, K. Fennelly, A. E. Van Dusen, and C. Collier, eds., *Public Records of the State of Connecticut,* 11 volumes (Hartford: Case, Lockwood and Brainard Company and Connecticut Printers, 1894–1967).

There are two general bibliographies available: Rheta Clark, David M. Roth, and Arthur E. Soderlind, compilers, *Connecticut Yesterday and Today: A Selected Bibliography for Connecticut Schools* (Hartford: Connecticut State Department of Education, 1974), and Robert E. Schnare, *Local Historical Resources in Connecticut: A Guide to their Use* (Darien: The Connecticut League of Historical Societies, 1975).

Pictorial treatments of Connecticut are included in Evan Hill, *et al., The Connecticut River* (Middletown: Wesleyan University Press, 1972); Marion Hooper, *et al., Life Along the Connecticut River* (Brattleboro, Vermont: Stephen Daye Press, 1939); Robert Wenkam, *New England* (Chicago: Rand, McNally & Company, 1974); and Editors of Yankee Magazine, compilers, *That New England* (Dublin, New Hampshire: Yankee, Incorporated, 1966).

The best and most recent single-volume survey of Connecticut history is Albert E. Van Dusen, *Connecticut* (New York: Random House, 1961). A good multivolume survey of the state is Harold J. Bingham, *History of Connecticut,* 4 volumes (New York: Lewis Historical Publishing Company, 1962). The five volumes in the Series in Connecticut History published in 1975 by the Pequot Press of Chester, Connecticut, and the Center for Connecticut Studies of Eastern Connecticut State College contain·narrative accounts of the principal forces and events in each period of Connecticut history as well as selections of various types of primary material: Albert E. Van Dusen, *Puritans Against the Wilderness: Connecticut History to 1763;* David

M. Roth and Freeman Meyer, *From Revolution to Constitution: Connecticut 1763 to 1818;* Janice Law Trecker, *Preachers, Rebels, and Traders: Connecticut 1818 to 1865;* Ruth O. M. Andersen, *From Yankee to American: Connecticut 1865 to 1914;* and Herbert F. Janick, Jr., *A Diverse People: Connecticut 1914 to the Present.* W. Storrs Lee, *The Yankees of Connecticut* (New York: Henry Holt and Company, 1957), and Odell Shepard, *Connecticut, Past and Present* (New York: Alfred A. Knopf, 1939) are interesting general analyses of Connecticut.

On colonial Connecticut, one could do no better than beginning with Charles McLean Andrews, *Connecticut's Place in Colonial History* (New Haven: Yale University Press, 1924), a slim but brilliant essay on the principal characteristics of early Connecticut. Seventeenth-century Connecticut is treated in Paul R. Lucas, *Valley of Discord: Church and Society Along the Connecticut River: 1636–1725* (Hanover, New Hampshire: The University Press of New England, 1976). The most thoughtful analysis of Connecticut in the first half of the eighteenth century is Richard L. Bushman, *From Puritan to Yankee: Character and the Social Order in Connecticut, 1690–1765* (Cambridge, Massachusetts: Harvard University Press, 1967), and the standard account of Connecticut in the decades leading up to the Revolution is Oscar Zeichner, *Connecticut's Years of Controversy, 1750–1776* (Hamden: Archon Books, 1970).

Those interested in Revolutionary Connecticut have available the volumes in the Connecticut Bicentennial Series under the editorship of Professor Glenn Weaver. The series, to continue into the 1980s, at present includes fifteen volumes from the Pequot Press and ten from the American Revolution Bicentennial Commission of Connecticut. The following fifteen books are from the Pequot Press: Thomas C. Barrow, *Connecticut Joins the Revolution* (1973); Christopher Collier, *Connecticut in the Continental Congress* (1973); North Callahan, *Connecticut's Revolutionary War Leaders* (1973); David O. White, *Connecticut's Black Soldiers, 1775–1783* (1973); Chester McArthur Destler, *Connecticut: The Provisions State* (1973); Robert A. East, *Connecticut's Loyalists* (1974); J. William Frost, *Connecticut Education in the Revolutionary Era* (1974); Louis Leonard Tucker, *Connecticut's Seminary of Sedition: Yale College* (1974); David M. Roth, *Connecticut's War Governor: Jonathan Trumbull* (1974); Robert F.

McDevitt, *Connecticut Attacked: A British Viewpoint, Tryon's Raid on Danbury* (1974); Bruce Colin Daniels, *Connecticut's First Family: William Pitkin and His Connections* (1975); Bruce P. Stark, *Connecticut Signer: William Williams* (1975); John T. Hayes, *Connecticut's Revolutionary Cavalry: Sheldon's Horse* (1975); Charles L. Cutler, *Connecticut's Revolutionary Press* (1975); and Catherine Fennelly, *Connecticut Women in the Revolutionary Era* (1975).

Available from the American Revolution Bicentennial Commission of Connecticut in Hartford are William Lamson Warren, *Connecticut Art and Architecture: Looking Backwards Two Hundred Years* (1976); Sheldon S. Cohen, *Connecticut's Loyalist Gadfly: The Reverend Samuel Andrew Peters* (1976); Wyman W. Parker, *Connecticut's Colonial and Continental Money* (1976); William F. Willingham, *Connecticut Revolutionary: Eliphalet Dyer* (1976); Larry R. Gerlach, *Connecticut Congressman: Samuel Huntington, 1731–1796* (1976); Jackson Turner Main, *Connecticut Society in the Era of the American Revolution* (1977); John Niven, *Connecticut Hero: Israel Putnam* (1977); Freeman W. Meyer, *Connecticut Congregationalism in the Revolutionary Era* (1977); Adam Ward Rome, *Connecticut's Cannon: The Salisbury Iron Furnace in the American Revolution* (1977); and John W. Ifkovic, *Connecticut's Nationalist Revolutionary: Jonathan Trumbull, Junior* (1977).

Studies of Connecticut since the Revolution include Richard J. Purcell, *Connecticut in Transition, 1775–1818* (Washington, D.C.: American Historical Association, 1918); Jarvis Means Morse, *A Neglected Period of Connecticut's History, 1818–1850* (New Haven: Yale University Press, 1933); John Niven, *Connecticut for the Union: The Role of the State in the Civil War* (New Haven: Yale University Press, 1965); and Frederick M. Heath, "Politics and Steady Habits: Issues and Elections in Connecticut, 1894–1914" (unpublished Ph.D. dissertation, Columbia University, 1965). An excellent treatment of Connecticut in recent decades is the essay on the state in Neal R. Peirce, *The New England States: People, Politics, and Power in the Six New England States* (New York: W. W. Norton and Company, 1976).

Biographical studies of Connecticut worthies include Glenn Weaver, *Jonathan Trumbull: Connecticut's Merchant Magistrate (1710–1785)* (Hartford: The Connecticut Historical Society, 1956); Christopher Collier, *Roger Sherman's Connecticut: Yankee Politics and the American Revolution* (Middletown: Wesleyan University Press, 1971); Lawrence Henry Gipson, *Jared Ingersoll: A Study of American Loyalism in Relation to British Colonial Government* (New Haven: Yale University Press, 1920); Henry Phelps Johnston, *Nathan Hale, 1776: Biography and Memorials* (New Haven: Yale University Press, 1914); Willard M. Wallace, *Traitorous Hero: The Life and Fortunes of Benedict Arnold* (Freeport, New York: Books for Libraries Press, 1970); Charles S. Hall, *Life and Letters of Samuel Holden Parsons* (New York: From the Archives of James Pugliese, 1968); Chester McArthur Destler, *Joshua Coit: American Federalist, 1758–1798* (Middletown: Wesleyan University Press, 1962); Edmund Fuller, *Prudence Crandall: An Incident of Racism in Nineteenth-Century Connecticut* (Middletown: Wesleyan University Press, 1971); Peter Tolis, *Elihu Burritt: Crusader for Brotherhood* (Hamden, Connecticut: Archon Books, 1968); Kathryn Kish Sklar, *Catharine Beecher: A Study in American Domesticity* (New Haven: Yale University Press, 1973); John Niven, *Gideon Welles: Lincoln's Secretary of the Navy* (New York: Oxford University Press, 1973); Irving Wallace, *The Fabulous Showman: The Life and Times of P. T. Barnum* (New York: Alfred A. Knopf, 1959); Justin Kaplan, *Mr. Clemens and Mark Twain: A Biography* (New York: Simon and Schuster, 1966); Curtiss S. Johnson, *Raymond E. Baldwin: Connecticut Statesman* (Chester: The Pequot Press, 1972); Edwin McNeil Dahill, "Connecticut's J. Henry Roraback" (unpublished Ph.D. dissertation, Teachers College, Columbia University, 1971); Sister Mary Hickson Murray, "Wilbur L. Cross: Connecticut Statesman and Humanitarian, 1930–1935" (unpublished Ph.D. dissertation, The University of Connecticut, 1973); and Joseph I. Lieberman, *The Power Broker: A Biography of John M. Bailey, Modern Political Boss* (Boston: Houghton Mifflin Company, 1966).

Connecticut is rich in first-rate town and county histories, a great many of which are cited in Robert E. Schnare, *Local Historical Resources in Connecticut: A Guide to Their Use* (Darien: The Connecticut League of Historical Societies, 1975). Still of use are the sixty pamphlets in the Tercentenary Pamphlet Series published in the 1930s by the Yale University Press under the editorial direction of Professors Charles M. Andrews and George M. Dutcher.

Index

Abel Porter and Company, 28
Aetna Insurance Co., 32
Allen, Ethan, 87
American Federation of Labor (AFL), 158
American Graphophone Co., 183
Americanization, 182, 183–185
American National Life & Trust Co., 163
American Protective Association (APA), 161–162
American Railway Union, 167
American Revolution. *See* Connecticut: Wartime activities
American Shakespeare Festival, 206
American Thread Company, 149
Ames Iron Works, 146
Amistad Case, 127
Andros, Sir Edmund, 14–15, 21, 62
Anglican church, 35–36, 51–52, 72, 82
Ansonia, 5, 153, 161
Ansonia Manufacturing Co., 177
Antietam, 139–140
Armenians, 151
Arnold, Benedict, 9, 84, 85–87
Austrians, 151
Automotive industry, 177, 179
Aviation industry, 177, 203

Bailey, John Moran, 214–216
Baldwin, Roger Sherman, 127
Baldwin, Simeon (gov.), 173, 180, 200–201, 202
Banking, 31, 193
Baptists, 50–51, 112
Barnes Engineering Company, 207
Bassick Company, 177
Black codes, 46
"Black Law," 131
Black Republicans, 136
Blacks: in colony, 45, 46; in 1800s, 126–131; in 1930s, 201; in World War

II, 204; in 1970s, 209, Black militants, 210–211
"Bloody Apple Tree," 10
Bloomfield, 209
Blue Laws, 53–54
Boston Tea Party, 79, 123
Branford, 24, 37
Brass industry, 28
"Bride's Brook," 11
Bridgeport: and whaling, 24; and banking, 31; and war supplies, 144, 176–177; manufacturing, 149, 177–178; population, 153; and APA, 161; in 1930s, 194–195; in 1970s, 210, 211
Bridgeport Brass, 183
Bristol, 21, 30
Broad Brook, 149
Browning, John M., 177
Buckingham, William A. (gov.), 128, 135–139
Bullard Engineering Co., 177
Bullet Hill School, 5
Bushnell, Rev. Horace, 7, 125
Busing, 211

Canaan, 119
Candee Rubber Company, 147
Canterbury, 119, 130–131
Carriage making, 147, 157
Catholics, 159–162, 213, 214
Cemetery Hill, 162
Champion, Henry (col.), 98–99
Chancellorsville, 141
Chance-Vought aircraft, 178, 203
Charles II, 6, 20, 62, 75
Charter Oak storm, 14
Charter of 1662: in Hartford, 7; hidden, 14; influence on land, 20, 75; influence on gov't., 62, 70, 83, 112
Christian Sharps Rifle Co., 146

225